Forget Me Not

Finding the Truth

Previous works by Valmai R. Harris:

1. **Forget Me Not**
2. **Forget Me Not – The Journey Continues**
3. **Forget Me Not – Journey's End**

Forget Me Not – Finding the Truth is the fourth book in the Forget Me Not series.

Copyright© 2023 Valmai R. Harris

ISBN: -13: 978-0-6450727-5-4

valmairuthharris@gmail.com

Cover design created by Joanne Livingstone:
joliving@westnet.com.au
Author photography: imaginepictures.com.au

All rights reserved. No part of this book may be reproduced or transmitted, in any form or by any means, electronic or mechanical, including photocopying, recording or by any information storage and retrieval system, without prior permission in writing from the author.

Produced and printed in Australia by IngramSpark

Forget Me Not
Finding the Truth

It is now 1920 and we are introduced to Nick Armitage, the stranger who finds his way into the lives of the DuBois family, bringing shadows and secrets of the past with him.
This is a work of fiction, and any similarity between my characters and persons living in that period, is purely coincidental. Certain names and place names have also been changed.

Valmai R. Harris.

Introduction

Charlotte stood silently beside the cot that had been her bed for the past thirty-two years. Her eyes skimmed the sparse room and stopped on the small suitcase that lay on the cot. Her worldly possessions were in there, and amongst the clothes she saw the tiny, knitted baby's jacket that some kind soul had given her when she entered the gates of the Convent. It was yellow with age, and Charlotte slowly picked it up, handling the soft wool as though it were fragile.

She breathed deeply as she began to disrobe, laying each article of her habit on the cot. In the case she found street clothing that had been acquired for her from a local charity shop, and slowly she began to dress. There was no mirror to see how she looked, but it was of little consequence when her friends would not be there to see her go. Charlotte ran her fingers through her short grey hair, and feeling the need to cover her head, found a blue felt hat amongst the contents of the case. The clothing she had entered the Convent in, were long gone; perhaps to some novice who had changed her mind at the last minute.

When she was ready, she closed the case, and stepping out into the dimly lit corridor, began her solitary walk through the building. She paused outside Sister Miriam's door, and thought she heard the faint sound of weeping.

"Good-bye, Sister Miriam," she whispered, before continuing on her way

As she crossed the grass to the gates, she was aware that somebody was watching her progress, but she dared not look back. It would be Sister Miriam, and her heart ached for the kindly soul she was leaving behind.

Outside the open gate she saw a black car. Clarence Bonner-Smythe was her only local contact with the outside world, and he had agreed to take her to his friend, Angela, and from there she would make her plans.

*

Beau replaced the receiver and leaned against the wall. "Jess!" he called

Jess appeared from the kitchen, baby Charlotte in her arms. "What is it, Beau?" She looked at his tear-stained face. "What's happened?"

"It's my sister Charlotte." He choked on the words.

"What's wrong with her?" Jess touched his arm.

"Nothing's wrong, Jess." He wiped his eyes with his sleeve. "She's coming here to be with us."

"What?"

"She's left the Convent, Jess; renounced her vows and wants to be with her family. She wants to be with us, Jess. Isn't that wonderful?"

"Yes, Beau." Jess had tears in her eyes. "I knew she didn't want to let you go."

Part One
Making Changes

Harrow Place, Sydney, September 1920
Nicholas Armitage

"Nicholas! Telephone!" The sharp female voice shattered the warm early spring air like a sudden gunshot.

A young man reclining on a striped deckchair at the lower end of the sloping garden, groaned as he uncurled his long frame. Dressed in cream flannels and sporting an impressive moustache, he cut a fine figure, with blonde hair curling around the collar of his shirt. He flicked his fingers through it now, as he ambled across to the enclosed tennis court where two young men, similarly attired, were hitting a tennis ball in a well-matched volley.

"Nick!" the young man called out, drawing attention from one of the players, who frowned as the ball whistled past his ear. He turned to the young man at the fence.

"What is it, Chris?" Nicholas Armitage flicked the racquet against his trousers, annoyance visible on his handsome bronzed features. "You know better than to interrupt a volley like that!"

"It's your mother, Nick." The young man shrugged. "You're wanted on the telephone."

"Blast! This had better be good!" Nick strode towards the gate in the fence, and thrusting the racquet at his companion, headed up the grass-covered hill towards the house. "You take my place, Chris!" he called over his shoulder.

Nick crossed the wide verandah of the rambling sandstone house and pulled open the wire door. His mother, Beatrice Armitage, stood in the entry hall, one hand on the telephone receiver, the other on her slender hip.

"You took your time," she said airily, handing her son the receiver. "It's Joe Hudson."

Nick scowled in her direction, as she turned and headed along the hallway, her footsteps echoing on the grey slate floor. Then he turned his attention to the telephone.

"This had better be good, Joe," he said bitingly. "You interrupted a serious tennis match."

A loud guffaw resounded through the earpiece. "I'm sorry about that, Nick," a strong American voice said loudly, "but I have a job for you, if you're interested."

There was silence for a moment, as Nick contemplated his answer.

"Nick? Are you still there?"

"Yes, Joe." Nick sighed. "What's the job and where is it?"

There was another loud laugh from the other end of the telephone. "Piqued your interest, have I?"

"Get on with it, Joe." Nick's handsome features were creased into a frown, his dark eyes hooded.

"Alright! Alright!" There was a slight pause before the voice continued. "Do you remember the case I had three years ago, where a doctor who had recently returned from the Western Front, went missing, and I found him eventually in Victoria, in the gold-mining town of Bendigo?"

"Yes, I vaguely remember it? Gone missing again, has he?" Nick held the telephone away from his ear as another loud guffaw sounded.

"No, but his name has come up again in the cold case of a young woman who went missing back in 1917 and who has not been seen since."

Nick pricked up his ears. "I'm listening. Is your doctor a suspect?"

"No, but it is a coincidence that one of the persons of interest was recently up on a charge of harassing the same Doctor DuBois and his wife. Firstly, he assaulted Mrs. DuBois, and then threw a brick through their bedroom window a few days later."

"Definitely the violent kind." Nick paused. "I need the beginning of this story, Joe."

"Right!" There was a pause. "Could we meet for lunch, say at Gray's Hotel in George Street?"

Nick looked at his watch. It was 11.30. "Alright. I can be there by twelve. I'll be in my tennis whites; I suppose that's acceptable?"

"Certainly, my boy! We're not dining at the Hilton." There was another laugh. "I can't afford the Hilton. See you at twelve!"

Nick replaced the receiver and hurried in the direction of the kitchen. "Mother!" he called out.

Beatrice appeared in the kitchen doorway; her slender form wrapped in a green pinafore. Steel-grey hair was swept up into a coil on the top of her head, and her haughty features were locked into an expression of resignation. "What is it this time, Nick?"

"I'm sorry, mother, but something important has come up, and I'm meeting Joe for lunch at Gray's Hotel in half an hour."

"What about your friends out there on the tennis court? What am I supposed to do with them?"

Nick bent and flicked a kiss on her cool cheek. "Feed them, mother." He flashed a smile in her direction. "You're good at that. I shan't be long." He patted her arm absently. "I'll duck out the front door, so they don't see me. This could mean a job down south, if I play my cards right."

"Are you planning on taking your father's car?"

"Naturally."

"You're lucky he didn't need it this morning then," said Beatrice meaningfully.

Nick shrugged. "Then I'd have caught the tram, mother. There's always a solution."

"Or borrowed one of your friends' cars perhaps?"

"Not likely."

Beatrice shook her head as her son hurried along the hallway to the front door. Her Nicholas was a mystery to both herself and his father, Hugh Armitage. A college graduate with high academic scores, Nicholas had chosen to attach himself to the blustering American Private Investigator, Joe Hudson. No amount of pleading and arguing could have persuaded the then twenty-nine-old to reconsider his decision. Hugh, a semi-retired defence lawyer, had tried every means at his disposal to encourage his son to follow in his footsteps, but the obstinate young Nicholas had chosen his own path. He was, by all accounts, good at his job.

The front door slammed, and sighing deeply, Beatrice returned to the kitchen. Nicholas would do precisely what he wanted to, and if it meant he was about to head south, then she had better make sure his clothes were in order. In the meantime, she had two young men to feed.

*

Nick hurried up the stone steps, and into the bar of Gray's Hotel. A young waiter with slicked down dark hair and a poor excuse for a moustache, greeted him with a smile.

"Do you have a booking, sir?" he asked politely.

Nick had no idea whether Joe had made a booking. "I - er - I'm meeting a friend here, name of Joe Hudson. My name is Nicholas Armitage."

"Ah, yes, Mr. Armitage." The young waiter inclined his head. "Mr. Hudson is expecting you. Follow me, please."

Nick followed the young man past the bar, where the lunchtime crowd was milling, and through a swing-door into the dining room. They crossed the room to a secluded table where Joe was hunched over a sheaf of papers. The young man politely waited while Nick pulled out a chair and sat heavily.

"Two beers, please," said Nick, and the young man scurried away.

Joe looked up from his scrutiny of the papers before him and smiled at Nick. He was a man in his late fifties, but the over-indulgence of alcohol and food had given him the appearance of being much older. His grey hair was long and unkempt, curling around the frayed collar of a white shirt that had not seen an iron for some time. Evidence of recently consumed food remained on the lapel of his grey suit. In spite of his unkempt appearance, his smile was wide, and blue eyes crinkled with humour as he looked up at Nick.

"Nick, my boy!" His voice was too loud. "Sorry to interrupt your tennis match."

Nick cringed, as other patrons turned to look in their direction. He shrugged. "That's alright, Joe. I was losing anyway. Now what is this all about? I thought you were in Melbourne."

"I was, and that's where I found this." Joe pushed a newspaper cutting in front of him.

Nick turned the cutting around and ran his eyes over it. It was from the Melbourne Age, and read:

> *Police are seeking information on the disappearance of a Miss Phyllis Powell, from Bendigo, Central Victoria, in 1917. Miss Powell has not been seen since then, and Police are offering a reward for information that may lead to her whereabouts.'*

Nick looked up at his companion. "Do you have any more information than this?"

Joe leaned forward and lowered his voice. "I took the liberty of detouring to Bendigo, before coming home, and called in at the Police Station." He sat back as the waiter arrived with their beers.

"Are you ready to order?" the waiter asked politely, as he pulled a notebook and pencil from the pocket of his black shirt.

"I'll have the pie and chips," said Joe, without consulting the menu.

Nick glanced at the menu, before smiling up at the young waiter. "Could I have a piece of grilled fish with some salad greens, please?"

The young man wrote swiftly in his notepad, before moving on to another table.

"Pie and chips, Joe?" Nick screwed up his nose at the thought of all that grease.

Joe was unperturbed. "I no longer have a woman nagging me to eat right," he shrugged, "so I eat what I like, and to hell with the consequences."

Nick frowned. "It's your body, Joe. Now, where were we?"

Joe leaned forward. "My visit with the local constabulary was very enlightening. The Chief Constable remembered me from my last visit and was extremely willing to share information about a certain young man by the name of Sidney O'Connor." He took a deep breath. "Apparently Miss Powell and this Mr. O'Connor were 'knocking about together', as he so indelicately put it, but here's the interesting bit." He licked his lips. "You know I told you that O'Connor had thrown a brick through the window of Doctor DuBois's house?"

"I don't see the connection but go on."

"O'Connor had a grievance against DuBois, on account of he blamed him for the loss of his job, but that's another story, and I don't think it has anything to do with the missing woman."

"You're beating about the bush, Joe. Can we get to the crux of the matter?"

"When O'Connor was apprehended for throwing the brick through the window, he was actually brought in by a one-time mate, a William Maitland, who incidentally had also been involved with the missing woman."

"I see. The plot thickens."

"Indeed, it does, because the missing woman had a young child."

There was silence for a moment as Nick processed the convoluted information. Finally, he looked across at Joe. "Whose child?"

"That is the pertinent question, Nick. We have two men, one missing woman and a young child, and that does not make for a happy situation."

"Does that mean the child is missing too?"

"Nobody seems to know, but we can presume that is the case."

"Who reported her missing?"

Joe shrugged. "Unfortunately, that information has not been recorded, for whatever reason."

"That's strange." Nick frowned. "So, where do I come into this? What do you want me to do?"

"What you do best, Nick."

"And that is?"

"Snoop around without being too obvious. A handsome young blade like you can circulate without drawing attention. You don't have that stamp of a crusty old detective, like me."

Nick laughed. "So, you want me to snoop, eh? Tell me, Joe, who's putting up the reward money?"

"The money is coming from police coffers. They want to find out what happened to her."

Conversation ceased, as the waiter appeared with their meals. Joe immediately set to work attacking his pie with a fork, while Nick watched on as the gravy oozed on to the plate. He shook his head in disbelief, as he picked up his own fork. The American had a strange way of eating, and Nick was relieved that they were not dining at the Hilton. He concentrated on his own meal, trying not to watch what was happening on the opposite side of the table.

Finally, he put down his knife and fork, wiped his mouth on a paper napkin and sat back, waiting for Joe to demolish the last of his chips, which he did after wiping them through the gravy. Nick had a sudden picture of his mother's face registering horror at Joe's lack of table manners.

Joe put down his fork, belched, and sat back with a sigh. "That was good," he muttered.

They were silent for a few moments, while the waiter returned, removed the dirty plates and asked politely if they required more drinks. Nick shook his head, while Joe drained his glass and nodded at the waiter.

"You realise, Joe," said Nick seriously, "that the young woman in question, may simply have decided to change her name and remove herself from her situation."

"Yes, that is always a possibility. She may not have been the victim of foul play, but it would be remiss of us not to find out for sure." Joe leaned forward. "This should be a good chance for you to prove yourself, Nick, in readiness for my retirement."

"Your retirement?" Nick laughed. "You're not seriously thinking of retiring, Joe?"

The older man nodded briefly. "I'm thinking of it."

Nick was silent. "Very well," he said slowly, "when do you want me to start?"

"As soon as it can be arranged." Joe became business-like. "You will be booked into a local hotel in Bendigo, as a journalist doing local interest stuff."

"You've got it all worked out, haven't you, Joe?" Nick was incredulous. "And what, pray, will you be doing back here, while I'm parading as a journalist down south?"

The waiter returned with Joe's beer.

"I might just go and see my old friend, Clarence Bonner-Smythe, and see what I can find out about Doctor DuBois. I remember at the time, he was reluctant to be found." He shrugged as he picked up his beer glass. "If he's still in Bendigo, maybe he's worth a second look." He drained his glass.

Nick drummed his fingers on the table. "Why a journalist, Joe?"

"Why?" Joe wiped a hand across his mouth. "You might get more response from the locals if they don't know what you're really up to."

Nick shrugged. "Right! Well, I'd better go home and give my parents the good news."

Joe grinned widely. "I'm sure they'll be ecstatic."

Nick's Journey

Nick broke the news to his parents that evening, as they sat in the comfort of a warm sitting room, sipping on glasses of red wine. A large red-setter dog lay on a mat at Nick's feet, absorbing the heat of a crackling fire. Although the days were warm, the evenings tended to be chilly, particularly in the wooded hills on the outskirts of the city.

Hugh Armitage stretched his long limbs and yawned. He was a large man with greying ginger hair and sporting an impressive moustache. Clad in a grey lounge coat, loose trousers and slippers, Hugh looked about as relaxed as a busy man could be after a long day in the city.

Beatrice looked across at him over the rim of her glass, and for a tender moment, wanted to stroke his hair. The moment passed, however, and she moved uncomfortably on the green floral lounge chair. They had never been that close, and she felt a warm flush creep up her neck to her cheeks. Looking quickly at her husband now, she was pleased to see that his eyes were shut. She relaxed against the chair and placed her cool glass against her face.

Nick saw the movement. "Are you too hot, mother?" he asked, as he moved his own chair back from the fire.

"Just a little," she replied softly, lowering her glass.

Nick rose and placed the copper fireguard on the hearth. "There! That should solve the problem."

Hugh opened one eye. "Who's too hot?" he muttered.

The dog hadn't stirred.

"It's alright, Hugh," said Beatrice, "Nick has remedied the situation."

Hugh grunted and closed his eye once more.

"I'm heading down to Victoria in a few days' time," said Nick absently.

There was silence for a few moments before Hugh spoke. "What's the Yank got you chasing now, Nicholas?" he asked dryly, his eyes still closed.

"A woman went missing from Bendigo in 1917, and the police are finally anxious to find out what happened to her. It seems she had a young child, too."

Hugh's eyes snapped open. "They've been missing for three years?"

"Apparently. Nobody has seen them, at any rate."

"That's terrible!" whispered Beatrice. "How can a young woman be missing that long, and nobody know where she is?"

"It happens, mother," said Nick smoothly. "Sometimes they don't want to be found."

Beatrice shook her head. "And Joe wants you to find her?"

"Joe wants me to find out what I can about certain people who were known to her at the time of her disappearance."

"In other words," said Hugh, "spy on them?"

"Precisely, or as Joe puts it, 'snoop around, without being too obvious.'"

"How long will you be gone?" The question came from Beatrice.

"I have no idea, mother." Nick shrugged. "It depends on what I find."

"So, I'll pack your suitcase with all the necessaries?"

Hugh frowned in Nick's direction. "Surely he can pack his own suitcase, Beatrice?" he growled.

"I'll do it, mother," said Nick hastily, wanting to avoid a confrontation between his parents.

"Of course you will." Hugh closed his eyes again. "When's supper, Beatrice?"

Beatrice rose quickly to her feet. "I'll get it now, Hugh."

As the door closed behind her, Hugh turned to his son.

"Isn't it time you found yourself a wife and settled down, Nicholas? You're over thirty years of age, for God's sake. It's time you had your own family."

Nick smiled absently as he eased himself on to the mat beside the sleeping dog.

And finish up like you two? I think not! "I haven't found the right girl, father."

"You never will, while you spend all your free time with the two layabouts you left here for your mother to feed, today."

"They're alright, father."

"Humph! What do they do, exactly?"

"Do?"

"Yes!" Hugh was becoming impatient. "How do they earn their living?"

Nick laughed as he fondled the dog's ears. "They have wealthy parents. They don't have to work."

"Playboys, eh?"

"Not exactly. Chris dabbles in the share market, and Duncan – well let's say that Duncan spends a lot of time and money in gambling establishments."

"In other words, they're playboys, Nick."

Nick shrugged. He didn't want to get into an argument with his father about his friends. He knew what they were, and although he didn't share their lack of enthusiasm for honest work, they were, after all, his friends. They'd been friends since college days.

Beatrice chose that moment to enter the room, much to Nick's relief. He got up to relieve her of the supper tray. The routine never changed.

*

"The hotel is called the Grey Goose, Nick, and it's only a short walk from the station." Nick and Joe were standing on the platform of Sydney's Central Station, as the train issued steam in front of them. "The publican is an amenable lady by the name of Mrs. O'Malley. I'm sure you will be able to charm information out of her." Joe grinned at Nick's sour expression. "You'll enjoy it, Nick." He gave the younger man a playful shove. "Just remember to keep me informed with anything you happen to glean from the locals. Oh, and make yourself known to Chief Constable Whitley at the Police Station." The whistle sounded, cutting off all conversation. "Good-bye, Nick!" He shouted.

"Good-bye, Joe!"

Nick stepped on to the train, and made his way along the narrow corridor, checking the number on his ticket as he walked. Joe had gone to great lengths to make sure he had a private compartment, for which he was extremely grateful. The number on the ticket was 10. Nick walked the length of the carriage before reaching compartment 10.

Sliding the door open he stepped inside, glancing around with a certain amount of curiosity. He had not travelled in a sleeper before and was surprised to see how much could be fitted into such a small space. There was an upper and a lower bunk, the lower not yet made up into a bed. A sliding door opposite the bunks revealed a foldaway basin and a toilet bowl. He had his own facilities.

Nick closed the sliding door, and after placing his suitcase on the bunk, pulled up the blind to let in some light. Beneath the window was a small folding table, and on it Nick saw a vase with a single rosebud, and a folded newspaper. He would be quite comfortable here, he thought.

A light tap at the door made him turn round, and a cheerful face appeared in the doorway.

"Good afternoon, sir," said a young man in a crisp white coat. "I'm Henry, and I am your steward for this trip. Anything you want, sir, just call on me."

"Thank-you, Henry. We change trains in Albury, I believe?"

"Yes, sir, which means you probably won't get much of a sleep this end of the journey."

"That's alright. I'm a light sleeper anyway. What time do we arrive in Albury?"

"Usually just before midnight, sir."

"So, it's hardly worth while creasing the sheets?"

"I wouldn't say that sir. Unlike some overnighters, we do boast comfortable bunks." His round face beamed with pleasure. "I'll prepare your bunk in about an hour's time, sir."

"Very well." Nick looked at his pocket watch. It was 4.10. "In that case I have time to head on down to the buffet car and have a meal."

"Very good, sir." The steward retreated, and Nick placed his suitcase up on the top bunk. Feeling in his coat pocket for his wallet, he left the compartment, sliding the door shut behind him.

Along the carriage, doors were closing as people made their way to the buffet car. Nick followed, treading carefully across the shuddering boards that covered the couplings.

Inside the buffet car it was warm, and the smell reminded Nick of his mother's kitchen on those rare occasions when she made meat pies. He waited his turn to be served and decided that a pasty and a cup of tea would have to suffice. There was one unoccupied table at the end of the carriage, so Nick made his way towards it. As he put down his tray, a voice sounded close to his ear.

"Do you mind if I share your table?" Nick looked up quickly, staring into startlingly blue eyes. The young woman smiled at him. "It is the last one."

Nick smiled back, a little self-consciously. "Yes, certainly." He pulled his tray forward as he sat.

The young woman sat opposite, and for a moment they stared at each other, until Nick dropped his gaze and began to stir sugar into his tea. His companion unwrapped her sandwiches and folded the paper neatly beside her plate.

Suddenly she reached a hand across the table. "Rebecca Tweed," she said, and waited for Nick to respond accordingly.

"Nick Armitage," he said finally, taking her outstretched hand.

"Nice to meet you." Her voice was warm, with the hint of an accent that Nick could not quite place. "And what takes you to Melbourne, Nick?"

"Oh, I'm heading up to Bendigo, actually." Nick shook a sauce bottle over his pasty, watching with dismay as the sauce spurted across his plate and on to the table.

The young woman stifled a giggle as she handed him a paper serviette. "Too much sauce?"

Nick had to smile - he had no choice. "You could say that." He mopped up the mess and placed the used serviette on his tray.

"Shall we start again?" the young woman was saying.

Nick glanced up at her and nodded sheepishly. "That sounds like a good idea."

Rebecca sat back on her chair, tilting her head slightly as she surveyed her companion. Nick felt uncomfortable under those incredibly blue eyes and felt the blood creeping up his neck. The woman opposite him was probably in her early twenties, with dark hair bobbed in the latest fashion, and partly covered with a bright red beret. Her lips, open now in a smile, were the same colour as her beret, and revealed even white teeth. A light smattering of freckles across the bridge of her nose, gave her an impish look that Nick found beguiling. Not often was he lost for words when in the company of an attractive woman, but he was now, and felt completely out of his depth.

Rebecca must have sensed his discomfort, for she turned her attention to her sandwiches, leaving Nick to wrestle with his pasty. After what seemed like a long and painful silence, Rebecca tried once more to initiate a conversation.

"So, Mr. Armitage, what's the attraction in Bendigo?" She wiped her mouth delicately on a serviette.

"Attraction?" Nick swallowed and coughed as pastry caught in his throat. This wasn't going at all well, and the blue eyes danced merrily, as though their owner was enjoying his discomfort. "There's no attraction. I'm looking for somebody."

That wasn't what he had intended to say; it sounded lame and a little foolish.

"Looking for somebody?" The blue eyes held his.

"Somebody who has been missing." *Come on, Nick; pull yourself together!*

"Oh!" There was a slight pause. "Are you a policeman?"

"No." Nick took a sip of his tea, knowing he had said too much. "No, I'm not a policeman."

"A private detective then?" Nick hesitated. "You are, aren't you? How exciting!"

Nick groaned inwardly as he thought of Joe. He would have relished the embarrassing moments his junior was experiencing and would have laughed loudly over the sauce incident.

"I wouldn't say it's exciting," said Nick with a shrug, "and I would appreciate it if you kept it to yourself."

Rebecca leaned forward, her eyes sparkling. "In my profession we would say 'off the record.'"

Nick groaned, audibly this time. "You're a journalist."

"No, I'm not a journalist - I'm a mere reporter with the Sydney Herald."

"Same thing," muttered Nick.

"Not really." She smiled. "And I *can* keep it to myself, if that's what you want." She stared at Nick for a long moment. "Actually, I might be able to help you, Mr. Armitage."

"In what way?" Nick's eyebrows drew together into a frown.

Rebecca leaned further forward, and Nick caught a whiff of her perfume - like sweet musk. "I'm heading to Melbourne to see my mother, and I expect that I will have time on my hands. I'll be in the position to check newspapers." She spread her well-manicured hands across the table.

"Why would you do that? I hardly know you, Miss Tweed."

"Let's just say I enjoy a good mystery, and I get the impression, Mr. Armitage, that this is your first solo job?" Her neat eyebrows arched slightly, catching Nick off-guard.

Why did he feel like an awkward schoolboy? Was he so transparent that she could see straight through him?

"I appreciate your interest, Miss Tweed, but I think I can manage this on my own."

Rebecca searched through her red handbag, and as though she hadn't heard him, produced a notebook and pencil. "Now, tell me all about this person who has been missing?"

"I don't think you quite understood me, Miss Tweed. I said…"

"I know what you said, but I also know that I can help you." The blue eyes were wide.

Nick folded his hands and rested his chin on them, surveying her over his fingers. "Are you always this forthright, Miss Tweed?" His brow folded into a scowl.

"I am." She grinned, unabashed. "And it's Rebecca, if you don't mind. Miss Tweed sounds so formal. Anyway, Nick, how do you know I'm a 'Miss'?"

"You're not wearing a ring," replied Nick dryly.

"That isn't always the case, you know?"

"Perhaps not, but I'm right this time."

Rebecca stroked the fur collar of her black wool coat and pursed her red lips as she surveyed Nick coolly. "We could make a good team, Nick, as we obviously both like solving mysteries."

Nick laughed as he shook his head. "I'm sorry, Rebecca, but I don't really know enough about this case to share with anyone, particularly someone I've just met."

Rebecca leaned over her notepad; pencil poised. "Tell me what you do know."

Nick rubbed his chin thoughtfully, afraid that he was about to make the biggest mistake of his short career. "This is strictly off the record, Rebecca." He reached into his jacket pocket and pulled out the newspaper cutting that Joe had given him. Unfolding it, he placed it on the table.

Rebecca quickly scanned the article before looking up at Nick. "Not much to go on, is it?"

Nick sighed. "I do have a little more information."

"Then let me hear it." The blue eyes were sparkling with anticipation.

"Before I do, can you tell me what your accent is? I've been puzzling over it."

She laughed gaily. "My mother came from New Zealand. I'm a Kiwi, Nick."

By now, the dining car was nearly empty, and as Nick told a perfect stranger the few facts that he did know about the missing woman, they finally found themselves alone. The only sound was the rattle of the carriage as the iron wheels turned beneath them.

Finally, Rebecca snapped shut her notebook, placed it in her handbag, and stood, stretching lithely.

"I think it's time I caught a few hours' sleep." She yawned behind her hand. "I believe we have to change trains in Albury?"

"Yes." Nick looked up at her. "Do you have a sleeper?"

"No." She paused. "Do you?"

"Yes."

Her eyes narrowed for a split second. "Lucky you," she said wryly, moving away from the table. "Goodnight, Nick. I'll see you in the morning. Sleep well."

Nick watched as she made her unsteady way along the moving carriage. At the end she stopped and turning, gave him a brief wave before sliding the door open. He heard the rushing sound of the train wheels as Rebecca stepped out on to that no-man's land between the carriages. The door slammed shut behind her, and he was alone.

Nick sat back on his chair, expelling a long breath. His head was spinning, and he found it hard to believe what had transpired over the past hour or so. Had he dreamt it? No, he couldn't have, because her perfume still lingered in his nostrils. Nick pressed his fingers into his eyes. Would he see her again, he wondered?

"Have you finished here, sir?" A voice sounded in his ear.

Nick looked up to see a young man, dressed in a railways uniform, smiling down at him.

"Yes," answered Nick hurriedly. "I'm sorry to keep you waiting."

"That's alright, sir."

Nick stood, and swaying slightly, headed for the door leading to the sleeper carriages. It had been a strange evening.

*

Nick spent the next few hours lying awake on the narrow bunk, feeling the vibration of the wheels, and pondering on the strangeness of his encounter with the irrepressible Rebecca Tweed. It was too much of a coincidence, and he wracked his brain, trying to find a solution. Had Joe set this up to keep an eye on him? No, Joe wouldn't do that... or would he? There was only one way to find out.

After falling asleep with these thoughts in his mind, Nick was awakened by the sound of a loud voice in the corridor.

"We'll soon be approaching Albury! Time to prepare for changing trains."

Nick struggled off the bunk, shrugged himself into his jacket, and after using the amenities, pulled up the blind to the outside world. There was nothing to see - not even moonlight.

After several minutes had passed, he felt the train slowing, and the whistle sounded sharply, indicating that a town was close by. It was time to go. Compartment doors slammed all along the corridor, and once more Nick joined the queue. This time they were all heading for the platform where they would be escorted to the Victorian side of the railway - a different gauge to the New South Wales line. Nick pondered on the logic of this. Surely it wouldn't be too difficult to unify the States Rail System.

Nick didn't catch sight of Rebecca during the transfer, and once on board the Victorian train, there was no chance to go looking for her. He was ushered to his compartment by the same steward, Henry, and found his bunk ready to fall into.

"I'm sorry, but there are no private amenities on this train," explained Henry, as Nick looked around for the sliding door. "There are toilets at each end of the carriage."

Nick nodded, and as Henry took his leave, he sat heavily on the bunk. He was weary, and even the thought of the rattling train probably wouldn't keep him awake during the remainder of the journey. Without removing his clothes, he lay down, and before long was asleep, all thoughts of Joe's possible deception, faded from his brain.

Nick's Arrival

Once in Melbourne, Nick made his way along the crowded Spencer Street station, hoping to catch a glimpse of Rebecca's red beret. She was nowhere to be seen. Nick felt that he had been successfully taken for a ride, with or without Joe's input. He would probably live to regret it.

A growling stomach drove him to search for the cafeteria. The previous night's meal had not satisfied his hunger, and the smell of frying bacon hastened his footsteps. Nick joined other hungry passengers, as they queued with trays, anxious to be fed. The air was warm and pungent, and when it came to his turn to be served, Nick ordered a full English breakfast. He knew that his mother would have been horrified to see what he had on his plate. What she didn't see, she couldn't worry about.

Juggling the tray and his suitcase, Nick made his way to an empty table where he sat and unwrapped the cutlery from its serviette. As he cut a slice of hot sausage, he heard a familiar voice beside him.

"Hello, Nick. Mind if I join you?"

It was déjà vu. Looking up, he saw Rebecca smiling down at him. He scrambled to his feet as she sat opposite, a cup of tea in one hand and a plate of toast in the other.

"This is becoming a bit of a habit," he muttered, as he resumed his seat.

"It is, isn't it?" She was eyeing his breakfast plate. "Hungry?"

"Yes." Nick swallowed hard on the sausage, before picking up his serviette and wiping his mouth. "I think you and I have a few things to discuss, Miss Tweed."

"Like what?" Rebecca took a delicate bite out of her toast.

"Like who sent you to check on me?"

"I beg your pardon? What do you mean, Nick?"

Nick sat back on his chair. "What happened last night was not simply coincidence - you were sent by my employer, Joe Hudson. Am I right?" The blue eyes surveyed him coolly, and for a fleeting second, he could see Joe in their depths. "You're Joe's daughter, aren't you?" The penny had finally dropped.

"Congratulations, Nick!" Rebecca carefully put her toast on the plate. "And what brought you to that conclusion?"

"I knew there was something not quite right, but I couldn't put my finger on it. Why did he send you to check on me? Didn't he trust me?"

"It wasn't that. I asked him if he had a job for me." She laughed. "We are more alike than we care to admit, Joe and me."

"Why the game? You could have simply introduced yourself as Rebecca Hudson."

The blue eyes looked down at her plate. "It's Amelia, actually - Amelia Hudson."

"Oh!"

Nick rubbed his chin thoughtfully. He had worked with Joe for five years and knew that he had a wife and daughter somewhere, but he rarely spoke of them. It was easy to see, looking at Amelia, that life with Joe could be a rollercoaster. Perhaps it was the same for her mother.

"I'm sorry, Nick. I never intended to deceive you, but I did enjoy the game, brief though it was."

"So you *are* a reporter?"

"Yes, that much is true."

"And you *are* going to see your mother?"

"Yes."

"I suppose I can forgive you, but I won't forgive Joe for agreeing to it."

"He'll laugh when I tell him what's happened."

"I'm sure he will." Nick cut off another slice of sausage. "Tell me, how did you know it was me?"

"I'm paid to know who's who, Nick." Her tone was conspiratorial.

"I see. Well, I'd like to finish my breakfast before it gets cold, if you don't mind."

"In spite of what's happened, Nick, do you still want my help with this case?"

Nick put down his fork and stared into the cool blue eyes. "I'll think about it."

Amelia smiled as she picked up her teacup. "Don't think about it for too long, Nick. I'm only here for two weeks."

*

Nick settled back against the leather seat of the train compartment and thought of all that had transpired over the past twenty-four hours. He was still smarting from the fact that Joe had said nothing to him, and that he had fallen for the ruse so easily. There was still a lot for him to learn.

He looked around the compartment at the people heading to Bendigo and further, and as the train rattled its way north, he made a mental note of each face, and determined where each was heading and for what purpose. The man opposite, with an unsmiling face and a pince-nez pressed firmly on his aristocratic nose, stared unblinking through the window, as trees and paddocks flashed by. He was an undertaker, Nick deduced, and his black suit bore testimony to many a pressing beneath a hot iron.

Beside the undertaker sat a young woman who tried to catch his eye several times throughout the journey, and each time he caught her looking at him, she shifted her gaze, her face suffusing with colour. She was not unattractive, but there was a nervous quality about her that reminded Nick of a bird about to take flight. She was possibly being chaperoned by the dowager-like woman seated beside her, and who spent most of the journey asleep.

Beside Nick sat a young couple who had eyes only for each other, and Nick uncomfortably deduced that they were on their honeymoon, as the young woman kept glancing down at her left hand, on which he saw a shiny gold wedding band.

Nobody spoke, and as the movement of the train became hypnotic, Nick felt the need to leave the confines of the compartment, for the solitude of the corridor. He excused himself and sliding the door open, stepped outside. He was not alone. Two men and a woman stood at the far end of the carriage, deep in animated discussion. Nick gave them a cursory glance. The woman began pacing the narrow corridor, a cigarette burning in her gloved hand, and when she saw Nick watching her, she blew a puff of smoke towards him, before turning to the men. They all looked in his direction, and for a moment, Nick thought there might be an altercation, but one man grabbed the woman by the arm, and shepherded her into a compartment. The other man gave Nick a final long look and followed them.

What was that all about? Nick took a deep breath and turned towards the window. The detective in him wanted to create a situation, but he decided that he was letting his imagination run away with him. They were probably having a family argument and resented his intrusion. He pressed his forehead against the glass, feeling the vibration of the wheels, and turned his thoughts to Rebecca. He couldn't think of her as Amelia – to him she would always be Rebecca.

Nick had left her at the station, as she had to hurry for another train to take her to her mother's. They had made no plans to meet again, but Nick assumed that Joe had already taken care of that. He laughed softly. Would she arrive unannounced one day, armed with a briefcase full of information? He couldn't depend on it, but he had to admit to himself that he would be pleased to see her again.

*

Nick returned to the compartment to retrieve his suitcase, as the train arrived at the Bendigo station. His fellow passengers were preparing to alight, and cases were being handed down from the luggage rack. The shy young woman who had been sitting opposite Nick, was struggling to reach her case.

"Here, let me get that for you." Nick reached for the case and received a warm flush in response.

"Thank-you," she said quietly, as the woman beside her glowered at him.

Grabbing the young woman by the arm, she escorted her hurriedly out of the compartment, and along the corridor to the exit.

That was a strange reaction, thought Nick. He was only trying to be helpful, not abduct the girl.

Nick decided to forget the two strange incidents, and as he made his way along the station platform, tried to remember Joe's instructions on how to get to the Grey Goose Hotel. He walked over the pedestrian bridge, out on to the street, and made a right turn.

Following the street up a slight incline, he stepped it out until he found himself at the hotel, white walls gleaming in the warm spring sunshine. He paused at a door with a sign which read: Ladies' Lounge and pushed tentatively on it. Beyond was a long passage, and to the right he saw the ladies' lounge. A little further on, and to the left was a swing door, behind which he could hear the heavy sound of men's voices. That had to be the bar.

Before he had a chance to push the door open, a voice greeted him from further along the passage.

"Can I help you, young man?" The cheery voice came from a plump woman, who shuffled towards him as she spoke.

Nick hastily removed his hat. "I'm looking for a Mrs. O'Malley," he said politely.

"That would be me." The woman had reached him and was studying him intently. "You wouldn't be the journalist from Sydney, by any chance?"

"Er – yes, I am the journalist from Sydney." Nick held out his hand. "I'm Nicholas Armitage."

"I'm so pleased to meet you, Mr. Armitage." Mrs. O'Malley shook his hand warmly. "We have a room ready for you, so if you'll follow me, I'll take you there now."

Nick followed Mrs. O'Malley, as she clumped heavily up the stairs, and along a corridor to the last room on the left. Opening the door, she ushered him in.

"This is your room, Mr. Armitage."

She was breathing heavily, and Nick hoped that she had her own room downstairs.

"Please, call me Nick, everyone does."

"Very well, Nick it is." She smiled at him. "Make yourself comfortable. The bathroom is along to your right, and I have to tell you that it is shared, so please don't leave any of your things in there."

Nick nodded, as he dropped his suitcase on to the bed. "Do you serve meals here?"

Mrs. O'Malley stopped, her hand on the door handle. "That depends, Nick. You can join the family (the staff, in other words) for breakfast in the Ladies Lounge, and that's at seven-thirty. If you're about at lunchtime, we do a tray of sandwiches for the locals, and at teatime, you're welcome to join the family again in the Lounge. You will have to let us know, of course, so we can plan for you."

"That sounds very accommodating, thank-you."

"We don't have a lot of guests staying over." She paused. "Until recently I was running the place myself, but now I have a partner in the business, and I think things might be about to change." She smiled. "When you come down to the bar, I think you'll understand what I mean."

The door closed behind her, and Nick was alone. He looked around the room. It was small in comparison to the room he had at the family home in Sydney, but it looked comfortable enough for a 'journalist'. Nick smiled to himself as he wondered how long that ruse would last.

Pushing his hand down on the bed, he tested the springs. Yes, it would be comfortable enough. The bed covering was brightly coloured and looked new, as were the cushions that were displayed on a deep lounge chair that stood beside the bed. A vase of fresh flowers sat on a small table by the window, which was open to let in the fresh air. Pretty lace curtains billowed softly, and as Nick stood meditating, he heard voices coming from below.

Stepping across to the window, he looked down into a walled courtyard, where two little girls were playing on the grass with a terrier dog. As he watched, one threw a ball to the dog. It bounded after the ball, grabbed it and returned it to the children, dropping it at their feet. They squealed with delight, and Nick smiled as they jumped with excitement.

As he watched, a woman came into view from the direction of the building. Her blonde hair was wrapped in a floral scarf, and her body was encased in a bright pink pinafore. She stood watching the children for a moment, her hands on her hips. It was a scene of perfect domesticity.

"Freya! Grace!" she called out. "It's time to come inside now."

The chubby little blonde turned at the sound of the woman's voice. "Do we have to, mummy?"

"Yes, Freya! And there will be no argument."

"But we don't want to, do we Grace?"

The other child stared up at the woman, and Nick saw her shake her head, golden curls bobbing.

"I see." The woman turned towards the building. "So you don't want a drink of lemonade?"

The blonde child jumped up and down, and Nick smiled as he saw her little fists clenched. She was not happy with the ultimatum.

The woman stepped out of his vision, but he heard her say, "Alright! Suit yourself."

Nick heard a door slam.

The two children stood where they were for a few moments, before running after the woman.

The door slammed again.

Nick turned his attention back to the garden, and his eyes lingered on two murals that had been painted on the outside wall. He saw a waterfall cascading down a hill, the sun reflecting on the mist that rose from it. The artist was good, he mused. Beside the waterfall was a poppet-head, painted in great detail. He recognised it as a symbol of goldmining and was probably a local structure.

As his eyes lingered on the paintings, there was a knock on his door.

"Come in," he said as he turned towards the sound.

The door opened slowly, and the woman he had seen in the yard, appeared. She smiled at him across the room - a sunny smile in a pretty face.

"Mr. Armitage?" She crossed the room, holding out her hand. "I'm Isobel Dalton – Izzy for short. I'm the resident cook and bottle washer of this establishment." She laughed gaily as they shook hands. "I've come to find out if you'll be joining us in the lounge for tea. I believe Jean has told you what usually happens here."

"If you mean Mrs. O'Malley, yes, she has. I'm pleased to meet you, Mrs. Dalton." At her puzzled expression he added quickly, "I saw you in the yard below, with the two children, so I put two and two together," he shrugged, "and made four."

"Very good, Mr. Armitage. You assumed correctly. My husband, Harry runs the bar. We've only recently become part owners of the hotel. Before that we had a mixed business in Swan Hill."

"That's a bit of a change, I would think."

Izzy shrugged. "It is, but it's what Harry loves, and as it happens, it's brought me closer to my sister, Jess, who lives just along the street. So, I can't complain." She smiled again. "Now, are you joining us for tea, or have you somewhere better to go?"

"No, I have nowhere better to go, and yes, I'd be very pleased to join you. I have to find out as much as I can about this town and what makes it tick."

"Then you've come to the right place. There's not much gets past Jean O'Malley." Laughing, Izzy headed for the door. "We'll see you at six-thirty, then?"

"Oh, before you go, Mrs. Dalton, can you tell me who painted the murals on the wall outside?"

"I did, Mr. Armitage, and please call me Izzy."

Nick's dark eyebrows were raised in surprise. "That's your work?"

"Don't sound so surprised, Mr. Armitage. I can do more than cook and clean, you know!"

"I can see that." Nick laughed. "They are very good, I must say. Are they local images?"

"Yes, of course." Izzy moved across to the window and pulled the curtain aside. "The Cascades you will find in our town's botanical gardens, and the poppet-head, well, there are a few of those around the town." Izzy flashed him that disarming smile, and then she was gone, the door closing quietly behind her.

Nick opened his suitcase. It seemed that Joe had chosen the right place for him to stay if it was information he was seeking. He was suddenly looking forward to the adventure.

*

At precisely six-thirty, Nick walked down the staircase and along the passage to the Ladies' Lounge. He had swapped his suit, collar and tie, for a pale blue open-neck shirt and a navy blazer. The bathroom had been free, and so he had shaved the dark stubble from his chin and tamed his thick thatch of black hair.

Laughter was erupting from the lounge as he stood in the doorway. The woman - Izzy - spotted him hovering and hurried towards him. She had removed the headscarf, allowing her short blonde hair to tumble free, and her bright red dress floated around her, reminding Nick of a nymph.

"There you are, Mr. Armitage!" She grabbed his arm. "Come and meet my husband." He was ushered towards a large man with a balding head, and an impressive handlebar moustache. Grinning widely, he extended his hand towards Nick, as Izzy introduced them. "Darling, I'd like you to meet Mr. Nick Armitage." She turned towards Nick. "Nick, this is my husband, Harry."

The two men shook hands, as Harry Dalton's voice boomed out: "Welcome to Bendigo, Nick!"

"Thank-you." Nick winced under the pressure of Harry's large hand.

"I believe you are writing an article about our wonderful town for the Sydney paper?"

"Er – yes, that's right." Nick flexed his fingers as they were released.

"Well, you've come to the right place for information, young man." Harry laughed. "Mrs. O'Malley can surely tell you all you need to know."

Jean O'Malley, who had been listening to the exchange, stepped forward, her cheeks flushed. "Don't believe everything this man tells you," she said gruffly. "I've been here a long time, but I wouldn't say I know everything."

Nick smiled warmly. "Whatever you can tell me about the people here, will certainly be useful." *How long was he going to have to play this game?*

"Hello!" A childish voice made Nick look down. The little blonde girl he'd seen in the courtyard was staring up at him, her blue eyes wide. "I'm Freya."

Nick bent and took her hand. "Hello, Freya. I'm Nick."

"Are you staying here?"

"Yes, I am."

"How long?"

"I don't know. Maybe a week?"

The child looked up at her mother, a frown creasing her brow. "How long is that, mummy?"

"It's seven days, Freya, now stop asking questions, and sit at the table, please."

The child pouted but said no more. Instead, she clambered on to a chair at the table, which had been set for tea.

Nick glanced around the room, noticing that the other child he had seen earlier was not present.

"There were two children in the yard." Nick didn't realise he had spoken aloud.

"That was Gracie, my sister Jess's little girl." Izzy Dalton was smiling at him. "She likes to play here with Freya, and it gives her mother a break. She has a young baby."

"Oh, I see." Nick smiled a little self-consciously.

"Now if you'd like to sit here beside Harry, I'll have tea on the table shortly."

"Plonk yourself down here, Nick." Harry had pulled out a chair for him. "We don't stand on ceremony here."

Jean O'Malley shook her head. "Harry's not a local yet," she said wryly, looking in Nick's direction. "Don't let him shock you."

"I'm not easily shocked, Mrs. O'Malley."

"Good!"

Joe Hudson

The doorbell to one of Sydney's inner city terrace houses clanged as Joe Hudson released it, and he stood back and waited. He looked at his watch. It was twenty minutes past five. Footsteps were heard on the other side of the door, and it opened to reveal the large, impressive form of Clarence Bonner-Smythe. He frowned as he looked through the screen door.

"Yes!" His voice boomed across the neighbourhood.

Joe removed his hat. "Mr. Bonner-Smythe, remember me? Joe Hudson, Private Investigator."

There was silence for a brief moment, before Clarence's face erupted into a smile.

"I believe I do," he laughed. "Come in! Come in!"

The screen door opened, and Joe stepped into the hallway. He had been here before - three years ago, in fact, when Clarence Bonner-Smythe had requested his assistance in tracking down his son-in-law, Beauregarde DuBois.

"What brings you to this neighbourhood?" Clarence led the way to the sitting room, where a fire crackled in the grate, and two comfortable armchairs were drawn up to the heat. "I take it that this is not a social call." The remark hung in the air for a moment.

"No." Joe sat at his host's request. "No, it's not entirely a social call."

Clarence sat heavily in the opposite armchair. "If it's not 'entirely' a social call, then what is it?"

Joe flexed his fingers and stared into the fire for a moment before looking at Clarence. "I need some information on your son-in-law."

"You mean Beau?"

"I do."

Clarence stared at his guest, his brow furrowed, and his lips pursed. "What sort of information?"

Joe looked back at the fire. "I believe it's about three years since you asked me to track him down?"

"Indeed, it is, but I must inform you that he is no longer my son-in-law." The two men looked at each other. "No. Beau has recently re-married and is now living in Victoria."

"Bendigo?"

"Yes. How did you know that?"

"Maybe I'd better explain."

"I think you had, and while you're doing that, I'll pour us a drink. What will you have, Joe?" Clarence heaved himself out of the armchair. "From memory, you are a beer man, am I right?"

Joe laughed. "Yes, I am." He delved into his coat pocket and retrieved a crumpled piece of paper. Straightening it out, he waited for Clarence to hand him a glass of beer.

Clarence took the paper, in exchange for the glass. "What's this then?"

"It's a case that's come to my attention - a young woman who hasn't been seen around the Bendigo area for three years."

Clarence read the newspaper article and frowned. "What's this to do with Beau?"

"Nothing at all, except that a person of interest is known to him, and recently the two were involved in an incident."

Clarence poured himself a glass of wine and returned to his seat. "How do you know all this?"

"I visited the police station in Bendigo and discovered that this person had assaulted Dr. DuBois's wife, and had then thrown a brick through their bedroom window."

Clarence raised his eyebrows. He knew about the incident. "You're talking about a certain Sid O'Connor, I believe?"

It was Joe's turn to be surprised. "You know him?"

"I know of him, and I am aware of the incident." Clarence placed his glass carefully on the small table beside his chair. "Perhaps I had better explain."

"That would be helpful."

Clarence settled back in the armchair, folded his hands on his lap, and looked fully at Joe.

"First of all, when Beau was returned to us three years ago, he was in bad shape, and spent a good six months recovering from the shellshock that had affected him during the war. His marriage to my daughter, Celia, was over, and she re-married." He cleared his throat, as he tried to remember the details. "Eventually he was able to regain his registration as a doctor, and he worked damned hard to assist the recovery of other soldiers who were suffering from the same complaint.

I remember he was in Melbourne, speaking at one of the hospitals about his work, and he visited Bendigo, primarily, I think, to see the woman who had befriended him during his time there. Her husband had been wounded in France." His brow puckered. "I'm not sure of the finer details, but her husband died of the Spanish Flu at the end of the war." He paused. "Beau kept in touch with her, and eventually asked her to marry him."

"He moved to Bendigo?"

"Not immediately. He came back here to continue his work for a time. Look, there's a lot of water gone under this bridge, and I don't know how much you need to know."

"What about his wife? How well did she know Sid O'Connor?"

"Jess?"

"Is that her name?"

"Yes." Clarence shrugged. "I don't know, but he had been her woodman in the past."

"They had history?"

"I suppose they did." Clarence stared into the fire. "What's the connection between Sid O'Connor and the missing woman?"

"They were a couple for a time before she suddenly disappeared."

"Suddenly?"

"Joe shrugged. "Well, nobody has seen her since then."

"You think Sid might have had something to do with it?"

"At this stage I can't say, but I know she did have a child."

"Oh? Sid's child?"

"We don't know that either, but I have a young colleague in Bendigo at present, and he will be looking into all those details." He added hastily, "Covertly, I might add."

"I see. How can I help?"

"If you remember anything at all that Doctor DuBois may have said about Sid O'Connor, I would be keen to know of it."

"Certainly." Clarence paused. "So, you're not implicating Beau in any way, in the disappearance of this young woman?"

"No, I'm not implicating Doctor DuBois in *any* way."

The front door slammed, and a woman's voice could be heard in the hallway.

"I'm sorry I'm late, Clarence!" There was a slight pause. "It's beginning to rain out there, and I'm afraid I got wet." They heard her laugh. "I forgot my umbrella, didn't I?"

A young woman appeared in the doorway, and her laugh subsided as she saw that Clarence was not alone. "Oh! I didn't realise you had company, Clarence."

"Angela, m'dear." Clarence rose from his chair. "This is Mr. Joe Hudson, Private Investigator."

Brown eyes widened, as Angela shook the water from her short dark hair. "Private Investigator?" She stepped quickly into the room. "Nothing's wrong, is it? Nobody's missing?"

Clarence took her arm and pressed her gently into the chair he had recently vacated. "Nobody you know, m'dear." He turned to Joe. "Joe, I'd like you to meet my dear friend, Angela Rickard. Angela and Jess are very good friends."

"Jess?" Angela spun around on the chair. "What's happened to Jess?"

"Nothing, m'dear." Clarence took her hands as they fluttered against her breast. "Calm down and Joe will explain to you why he's here."

Angela gulped loudly as she turned slowly to face Joe. "I'm listening."

*

Angela slumped back in her chair as she heard the front door close. A few seconds ticked by before she heard Clarence re-enter the room. He walked straight to the sideboard and poured himself a glass of wine.

"What do you suppose he was really saying?" whispered Angela. "That Beau is indeed implicated?"

"No." Clarence shook his head as he sat opposite Angela. "I think he's just trying to establish some facts about Beau's relationship with the notorious Sid O'Connor." Clarence took a sip of wine. "The more I hear about that man, the less I like him."

"Poor Jess! She doesn't need any more drama in her life. She has a new baby, and that should be enough for her to deal with." Angela sighed heavily. "So this Joe Hudson has a colleague in Bendigo at present, snooping around looking for incriminating information." It was a statement rather than a question.

"I believe so, but 'under cover', as they so politely put it."

"Should I telephone Jess and tell her what's going on?"

Clarence looked up, startled. "No, m'dear. Let's leave it to Joe and his offsider."

Angela smiled mischievously. "Why, Clarence, it wasn't so long ago that you did your own sleuthing and chose to ignore the authorities."

Clarence coloured slightly. "That was different. We were looking for Beau, and it wasn't three years after he had last been seen. It was only a week."

Angela's brow furrowed. "Why do you think it's taken this long to go looking for her? I mean, she must have some family somewhere." She shrugged.

"Not necessarily, m'dear. Not everybody is that fortunate."

"Friends? Workmates? Neighbours?"

"Apparently not." Clarence leaned over and patted her knee. "Anyway, it's not for us to go delving this time." He smiled at her worried expression.

"I'm concerned for Jess and Beau. They don't need to be implicated in something shoddy."

"I'm sure they won't be. Now, what's for tea, eh? Celia has decided to stay at home tonight."

"Good!"

Clarence's daughter, Celia, was more than Angela could cope with at this time. Since her husband's untimely death, the previous year, Celia had been a constant drain on her father and Angela, as she negotiated life without Matthew. Her role as the new head of Matthew's Medical Practice, daunted her from time to time, and she would cry on her father's shoulder, pleading for him to interfere when situations became too much for her. Angela was aware that Celia's personality had a lot to do with the way situations flared up from time to time. Diplomacy was not her strong point.

Angela sighed. Yes, she could do without Celia's presence this evening.

"We're having chicken in mustard sauce, when I get myself organised." Angela rose to her feet, but Clarence placed a hand on her arm.

"Why don't we go to Mario's?" He smiled indulgently. "You've probably been cooking all day at the patisserie."

Angela's body relaxed. Mario's was an expensive restaurant on the waterfront, and one of Clarence's favourite places to dine. "That sounds like heaven, Clarence, and yes, I have been cooking all day. Business is starting to pick up again after the flu epidemic."

"Good! I'll get my hat."

*

Joe climbed the steps to his inner city office and fumbled in his jacket pocket for the keys. The evening was approaching fast, and the rain had set in. After running to catch a crowded tram from the Bonner-Smythe residence, he was soaked. Water dripped from his hat, making rivulets down his chin. Joe brushed impatiently at his wet face, before choosing the right key for the lock. The door opened with an ominous creak. The dark room swallowed him immediately, and he felt for the light switch on the wall beside the door. Feeble light wavered and sputtered before casting an eerie glow over the crowded space that Joe called his office. He shut the door with a bang.

The desk that dominated the small room was overflowing with papers, as was the shelving that made up much of the rear wall. Joe threw his hat and keys on the desk and sat heavily on the swivel chair.

"I must clean up some of this mess!" he muttered to himself, as he cleared a small space on the desk. Emptying his pockets of the small pieces of paper that had been crumpled there, he searched for the one piece that had a telephone number on it. There it was. He straightened it out as he thought about Nick's opinion of his methods. Disastrous!

Turning in his chair, Joe reached for the telephone that hung on the wall alongside the overflowing shelving. He peered at the number on the paper. Water had smudged the ink and so the numbers were almost illegible. However, Joe prided himself on his ability to remember numbers, and the Grey Goose Hotel was one of them. He grabbed the receiver and turned the handle vigorously.

After the lengthy process of going through the Sydney Exchange and then the Bendigo Exchange, Joe finally heard a loud male voice issuing from the earpiece. He dragged it away from his ear.

"Grey Goose Hotel! Harry Dalton speaking!" Joe hesitated for a moment. "Hello! Anybody there!"

"Er- yes." Joe paused again. "I'd like to speak with Nick Armitage, if he's there, please."

"Certainly! Who will I say is calling? His boss?"

"Yes, that's right. Is he there?"

"He certainly is! He's having tea with us. I'll get him for you."

"Thank-you."

Joe waited until finally he heard Nick's voice. "Joe! How are you?"

"Well enough," he muttered. "You've arrived safely, obviously."

Joe heard Nick laugh. "I've only just arrived, Joe. You don't expect me to have anything for you yet, surely?"

"No, of course not. I just thought I'd let you know that I've been to see Mr. Bonner-Smythe."

"Did he tell you anything of any use?"

"Not really, but it does appear that Mrs. DuBois has a history with the same Sid O'Connor. Her name's Jess, by the way, and she has a young baby. DuBois is a doctor in the town, so he should be easy enough to track down."

"I dare say he will." Nick paused. "By the way, Joe, I met your daughter on the train coming down from Sydney." Joe was silent. "Joe, did you hear me? I said I met Amelia."

"I heard you, Nick." Joe laughed suddenly. "You worked that out quickly."

"Are you extending?" a female voice interrupted.

"Yeah," said Joe quickly.

"Honestly, Joe, did you have to go to such lengths to make sure I could handle the job?"

"You sound a bit miffed, Nick."

"No, not really, but it has complicated things. Amelia is determined to help me…"

There was a long stretch of silence.

"Nick! Are you there, Nick? Damned fool things these telephones!"

"Yes, I'm here, Joe." Nick had lowered his voice. "Mrs. Dalton, the publican's wife, just walked by. How long do you want me to keep up this 'journalist' thing?"

"Well, if you think people are not going to clam up on you, I guess it's up to you."

"Thank-you, Joe. Now we are going to be cut off any second, so I'll say goodnight."

"Yeah, okay Nick. I'll wait to hear from you."

"Good idea."

The line went dead.

Joe replaced the receiver and turned back to the mess on his desk. He wanted to speak with Amelia, but he would have to wait until she telephoned him. He suspected that his ex-wife would not be impressed to receive a call from him.

In the meantime, his stomach was growling, so it was time for him to visit a nearby pub and refuel the inner man. Joe picked up his hat from the desk, grabbed his keys and headed towards the door. As he was about to switch off the light, the telephone rang.

It was a call from Melbourne. He waited, knowing that it would be Amelia.

"Joe?"

Joe ground his teeth. *Why couldn't she call him 'dad' like every other daughter?*

"Yes, Amelia? How did you know I would be here?"

There was a faint laugh. "You're always there."

"Point taken." Joe pulled the chair towards him and sat heavily. "So, you've met Nick already?"

Amelia laughed. "I have, and I can see why you've kept him from me all this time."

"Yeah, well you do have a reputation. I don't know what possessed me to let you two handle this job. I must have rocks in my head."

"You're getting old, Joe, that's your problem. You can't keep up the pace anymore."

"And you have no respect for your elders." There was a bite in his tone.

"Since when did you earn my respect, Joe?"

"Humph! I guess I asked for that."

"I had a good teacher, Joe. Remember?"

"Yeah."

"Are you extending?" a cheerful voice interrupted.

"Yes," said Amelia swiftly. "Joe, I'm planning on a visit to the Registrar of Births, deaths and marriages tomorrow, to check on a few things. Is there anything else you can tell me about Phyllis Powell? Was she married?"

"I don't believe so. According to the Bendigo Police, her relationships were all casual."

"That doesn't help me much. When was she last seen in Bendigo?"

"Early 1917." There was silence at the other end of the line. "When are you meeting up with Nick?"

"When I've got something concrete to give him."

"Keep in mind, Amelia, that you are there to work with him, not to sleep with him."

Amelia laughed softly. "I'll keep that in mind."

"Incidentally, Nick wants to drop the 'journalist' thing, as he put it."

"Fair enough. He's a snoop, not a journalist."

"I thought they were the same thing."

"No, not really. Anyway, before we're cut off, I'll let you know if I find anything more about the missing woman. Goodbye, Joe." There was a pause. "Mother sends her love."

The line crackled, and before Joe could respond to the last comment, it went dead. Joe replaced the receiver with a thump. *Sends her love, my eye!* He gritted his teeth. He and Maud had not been together for a very long time. On the odd occasion when there was contact, it was never without tension.

As he picked up his hat and keys for the second time, Joe thought about the days, thirty years ago, when he met the glamorous waitress, Maud Tilapia, with her stunning dark looks and smouldering eyes. They had fallen immediately in love, and for a few years enjoyed a passionate but volatile relationship. When Amelia arrived, the passion waned, but the fiery arguments continued until the day he walked away, leaving everything behind him.

Amelia hated him for a long time, until she was mature enough to understand that not all marriages were made in heaven. She resumed a distant relationship with him as she followed her own career path in a similar direction to his.

"The apple didn't fall very far from the tree, did it, Amelia?" he remembered saying to her once.

Joe pulled his coat around him as he headed out into the wet night.

Collecting Information

The following morning, after a refreshing night's sleep, Nick made his way to the Lounge for breakfast. Izzy Dalton was coming from the kitchen, a large saucepan in her hands.

"Here, let me carry that for you," said Nick as he reached for the saucepan.

"Careful!" Izzy warned. "It's very hot."

"Porridge, if I'm not mistaken." Nick grinned as he sniffed the air.

"I hope you like porridge." Izzy followed him to the lounge. "Just put it on the table over there." She pointed to a long table, set with plates, cutlery and bowls of stewed fruit.

"It looks and smells delicious," said Nick, as he placed the large saucepan carefully on the table.

"I hope you're hungry, Nick." Harry Dalton appeared in the doorway, rubbing his hands together as he surveyed the table. "Isobel, where are the bread rolls?"

"They're coming," she said lightly, as she flicked a tea towel at him. "Have patience, Harry."

Harry winked at Nick. "Just stirring the pot, Nick," he laughed. "You'll get used to us, if you stick around long enough."

Shaking her head, Izzy headed for the door. "Find a seat, Nick, and try to ignore whatever Harry says to you. I'll be back in a moment with the bread, and Jean, and Freya, if I can find her."

"Freya's outside with the dog," offered Harry, as he served himself a bowl of stewed apples.

"In that case, Harry," said Izzy sweetly, "would you mind bringing her in for breakfast?"

Harry hesitated, before placing his bowl on the table. "If you insist, my dear."

"I do."

Nick smiled to himself as he pulled a chair out from the table and sat. He thought of his parents, and the formal breakfasts at home, where his father was usually absorbed in the morning newspaper, and any conversation was as a result of something he had just read. His mother was more often than not, pre-occupied with making sure that the eggs were cooked to Hugh's liking, and that the toast was not burnt. Nick felt sure that breakfast here at the Grey Goose would be a far cry from those he was used to.

Izzy Dalton appeared with Jean, and behind them, Nick could hear Harry chastising his daughter.

"No, Freya!" Harry was saying loudly, "I've told you before that the water in Mack's bowl is not for you to wash your hands in. Now, off to the bathroom, and wash them properly!"

"Good morning, Nick!" Jean O'Malley smiled broadly at him. "Freya is up to her usual trick, I see."

Izzy raised her eyebrows. "Strong-willed, just like her father," she said airily.

Jean sent her a withering look. "Humph! Her mother more likely." She turned to Nick. "Don't let the breakfast get cold, while we argue the point."

"Who's arguing?" Izzy dropped a pile of warm bread rolls on to a large plate. "Help yourself, Nick. We don't stand on ceremony here." *Where had he heard that before?*

Jean raised her eyebrows, muttered, "We need butter and jam," and shuffled back to the kitchen, passing Harry and Freya on the way in.

"Are we clean now?" Izzy grabbed her daughter's hands and turned them over to inspect them. "Right! Sit at the table, Freya, and I'll get your porridge."

Nick, feeling somewhat bemused, waited while Izzy served a portion for Freya, and then he reached for a bowl. He hesitated a moment longer than necessary.

"Dive in!" said Harry, giving him a nudge. "There's plenty there."

Jean returned at that moment with a tray, on which she had butter, strawberry jam, a jug of cream and a bowl of sugar. "There! That should do it," she said as she set the tray on the table.

After a few minutes of plate shuffling and serving, everyone was finally seated, and breakfast began in earnest. Harry opened the conversation with an enquiry as to Nick's first night in a country pub.

"I was very comfortable, thank-you," Nick replied, after swallowing a mouthful of hot porridge.

"Normally we would have eggs," said Jean solemnly, "but Ben's chooks are not laying at present."

"Ben is our nephew," said Izzy, in answer to Nick's puzzled look. "My sister's boy? They live just up the street, and Ben likes to earn a little pocket-money, by supplying us with eggs."

"Oh, I see."

"He's ten-years-old and quite the little businessman." Izzy smiled at Nick. "If you want to write about local families, and how they survived the war, look no further than my sister, Jess, and her three children. Their father died of the Spanish Flu, over in England, just after the Armistice." Izzy wrenched a bread roll apart, and Nick watched as she scraped butter on to it. There was anger in her movements. "It wasn't easy for them; I can tell you!"

"Now, now Izzy!" Harry tried to placate his wife. "I thought we'd all moved on from there."

"We have," said Izzy sharply, "but if Nick wants a human-interest story, there's one right here."

"I'll keep that in mind." Nick put down his spoon. Joe had said that DuBois's wife was called Jess, and that she had a young baby. His job might have suddenly become easy.

*

Nick spent the morning walking the streets of Bendigo, amazed by the architectural splendour of the buildings in the centre of the town. Standing beside the grand Shamrock Hotel, he gazed across the busy street towards the Courthouse and the Post Office, solid granite structures, built to withstand the test of time. As he looked, the Post Office clock began to strike the hour. It was ten o'clock.

Nick shifted his gaze left towards what looked like botanical gardens and decided that he wanted to check out the Cascades. Sprinting across the wide street, and dodging a tram and several vehicles, he made it safely to the other side. He passed the Post Office with its clock still reverberating and turned the corner into a small street that led him to a creek, spanned by a wrought-iron bridge. This brought him into parkland with Elm trees, winding gravel paths and garden beds clothed in vibrant spring colours. Rosalind Park, he mused. Somewhere in here he hoped to find the Cascades that Izzy Dalton had replicated on the wall of the hotel. Nick strode across the grass towards a steep rise that would surely be an ideal place for water to tumble.

As he got closer he heard water bubbling and gurgling as it made its way down a man-made rocky cascade. Nick ran up the hill to get a better view, and it was just as Izzy Dalton had painted it, with the mist rising, the pond at the bottom of the hill and water spouting from a glistening fountain. Several people were seated on the grass, enjoying the vapours created by the movement of the water. It was mesmerizing. Nick was tempted to remove his shoes and socks and plunge his bare feet into the cooling flow, but he opted to join those who were seated on the grass and closed his eyes for half an hour. He knew he had been there that long, because the Post Office clock chimed the half hour. Reluctantly he stood, brushed the grass from his trousers and headed back down the hill. He had work to do.

*

Half an hour later, Nick sat in the bar of the Grey Goose, thumbing his way idly through the local newspaper. Harry and Jean were behind the bar, and several customers were seated at the counter, chatting amicably with the publicans. Harry brought him a beer, as he sat at one of the small tables by a window.

"Thirsty, Nick?" He placed the glass carefully on the table.

"Thank-you, Harry. Yes, I am, rather. Sightseeing is hot work."

Harry grinned. "Checking out our town, eh?"

"It's a very beautiful town." Nick moved the newspaper away from the glass. "I didn't expect to see such grand buildings."

"They're grand, alright," said Harry proudly. "Did you see the gardens?"

"Yes, and the cascades that your wife has painted on the wall outside."

Harry grinned. "Izzy would love to be let loose with a paintbrush all around this place, but I have to pull the reins." He chuckled. "You should have seen our shop in Swan Hill. I'm sure the customers came purely to see Izzy's work."

"She's very good."

"Isn't she?"

Harry moved away towards the next table, and Nick turned back to his newspaper. As he did, a tall young man swaggered through the main doors, and seated himself at the bar. Jean O'Malley greeted him warmly, and Nick pricked up his ears as he heard their exchange.

"Well, if it's not Billy Maitland!" she exclaimed. "Don't see you so often these days, Billy."

"Got extra shifts at the rail yards, Mrs. O'Malley." Nick noticed that his voice was very husky.

"Oh! Working you hard, are they?"

"Yeah."

"What about your mate, Sid? Haven't seen him for a while, either."

"Nah! Albie's keepin' him out of mischief at the wood yard."

Jean pushed a beer glass towards Billy. "Beau did the right thing getting Albie Blake to take Sid under his wing."

"Yeah, he did." Billy shrugged, before lifting his beer.

"It's good to see that you two are mates again. There was a lot of ill-feeling for a long time."

"Yeah." Billy downed his beer, slapped some money on the bar, and stood to leave. "Better get goin'. Thanks, Mrs. O'Malley. I'll be back for some sandwiches later."

Jean nodded as she picked up the empty glass. "Sure, Billy."

Harry moved back behind the bar. "Maitland was in a hurry today?"

"He's doing extra time at the rail yards."

Nick drained his glass and headed across to the bar.

"Same again, Nick?" Jean held up the glass.

"No, thank-you, Mrs. O'Malley." He paused. "That young man who was just here - "

"Billy Maitland?"

Nick nodded. "What's wrong with his voice?"

Jean picked up a cloth and began wiping the top of the bar. "He was gassed during the war." Her hand stopped suddenly, and she pointed a finger at Nick. "Now there's someone who could tell you a good story. He was one of the few of our young men to make it home from the war. He's had some experiences; I can tell you."

"Thank-you, Mrs. O'Malley. I'll probably follow up on that."

"It will be worth your while, I'm sure." As Nick turned to leave, she called after him. "Sandwiches will be out soon, if you're interested."

Nick waved a hand. "I need to go out, but I'll be back a little later."

"Righto! I'll keep you some."

"Thanks, Mrs. O'Malley."

"Call me Jean!"

Nick smiled in her direction before heading out the door and on to the street.

*

Nick jogged in the direction of the town. He needed to speak with Joe and using the telephone at the hotel was not an option. Hoping that the Post Office had a public telephone, Nick headed in that direction, dodging the traffic as he crossed the streets. Hopefully Joe would be in his office. He looked quickly at his watch, just as the Post Office clock chimed the three-quarter hour. He needed to hurry if he was to catch Joe before he headed to the nearest pub for lunch.

Bounding up the Post Office steps, Nick looked around for a public telephone. There were no obvious signs of one, so he pushed open the heavy doors and stepped inside. The clerk who was standing behind the massive wooden counter smiled at him as he approached.

"Yes, sir, what can I do for you today?"

"Do you have a public telephone?" enquired Nick, a little breathlessly.

"We do, sir." He pointed towards the far wall. "Over there, sir. You can pay me for your call when you've finished. Is it a local call, sir?"

"No, Sydney."

"Ah! You do know how to operate these things, do you, sir?"

Nick smiled. "Yes, I do."

"Goodo, sir." The clerk looked relieved. "I'll leave you to it."

Nick hurried across to where the telephone hung on the wall, and lifting the receiver, gave the handle a quick turn.

"Bendigo telephone exchange," said a bright female voice. "How can I help you?"

"I want to put a call through to Sydney," replied Nick.

"Certainly, sir. Hold the line, please."

Nick waited and eventually heard another female voice asking for the number. Nick gave her Joe's number and prayed silently that he was there to take the call.

The moments ticked by, and Nick was about to give up when he heard Joe's loud voice.

"Joe Hudson speaking."

"Joe, it's Nick. I have some news for you."

"Already? Wonderful! Let me hear it."

"Its not wonderful news," said Nick hurriedly, "but I do seem to have stumbled across all our key players in an extraordinary stroke of luck. I'll continue to play the part you've given me for the time being, in the hope that I can flush out the information you want."

"Excellent! Has Amelia landed on your doorstep yet?"

"No, but I fully expect that she will. Have you spoken with her?"

"Yes, she called me after I'd spoken to you last night." Joe laughed. "Don't discount her, Nick."

"That would be foolish, Joe."

"She was going to check the Registry of births, deaths and marriages, to see if anything comes up there. Keep digging, Nick, and let me know what you find."

"Of course."

"Are you extending?"

"No," said Nick sharply. "I'll talk to you soon, Joe."

"Sure thing, Nick."

The line went dead. Nick searched in his pockets for loose change and headed to the counter.

"How much?" he asked the clerk.

"Two and sixpence, sir."

Nick found the right change, handed it to the clerk, and with a smile, crossed the squeaky linoleum floor to the door.

Soon he was sprinting back along the streets that had suddenly become familiar to him, and within minutes was pushing open the door of the Grey Goose. Jean O'Malley greeted him with a smile.

"Just in time, Nick. Cheese and pickle sandwiches today."

"Lovely."

"Beer, Nick?" shouted Harry.

"Thanks, Harry."

Breathing heavily, Nick sat at the nearest table. He wasn't as fit as he thought he was. It was time to take up some running again. Pounding the streets of Bendigo might be a little different to pounding the streets of Sydney.

Izzy Dalton appeared beside him, a tray of fresh sandwiches in her hands. "You look as though you could do with some sustenance," she laughed.

Nick smiled wryly. "I used to run every morning, but I think I'm out of practise."

"There's some lovely bushland to run in, not far from here," said Izzy as she placed two rounds of sandwiches on a plate and slid them towards Nick. "Past the railway station, and head east."

Nick nodded as he picked up a sandwich. "I'll remember that."

The sound of a childish squeal at the door, made Izzy turn. Nick looked up to see the golden-haired little girl he'd seen the day before. A woman stood behind her, and they waited for Izzy to make her way towards them, after placing the tray of sandwiches on the bar. The woman had golden hair, just like the child, and Izzy greeted her with a warm hug. Nick couldn't hear what was said, but he presumed the woman must be Jess, Izzy's sister. He watched as Izzy shepherded her sister and niece out into the passage, closing the door behind her.

"That was Izzy's sister, Jess." Harry appeared beside Nick and placed a beer glass in front of him.

"I thought she must be," replied Nick.

Harry frowned. "How did you figure that out? They don't even look alike."

Nick smiled at Harry's bemused expression. "I saw the child playing with Freya yesterday. She's like her mother."

"Oh." Harry grinned. "I thought you must have been exceptionally clever to work that one out, but of course, as a journalist, you probably have to put two and two together and make four."

"Exactly."

Harry moved away from the table, leaving Nick to resume his lunch. Yes, two and two always had to make four in his line of work. As he pondered on exactly what was his line of work, the door opened and Billy Maitland sauntered in. Nick watched him grab a handful of sandwiches from the tray that Izzy had left on the bar, and seeing him looking around for somewhere to sit, Nick beckoned him over. It was time to strike while the iron was hot.

Billy sat opposite Nick, who slid a plate across the table towards him.

"Thanks, mate." Blue eyes stared at Nick. "You're new around 'ere."

"Yes, I am." Nick held out his hand. "Nick Armitage."

Billy wiped a grubby hand down the blue boiler suit he was wearing, before shaking Nick's hand.

"Billy Maitland," he rasped.

"Pleased to meet you, Billy."

Billy picked up a sandwich. "Where're ya from, Nick?"

"Sydney."

"Blimey! You're a long way from 'ome." Billy munched on his sandwich. "What brings ya t' Bendigo?"

"My job."

"Which is?"

"I'm a journalist."

Billy choked and thumped himself on the chest. "A journalist?"

"I'm here to write a story about the people of this post-war town." Nick paused. "Mrs. O'Malley tells me that you were gassed during the war, and that's how you lost your voice." Billy was eyeing him suspiciously. "I was in here when you came in earlier, and I overheard your conversation with Mrs.

O'Malley."

Billy put the half-eaten sandwich on the plate. "I s'pose that's how you get your information – listenin' to people's conversations." Nick winced at the indignation in his tone.

"Not usually, Billy. I'm more circumspect than that. I like to get my information firsthand."

"Want a beer, Billy?" Harry called out from behind the bar.

"Haven't got time, Harry." Billy picked up the half-eaten sandwich. "So ya wanna know about my war experiences, do ya?"

"Not exactly, Billy. I'd like to know how it's been for you since you returned home – how you've been accepted back into the community - your friends - that kind of thing."

"Uh-huh." Billy swallowed the last of his sandwich and wiped a hand across his mouth. "I gotta go to work now, (the late shift) but I can talk to ya tomorrow mornin' if ya like?"

"I'd like that, Billy." The younger man stood up to leave. "Shall we say here at ten o'clock?"

"Yeah, sure. See ya then." Billy leaned over the table before heading for the door. "Ya might wanna bring a pencil and some paper."

Nick smiled. "I'll do that, Billy."

The Gathering

Izzy and Jess sat on chairs in the courtyard, sipping on lemonade while they watched their little girls play with Mack. The sun was warm on their faces, and the perimeter wall offered protection from the wind. Izzy sat back with a sigh of contentment.

"I haven't felt this relaxed for a long time, Jess." She sipped lazily on her lemonade. "Harry and I did the right thing moving here." Her eyes were closed when she spoke again. "Are you glad we moved here?"

Jess turned, startled by the question. "Of course, Izzy. Why wouldn't I be?"

Izzy shrugged; her eyes still closed. "I don't know. I thought maybe you find me too overbearing now that I'm just down the road." Her eyes flicked open.

"Don't be silly." Jess's green eyes were suddenly shadowed. "It's wonderful having you here and…"

"And what?" Izzy put her glass on the grass beside her chair. "Come on, Jess, out with it?"

"I was going to say and having Beau's sister, Charlotte, here as well, has certainly been…shall we say, interesting."

"Interesting?" Izzy swivelled to look at her sister. "Is everything alright, Jess? I mean Charlotte spent the past thirty-two years in a Convent, living as a Nun. I suppose that must bring its issues."

"Not exactly, Izzy, but the house is rather crowded, and at times I feel a little overwhelmed."

Izzy sat back. "That's because you've just had a baby, Jess. Come to think of it, where is she?"

Jess sighed. "Charlotte is looking after her."

Izzy laughed. "A little confusing, isn't it? Two Charlotte's in the same house."

"It is rather. We've decided to call the baby Lottie, while Charlotte is still with us."

"That's a good idea, Jess. Has Charlotte thought about looking for work?"

"Yes, but what can she do? She has religious training, but not much else."

"Can't Beau get her a job at the hospital, as a sort of Chaplain?" Izzy spread her hands. "I can see her gliding through the wards, offering comfort to the sick."

"Don't let Charlotte hear you say that – gliding, indeed!"

"Well, you have to admit that she does seem to glide when she walks. It must be from having to be quiet all the time." Izzy shuddered. "I can't imagine anything worse."

"No, I daresay you can't."

The sisters were quiet for a time, as the happy shrieks of their offspring sounded around them.

"I've just had a thought," said Izzy suddenly.

Jess groaned. She knew where her sister's thoughts sometimes led. "I don't think I want to hear it."

"How well does Charlotte get on with Charles?"

Jess sat bolt upright. "No, Izzy! Absolutely not! Have you no shame?"

A wet tennis ball landed in Izzy's lap. She picked it up gingerly and threw it towards the garden wall. The terrier tore after it, followed by the two giggling children.

"Hear me out, Jess," said Izzy patiently. "I haven't finished."

"I know what you were going to say, and I absolutely forbid it! Charles is still reeling from the shock of losing Margaret. How can you…"

"Jess!" Izzy interrupted. "I'm not suggesting that we throw them into each other's arms."

"Aren't you?" Jess's tone was sharp.

"No, I'm not. I thought maybe Charlotte could do some housekeeping for Charles."

"He already has Audrey Maitland, and that's as far as I'm going with this conversation, Izzy." Jess stood up quickly, brushing her skirt as she turned to leave.

"Sit down, Jess." Izzy grabbed her arm, forcing her back to the chair. "Alright, so that's a dead end. We'll think of something to occupy Charlotte. I have something else to discuss with you."

Jess was forced back on to the chair. "What!"

"We have a young man staying here at present, and…"

"Who are you going to match-make him with?" interrupted Jess icily.

Izzy frowned. "Nobody." She was losing patience with her sister. "He's a journalist from Sydney, and he's here to write a story about the people of this town."

"And?"

"I told him he could look no further than around here. I told him that your story about the war and how it affected you, was worth telling."

Jess rounded on her sister. "Izzy, you didn't?"

The tennis ball skimmed across the grass towards them, and Izzy scooped it up, throwing it as hard as she could. "Yes, I did."

"Honestly, Izzy, you can be so exasperating at times!"

"I know." Izzy gave her sister a nudge. "He's rather handsome, Jess." She giggled. "Actually, if Charlotte is prepared to look after the children this evening, you and Beau come for tea and meet him. His name is Nick Armitage and he's very charming."

"I'm sure he is." Jess raised her eyes skyward. "What time?"

"Six-thirty, when all the regulars have gone." Izzy laughed. "You will like him, Jess. He's inside now, talking to Billy Maitland." She sat back on her chair. "It will be such fun. Now I have to think of something special to have for tea."

*

Nick changed his shirt for a white one with a buttoned-down collar. They were having guests for tea, and he needed to look a little less casual. He surveyed his reflection in the bathroom mirror. Would he pass as a journalist, he wondered? Investigative journalism was the field he had suddenly found himself in, and tonight would prove his capabilities. The DuBois's would be dining with them, and he had to get the question-and-answer mix right, or they might become suspicious of his motives. Tonight, he had to keep it within the bounds of 'general information'. It could turn out to be a very interesting evening.

After taming his unruly dark hair, and dabbing on a splash of cologne, Nick picked up his towel and toiletry bag and sauntered back to his room. It was nearly six-thirty, and Harry would have tipped the last of the drinkers on to the street. Hurrying footsteps along the passage outside his room meant that Harry was probably on his way to change clothes for the evening. Nick waited for a few moments before stepping out of his room and making his way to the staircase. The sound of laughter reached his ears. Trying to remember the last time there was laughter in his own household, Nick headed for the Lounge. He stopped at the door, and three pairs of eyes turned to look in his direction.

Izzy Dalton, resplendent in a bright pink flowing gown, moved towards him, smiling broadly.

"Nick!" she exclaimed. "Come and meet my sister and brother-in-law."

Nick felt his arm securely held as he was led across the room to where a man and woman stood watching him. The man was slightly built, clean-shaven and grey-haired, but it was the scar running down his face that took Nick by surprise. He tried not to stare at it as they shook hands.

"Nick Armitage, this is my brother-in-law, Beau DuBois, and my sister, Jess," Izzy was saying.

"I'm pleased to meet you both."

"Likewise," said Beau pleasantly.

Nick turned towards Jess and was met with an intense stare. He shook her hand warmly, sensing uncertainty in those green eyes. He would have to put her at her ease.

"I suppose Mrs. Dalton has told you that I'm a journalist, here on a mission." Nick smiled at her anxious face. "Have no fear. I'm not here to give you the third degree. Conversation is all I need."

"Relax, Jess." Izzy squeezed her arm. "Didn't I tell you that Nick is charming?"

Nick raised his eyebrows. "Charming?" he laughed. "Don't believe everything you hear, Jess."

"I don't," said Jess tightly.

Izzy, sensing the tension in her sister, steered her towards the table. "It will be alright, Jess," she whispered, as she glanced apologetically at Nick.

He turned to Beau, whose eyes were on his wife. "What do you do, Beau?"

Beau frowned briefly. "I'm a doctor, Nick."

"Excellent! Then you'd have some stories to tell, I imagine?"

The grey eyes flickered. "I'm sorry, Nick, but if it's medical information you want, I can't help you."

"No! No!" Nick felt suddenly embarrassed. "I'm not fishing for that kind of information." He paused. "We seem to have started off on the wrong foot. Let's begin again, shall we? How long have you been practising here?"

"Not long. I was previously in Sydney."

"Sydney, eh? Whereabouts?"

"I worked at a facility called Serendipity Lodge."

"I've heard of that. Isn't that where they treat returning soldiers who have ongoing - problems?"

Beau nodded. "It is. I was also a patient there at one time."

Nick's eyes widened. "Really?" He lowered his voice. "That —er- that scar on your face -"

"A war injury."

"Are you prepared to talk about it?"

"No, I'm sorry."

Nick shrugged. "I shouldn't have asked." He saw Jess watching him from across the room. "Perhaps we should join your wife."

At that moment Jean and Harry appeared, laden with trays of food.

"Time to eat!" Jean began arranging the dishes on the table. "Come on! It will soon get cold. Where's Freya?" She looked around the room.

"She's playing in your sitting room, Jean," said Izzy. "I'll get her."

Nick found himself seated beside Beau, with Jess across the table. He smiled at her, and received a half smile in return, before she looked down at her plate. He would have to be very careful with her, he realised. She didn't trust him, which was probably understandable. The two sisters were not alike, he deduced as he watched the two of them ladling stew on to their plates. Izzy was the outgoing one, whose smile was infectious, even now as she served her daughter. Jess was the quiet one; the one who could be resentful of his intrusion into their lives.

"There you are, Freya!" Izzy sat beside Jess. "Eat every mouthful, understand?"

Freya nodded her blonde head. Nick winked at her and received a wide grin in response.

Soon only the clatter of cutlery could be heard in the Lounge, as everyone concentrated on the food.

Harry was the one who finally broke the silence when he sat back and wiped a serviette across his mouth. "That was good. Thank-you, ladies." He looked across at Nick. "We have fine cooks in the country, don't you agree, Nick?"

"I certainly do."

Jean, who was seated alongside Nick, snorted loudly. "I can't take any credit for tonight's meal," she said, looking in Izzy's direction. "That was Isobel's creation."

"Well, I can't take credit for what's to follow." Izzy glanced at Jess. "My dear sister has made her famous scones for us to enjoy with a cup of tea. Jess is the only one who knows how to make scones. She tells me I'm too heavy-handed, and I finish up with rocks."

Everyone laughed, including Jess, and Nick noticed how her throat suffused with colour. Beau was watching her intently.

"I've tried to teach you, Izzy," said Jess quietly, "but you do like to attack the dough."

Izzy shrugged. "Oh, well, I can't be good at everything."

"You're a darned good artist," said Nick, and the others murmured their agreement. "I went to see the Cascades today. You have captured them brilliantly, Izzy. They are quite delightful."

"I'm so glad you think so." Izzy began to gather up the dirty plates. "I would like to do a lot more painting, but Harry thinks the mural in here is enough." All eyes turned to the end wall with its poppet-head and crouching miner with his gold pan. "So, I have to be content with that."

"Why Bendigo, Nick?" The question came suddenly from Beau, as Izzy hurried from the room. Grey eyes were studying him carefully. "It's a long way from Sydney."

Nick met his gaze. "Yes, it is, but Bendigo has such a rich history of gold and the Chinese migrants, and of course its magnificent architecture."

"But the people here are no different to those living in towns much closer to Sydney." Beau's grey eyes were watching him closely. "They are all adapting to post-war life."

"That's true." Nick shifted uncomfortably on his seat.

"So why Bendigo?"

"We go where we are sent, Beau." Nick shrugged. "My editor pointed to a spot on the map and said 'that's where you're going, Nick.'"

Beau frowned and was about to speak again when Izzy arrived with a tray of scones, jam and cream.

"Here we are! Tuck in, everybody."

The conversation stopped, while they all enjoyed Jess's scones. Nick felt

DuBois's eyes on him as he spread strawberry jam on the feather light scone. He had a feeling that here was a man who was perceptive enough to see through his little charade - a protective husband to a wife who had been through a lot over the past few years.

Nick smiled at Jess. "I must say I have not tasted such delicious scones before. I applaud you, Jess." He clapped his hands lightly.

Jess smiled. "Thank-you, Mr. Armitage."

"Call me Nick, please?" Nick put down his knife. "Your sister tells me, Jess, that your first husband died of the Spanish Flu, contracted overseas at the end of the war?"

"That's right." Jess glanced quickly in Beau's direction. His jaw was set.

"That must have been hard for you?"

"It was, but I have a lot of friends, and of course Jack's parents have always been very supportive."

"Jack was your husband?"

All eyes were focused on Jess. "Yes."

"Did you at any time, feel vulnerable, knowing that you were now a woman on her own, with three children, I believe?" Nick heard Beau suck in his breath, but he couldn't back down now.

"Yes," said Jess tightly. "There were occasions when I did realise my vulnerability."

"There certainly were, Jess!" Izzy took the bait. "Tell Nick about that terrible man, Sid O'Connor, who confronted you on several occasions, and even stole blankets from your sleep-out! Can you imagine that Nick? Stealing blankets from a client?"

"Client?"

"Yes! Sid delivered wood to Jess for many years."

Nick looked squarely at Jess, whose discomfort was obvious. "So you'd known this man for some time, Jess?"

Beau spoke quietly. "You don't have to do this, Jess."

"It's alright, Beau." She reached across the table and squeezed his hand, before shifting her gaze to Nick. "Yes."

"Did you have trouble with him before your husband went away?"

"No."

"So he treated you differently once you were on your own?"

"He did."

"He's a changed man now, Nick," interrupted Jean. "He's had his come-uppence. A spell in jail, and a day in Court changed his attitude."

"Oh, really?" Nick's interest was piqued. "Does that have any relevance to my questions?"

"No!" said Beau sharply. "I think it's time we went home, Jess." He pushed back his chair.

"You're leaving already?" Izzy sounded disappointed. "I thought we could all move to Jean's sitting room; it's more comfortable in there. Besides, this is getting interesting."

"I'm sorry, Izzy." Beau smiled tightly. "Charlotte is looking after all the children, and it's time to relieve her of her duties." He turned to Jean. "Thank-you for the hospitality, Jean, and you too, Izzy."

"But surely..." began Izzy.

"Good night, everyone." Beau turned to Nick. "I hope you get the information you need, Nick, but I'm afraid we cannot be involved in your research."

"That's a pity, Beau." Nick felt the disappointment rise in his chest. DuBois was not going to be easy to manipulate, and that was unfortunate.

Jess pushed her chair back and stood. "Goodnight, everyone. The meal was lovely, Izzy. I'll see you tomorrow." She looked at Nick. "I'm sorry we couldn't be more help to you, Nick."

Nick shrugged off the disappointment. "That's alright, Jess. I understand."

Silence fell on the remainder of the group as Jess and Beau made their exit. Izzy was the first to speak after they heard the main door close.

"What's got into Beau? I've never seen him like that before. I'm so sorry, Nick. I thought they would be happy to share their experiences with you."

"Not this one, obviously."

"No." Izzy frowned. "Oh well, we can all adjourn to the sitting room where perhaps Jean can throw some light on those incidents."

"Not without Beau's permission," said Jean stiffly. "I wouldn't do that to him or Jess."

"Let's not get uptight about this please?" Nick had to defuse the situation. "I'm sure there are other stories that I can gather."

"I'm sure there are."

*

Jess and Beau hurried along the dark street, their footsteps echoing on the asphalt. They were silent for a few moments before Jess turned to her husband.

"You're not taken with Mr. Armitage, are you, Beau?"

"Let's say I'm not taken in by him, Jess. There is a difference."

"Oh?"

"There's something about him I can't quite put my finger on."

"Perhaps you've met him in Sydney."

"I don't know. It's an odd feeling I have." Beau stopped walking and looked at Jess. "Call it an intuition, and I'd rather you had nothing more to do with him."

"Was he in the army?"

Beau laughed. "Mr. Armitage has never seen combat, Jess."

"How do you know that?"

"I just know."

"Intuition again?"

"Hm, possibly." Beau slid his arms around her, holding her close.

"Izzy seems quite taken by him. She called him 'charming'." Jess wound her arms around his neck.

"Yes, I can quite believe that. Harry needs to be careful."

Jess gasped. "Beau! What are you saying? Izzy wouldn't…"

"No, I'm sure she wouldn't." He kissed her lightly. "Come on, we'd better get home before Charlotte comes looking for us."

"How long do you think she's going to want to stay with us, Beau?"

"What do you mean?" Beau tilted his head back, surveying Jess in the watery glow of a streetlight.

"Don't get me wrong, Beau. I'm very fond of Charlotte, and she's a wonderful help with the children but…"

"But what, Jess?" His tone sent a shudder down Jess's spine.

"The house is too small for all of us."

Beau was silent, and Jess slowly released her arms from around his neck. She had hit a raw nerve.

"I didn't know you felt this way, Jess."

"I've not voiced it before. She can't spend another winter in the sleep-out. It's too cold."

Beau gave a short mirthless laugh. "Jess, Charlotte spent thirty-two years in a Convent. She's used to cold conditions."

"That may be so, Beau, but she shouldn't have to endure the cold now. I don't want her to."

"So what do you suggest?"

Jess shrugged. "Can we afford to do some improvements and make the room more liveable?"

There was silence before Beau answered. "Possibly."

"Think about it, Beau, please?"

He smiled suddenly. "Alright, I'll think about it." He tucked her arm in his. "In the meantime, promise me that you won't put my sister out on the street?"

"Beau!" Jess was horrified. "As if I would!"

They walked on to the gate, where Jess pulled Beau to a stop.

"How would Charlotte go as a hospital Chaplain?"

"What?"

"How would Charlotte go…?"

"I know! I heard you, Jess."

"She would be very good at it, and she has excellent nursing skills. She proved that when she cared for you after your…disappearance."

"Are you saying that she needs a job, Jess?"

Jess placed her hands on his chest. "All I'm saying, Beau, is that Charlotte needs to put her skills to work somewhere."

"So, you're giving me something else to think about?"

Jess smiled in the darkness. "I suppose I am."

The front door opened, and light spilled on to them. Charlotte stood there, tall and elegant, the baby snuffling softly in her arms.

"Good! You're home. It's time this child was fed, Jess. I'm no good to her."

Jess opened the front gate. "I'm coming, Charlotte."

Nick and Billy

Nick walked into the Lounge next morning, ready for breakfast. The previous evening had drawn to a rapid close once Beau and Jess had made their untimely exit. Conversation had waned, and Nick made the excuse that he had to write up some notes. Izzy had to put Freya to bed and Harry had some preparation to do before the morning's opening. So Jean had taken herself off to her sitting room to drink her nightcap alone.

The breakfast room was empty when Nick walked in, but the table was set with covered dishes, and the aroma was tempting indeed. Nick lifted each lid and found cooked tomatoes in one, scrambled eggs in another (Ben's chooks had obviously been busy), porridge in another and lastly slices of toast.

"Help yourself, Nick!" Izzy bustled into the room as he was deciding what to have first.

"It all looks delicious, Izzy. I suppose I'd better start with porridge." He grinned at her. "If my mother were here, she would be pleasantly surprised."

"Why? Does she not think we can do breakfast here in the country?"

"My mother is a little class conscious, Izzy." He laughed. "She has no reason to be. Father is a Lawyer, but he bypasses the social graces whenever he can. He prefers to spend his free time roaming the countryside with his dog."

"Oh! They sound like a well-matched couple."

Nick spooned porridge into a warmed bowl. "They tolerate one another, Izzy. One can't do without the other."

"Do you have any brothers or sisters?" Izzy was dishing out tomatoes on to slices of toast.

"Good gracious, no!" Nick feigned shock. "One was enough for mother."

Izzy sighed. "I would love another child, but I was lucky to have Freya, so I have to be content."

"And your sister, she has four children?"

Izzy dished another plate with eggs and toast. "Yes. She and Jack had three, and now she has baby Charlotte, (or Lottie as they're calling her) named after Beau's sister."

"I see." Nick sat and began spooning honey on to his porridge. "Beau's sister lives with them?"

"Yes, she does. It's a long story, Nick, and a very interesting one, but I'm afraid after last night, I can't say anything." Izzy picked up the two plates. "It was very disappointing seeing Beau's reaction last night." She shrugged. "Anyway, I'd better get these breakfasts to Jean and Harry. They haven't got time to eat with us this morning."

Izzy bustled out of the room, and Nick settled down to enjoy a quiet breakfast. He was meeting with Billy Maitland at ten, and maybe that would make up for the lack of information he had received the previous evening. Sid O'Connor certainly sounded like a character to be wary of, but it remained to be seen how much Billy would be prepared to say. The two had obviously been mates in the past, had a falling-out and were now friends again. Did the missing girl feature in any of this? Nick was anxious to know, and his experience with DuBois had increased his curiosity somewhat.

He pushed aside his empty porridge bowl and reached for the tomatoes and eggs. Smiling to himself he pictured his mother's disdainful expression as he described his lodgings to her. The more he worked with Joe, the more he could see himself becoming like him.

Thoughts of Joe immediately brought Amelia to mind, and he wondered briefly whether she would suddenly turn up. How was he going to explain her if she did? He sprinkled salt on his tomatoes and shrugged away the thought. That was something he would have to deal with if it happened.

Izzy came back into the room, Freya in tow. Lifting the child on to the chair next to Nick, she sighed loudly.

"Life is always interesting here, Nick." She reached across the table to the porridge dish and began to serve some into a bowl for Freya.

"Why is that Izzy? Has something happened?"

"Nothing that Harry can't handle, I'm sure." Nick waited for her to continue, but she finished serving Freya's breakfast. "I want you to eat all of that, Freya, or you are not going to play with Grace. Is that understood?" The child nodded sulkily. "Now, where were we?" Izzy turned her attention back to Nick.

"You were saying that there's nothing Harry can't handle, or words to that effect."

"Yes, I was, wasn't I?" Izzy served herself a plate of eggs and tomatoes and sat on the other side of Nick. "Jean's son, Rodney, arrived unexpectedly this morning. That can only spell trouble!"

"Oh?" Nick buttered another slice of toast.

"Oh, yes! Rodney worked here during the war, to help his mother out. Jean couldn't find a barman at the time." Izzy took a mouthful of egg and tomatoes. "That was alright until Rodney started stealing money from the till, to pay gambling debts." She looked at Nick. "Jean was outraged, naturally, and gave him his marching orders, telling him she never wanted to see him again. I wonder what's brought him back this time?"

"Needs more money, probably," offered Nick.

"He won't get it; I can assure you. When Harry and I came on board with the hotel, Jean was adamant that Rodney would not get another penny from her, not now or after she's gone."

Freya pushed her bowl away, and her shrill voice cut through the conversation.

"I've finished, mummy! Can I go to Grace's now?"

Izzy leaned across Nick and grabbed the moving bowl before it came to the edge of the table.

"That's a very good girl, Freya. You may leave the table, but you're not to go to Grace's until I'm ready to take you. Understood?"

"But you said…"

"I know what I said, but…" Raised voices could be heard coming from the direction of the Bar. Izzy glanced quickly at Nick. "It sounds like a storm is brewing." She rose from her chair. "Alright, Freya, I'll take you to Grace's now. I'm sorry, Nick. You'll have to finish your breakfast alone."

"Is there anything I can do?" Nick sensed her concern.

"Stay out of the way." Izzy grabbed Freya by the arm and hurried her from the room.

"I'll clear up the dishes!" Nick called after her retreating figure.

"Thank-you!"

They were gone, leaving Nick staring at the discarded breakfast dishes. *Never a dull moment* he thought as he began stacking the dirty plates. Oh well, it was an hour before he had to meet with Billy Maitland, so he might as well make himself useful.

Heading along the passage towards the kitchen, Nick heard Jean's voice, tight with anger.

"I'm not interested in your sob story, Rodney! I told you before that I don't want you darkening my door again. As far as I'm concerned you are no longer my son, and I will not have you coming here disturbing the peace. Harry and I are the joint owners of this establishment. You have no entitlement whatsoever!"

There was silence while Nick waited for an explosion from Jean's son. There was none, but he heard Harry trying to smooth out a tense situation.

"It would be a good idea, Rodney, if you went quietly, and stopped upsetting your mother. She is not going to change her mind."

"My mother! You heard her disown me." There was a long pause. "Alright, I'll go, but I promise you both, you haven't heard the last of this!"

Nick stepped hurriedly aside as a figure burst through the bar door, nearly toppling him over. The passage door slammed shut after Rodney's retreating figure, and Nick turned to see Jean and Harry regarding him, their expressions bleak.

"I'm sorry," he muttered. "I was heading to the kitchen with the breakfast dishes." He shrugged lamely. "Izzy's taken Freya to play with Grace."

Harry nodded slowly. "I'm sorry you had to witness that, Nick." He looked at Jean, who was dabbing her eyes on her apron. "Just a domestic dispute we'll have to sort out."

"He won't get his hands on this hotel, Harry! He won't!"

"Of course he won't, Jean. It's not possible."

"Anything's possible with Rodney."

Nick stood awkwardly, dishes in his hands. "I'd better get rid of these," he said, although he sensed nobody was listening.

Nick headed for the kitchen. There were stories at every turn in this place, he thought. It might pay him to stick around for a while. He looked at his watch. In the meantime, he had forty-five minutes before Billy Maitland arrived, so what better way to fill those minutes than washing dishes. He smiled to himself as he pushed the plug into the sink. His mother would be shocked to see him in this role. It wasn't something he would normally do or be expected to do. Turning on the tap, he discovered the water was cold. As he looked around for an alternative, he heard Izzy's voice beside him.

"Here, let me do that. I can see you're not used to domestic duties." She laughed.

"You're right there." He grinned at her. "I can dry them if that's any help."

"Alright." Izzy nodded towards the door. "You'll find a tea towel behind the door." As Nick followed her instructions, she whispered, "Has Rodney gone?"

"Yes, he has, but I got the feeling that he'll be back."

"Oh dear! This is something Jean does not need."

*

Nick sauntered into the bar at ten o'clock. Harry was there alone, arranging glasses on a tray. Jean was nowhere to be seen, and the trickle of regulars had not yet begun.

"Beer, Nick?"

"No thanks, Harry. It's a bit early for me, but I'll have a lemonade, please." He delved into his pocket for money. "On second thoughts, make that two?"

Harry cocked an eyebrow at him. "Two lemonades?"

"Yes, please. Billy Maitland is coming to talk with me shortly."

Harry laughed. "Billy would probably prefer a beer."

"That may be so, Harry," said Nick, placing coins on the bar, "but it's lemonade he'll be getting."

"Righto!"

Nick moved to a table at the corner of the bar, where they would not be disturbed. Remembering Billy's last instructions to him, he placed a notepad and pencil on the table and then sat back to wait.

It wasn't long before Billy ambled through the door and headed in his direction. He was dressed for work, in a blue boiler suit. Smiling at Nick, he sat opposite him.

"Good mornin', Nick." His gravelly voice broke the silence.

"Good morning, Billy," replied Nick pleasantly. "I'm very pleased to see you, and on time."

"Thank the army for that."

Harry appeared at their elbows and placed the lemonades on coasters in front of them. Billy looked up at Harry, his expression puzzled.

"Lemonade, Harry?" he rasped.

"It's on your friend here, Billy."

"Oh!" Billy glanced across at Nick. "Thanks, mate."

"It's too early for beer, Billy." Nick was smiling at him.

"Never too early f'beer, mate." Billy picked up the glass. "But this'll do fine."

Nick watched as Billy downed the lemonade in one long swig. Then wiping a hand across his mouth, he called out to Harry.

"Now I'll 'ave a beer, Harry!" He grinned at Nick. "Where do you wanna start, Nick?"

Nick shook his head. "Perhaps with your voice, Billy?"

Billy frowned. "I thought ya didn't wanna talk about the war, Nick."

"I don't, but for my readers to have the right perception of you, it might be a good idea to explain what happened to you."

Billy shrugged as Harry placed a beer glass in front of him. "Thanks, Harry." He stared at Nick for a long moment. "I was one o' the lucky ones. Some o' me mates had their throats burnt out with the gas that those mongrels were pitchin' at us." He blinked rapidly. "I was slow at getting' me mask on, an' suffered the consequence." He stopped. "Me brother Frank was killed, right before me eyes."

"Gas?"

"No, 'e was shot." Billy took a swig of beer. "It was no picnic out there, mate, I c'n tell ya." He leaned across the table. "How come you didn't get to fight?"

"I would have, Billy, but I wasn't called."

"Ya coulda volunteered." Billy's blue eyes bored into Nick.

"I know." Nick dropped his gaze, sorry now that he had opened the conversation with the war.

"Why didn't ya?"

"In hindsight, Billy, I know I should have, but they were looking for younger men."

Billy squinted at him. "How old are ya?"

"I'm thirty-two, Billy."

"My mate Jack, 'e was thirty-two an' it didn't stop 'im." He wiped a hand roughly across his eyes. "Trouble is, 'e didn't come 'ome, either."

"I'm sorry, Billy."

Billy sat back. "Yeah, expect you are. Anyway, that's enough about the war. What else d' you wanna know?"

Nick was somewhat at a loss. He had been condemned for his inaction, and he couldn't tell Billy that his father had paid for his freedom. It all seemed so wrong now. He shook away the thoughts that were emerging and tried to focus on the job he had to do.

"First of all, Billy, (I'm afraid I have to ask you this) how old were you when you were called up?"

"Nineteen. Me brother, Frank, was twenty-one."

"That's young."

Billy laughed harshly. "There were seventeen-year-olds who got away with it."

"So, when you came home you were how old?"

"Twenty-one."

Nick was taking notes now. "What was it like when you came home? Was it easy to get a job?"

"I was lucky, I suppose. I went back to the railway workshop."

"Was that easy?"

"What do ya mean, easy? It's bloody 'ard work."

Nick smiled. "I mean, was it easy to settle into a regular job?"

"I s'pose so. Like I said, I was one o' the lucky ones. The war didn't mess with me brain, like it did with a lot o' the others." He laughed. "That's probably because I don't 'ave a brain."

"I don't believe that for one moment, Billy."

The blue eyes flickered. "Don't ya?"

"No, I don't. What about your mates, Billy?"

"Which ones? The ones I fought with or the ones who chose to stay behind?"

Nick toyed with the pencil. "Let's start with the ones you fought with."

Billy shrugged. "Only two of us came 'ome – the most unlikely two."

"What makes you say that Billy?"

"Martin an' me were always in trouble, an' even our Sergeant was amazed that we both survived."

"And your friend, Martin, does he live around here?"

"Nope." Billy shook his head. "Martin went back t' France, t' help with the rebuildin'. He married a girl from over there, too."

Nick was scribbling on the pad. "And what about your mates who didn't fight? How did they accept you when you came home?"

"Don't 'ave too many mates who didn't sign up." His brow creased. "Unless ya wanna count Sid, who wouldn't 'ave signed up anyway."

"Sid?"

Billy's lip curled slightly. "Yeah, O'Connor. Biggest coward out!"

"And you're still friends?"

Billy laughed. "I put up with 'im. Known 'im since we were at school. Always was a crafty little bugger. We 'ad a fallin' out when I was in the trainin' camp, but as it turns out 'e did me a big favour."

"Oh? How's that?"

Billy moved restlessly on his seat. "It doesn't matter now, an' you wouldn't wanna hear about it anyway." He looked up at the bar clock. "I can't stay much longer. Gotta do some messages for me ma before I go t' work."

"What did he do, Billy?" Nick persisted, sensing that at last he was getting somewhere.

Billy stood up. "'E stole me girl, that's what 'e did."

"You were training to fight for your country, and he did that to you? That sounds like betrayal, Billy."

"It sure was." He shrugged. "Anyway, as it turns out, 'e was welcome to 'er." Billy leaned forward. "Turns out she was a tramp, an' I was better off without 'er."

Nick decided to go in, boots and all. "Does she live around here? Do you still see her?"

Billy screwed up his face. "Dunno where she is. I don't think Sid knows where she is, either. Like I said, she was a tramp. Good riddance, I say." He paused. "Anything else ya wanna know?"

"Not at the moment, Billy." Nick smiled up at the younger man. "But I might want to talk to you again."

"Sure." Billy moved away from the table. "See ya, Nick. Hope I was helpful."

"Before you go, Billy, is there any chance I can talk to Sid?"

"Talk t' Sid?" Billy's face screwed into a frown. "What would ya wanna do that for?"

Nick spread his hands. "There are two sides to every story, Billy."

"Yeah!" Billy laughed. "Ya won't get the truth from O'Connor, Nick. 'E couldn't lie straight in bed." He turned to go. "If ya wait around long enough, 'e'll probably come in 'ere. Ya can't miss 'im. Ugly as a hat full o' monkeys." Billy laughed as he headed for the door. "Thanks for the lemonade, Nick."

Nick sat back on the chair and exhaled loudly. Harry, who had been covertly watching the exchange, left the bar and sauntered over on the pretext of retrieving the glasses. He sat on the chair that Billy had vacated, took a quick look towards the bar where two men were drinking and sharing a joke, then focused his gaze on Nick. Leaning forward he spoke quietly.

"What are you really here for, Nick?" He steadied his gaze.

"What do you mean, Harry?" Nick narrowed his eyes.

"All these questions seem to be pointing in one direction, and that is Sid O'Connor. I don't think you're a journalist at all." The words hung heavily between them. "Are you a policeman?"

Nick sat back. "No, Harry, I'm not."

"What then?" Harry spread his hands. "A detective?"

Nick leaned forward now, so that their faces were inches apart. "I'm a Private Investigator, Harry, and I'm obviously not doing a very good job, if you've sussed me out already."

"The conversation last night set me thinking, and then overhearing what you were saying to Billy, well, I thought there must be more to it than a story for a Sydney newspaper. What has Sid done that you're asking questions about him?"

"I'm not sure that he has done anything, but I have been sent here to look into the disappearance of a young woman by the name of Phyllis Powell, back in 1917."

Harry shrugged. "I don't know the name, but then, I wasn't here in 1917." He squinted. "Is that the girl Billy was talking about?"

"Yes. It seems that O'Connor was the last person to have dealings with her in this area."

"Oh! So why the cloak and dagger, Nick?"

"My boss thought it might send people running in the opposite direction if they knew what I was really here for."

"So what have Jess and Beau got to do with it?"

Nick sighed. "Harry, my boss is the investigator who came looking for Beau about the same time."

Harry's face registered shock. "You're not saying that…"

"No, Harry, I'm not, but both Jess and Beau have had dealings with the same Mr. O'Connor."

"Phew!" Harry sat back. "I can't take all this in, Nick."

"Harry, can I ask you to say nothing about this for the time being? If O'Connor gets wind of it, he might disappear."

"Very well, but have a care, Nick. This is not a big town, and word does get around."

"Thank-you, Harry, I'll remember that." Nick watched as Harry pushed back his chair. "In the meantime, you have your own problems to sort out."

"You're not wrong there, Nick!"

Jess and Charlotte

Nick needed to update Joe on what was happening, so after telling Jean that he would grab a bite of lunch in the town, he headed out and made his way in that direction. He had not gone far when he looked up and saw Jess DuBois seated on a front verandah, in the sunshine, her baby in her arms.

She didn't see him approach, as she was smiling down at the child who hiccoughed suddenly, making her mother laugh.

"Hello, Jess."

She looked up, startled by the sound. Nick was standing on the footpath outside the gate. He raised his hat, but at the sight of him, her smile vanished, and she frowned.

"Hello, Nick. What are you doing here?"

"I was passing, actually, and I saw you sitting there, absorbed in your little one."

Jess did not invite him in, which was not a surprise to Nick.

"I shouldn't be talking to you, Nick. My husband wouldn't like it."

He frowned and wrapped his hands around the top of the gate. "Why is that Jess?"

Jess pulled the blanket tightly around her child. "We have had a lot of things to deal with recently, Nick, and Beau doesn't want me upset. I have the baby to think of and raking over past incidents is not going to help anybody."

"Was it my questions or was it me that your husband objected to?"

The front wire door opened, saving Jess from answering, and a tall woman stepped on to the verandah. Nick raised his hat politely.

"Ah! There you are, Jess." As she spoke, the woman's grey eyes held Nick's for a moment. "Who are you?" she asked stiffly.

"I'm Nick Armitage, ma'am, and you must be Doctor DuBois's sister, if I am not mistaken."

"I am." Charlotte flicked her gaze across to Jess, as though dismissing him. "I'm going to the Post Office, Jess, if there's anything you want in town."

"No, there's nothing I want, thanks Charlotte." Jess looked down at her now sleeping child. "Mr. Armitage was just leaving."

He had been dismissed, but Nick was not so easily put off. He smiled at the two women and opened the gate as Charlotte DuBois swept down the steps and on to the footpath.

"Perhaps I could accompany you, Miss DuBois, as I am going to the Post Office myself."

Cool grey eyes surveyed him. "I don't really need your company, Mr. Armitage, but if we're both going in the same direction, then I can't stop you, can I?"

Nick looked up to see Jess trying to hide a smile. "No, I don't suppose you can," he said, as he fell into step beside Charlotte.

They walked quickly, and Nick was surprised at the athleticism of the woman who must have been in her fifties he gathered. Her grey silk dress swept the ground as she walked, and she looked directly ahead, her back ramrod straight. Nick almost had to jog to keep up with her.

They slowed down to negotiate a corner of the street, and Nick cast a furtive glance in her direction. Was that a smile he saw on her lips? An approaching vehicle made them both stop, and when it had passed by, Charlotte resumed her rapid pace.

"Tell me, Miss DuBois," Nick was almost panting, "where did you learn to walk so fast?"

"Having trouble keeping up, Mr. Armitage?" She was smiling now.

"You could say that. Most ladies I know are content to stroll."

"I am not 'most ladies', Mr. Armitage." She had stopped to negotiate another corner. "I spent a good many years in a Convent, where if we didn't keep up, we were chastised."

"A Convent? As a nun?"

Charlotte turned to face him now, the smile gone. "Oh dear! You're a journalist, aren't you, Mr. Armitage? I shouldn't be talking to you."

They had reached the Charing Cross corner, where the fountain gleamed in the sunlight, and traffic moved in several directions at once. Charlotte picked up her skirts and stepped out into the traffic, weaving her way across to the other side of the roadway. Nick followed, as horns blared, and angry motorists shouted at them.

They made it safely to the footpath, where Charlotte smoothed her dress before heading in the direction of the Post Office. At the foot of the steps, she stopped. Nick stopped beside her.

"So, you renounced your vows and joined the outside world, Miss DuBois?"

They stared at each other for a long moment before Charlotte grabbed her skirts and marched up the steps. At the top she turned.

"This is where we part company, Mr. Armitage. Good day to you."

Nick watched her push open the heavy door before disappearing into the building. He waited at the foot of the steps; his thoughts scattered. His conversation with Joe would have to wait until she had left the building. He needed to ask Joe about DuBois's sister, but something niggled in the back of his head that maybe this was a diversion that he should do well to ignore. Still, he was intrigued that a woman of Charlotte's age should suddenly venture into the world, away from the security of a closed order. He could picture her now, dressed in her black habit, rosary beads swinging at her hip as she strode the stark halls of some remote convent.

Charlotte appeared beside him. "I thought you were going to the Post

Office, Mr. Armitage?"

He started. "I was – I am."

"It's just up the steps." His discomfort was amusing her.

"I know." He lifted his hat. "Good-day to you, Miss DuBois."

As he headed up the steps, Nick sensed that she was watching him, and he could hear the laughter as she related their conversation to the DuBois's. He pushed open the heavy door and strode across to the telephone. The Clerk smiled at him from behind the counter.

After waiting several minutes, Nick eventually heard Joe's voice.

"Joe Hudson."

"Joe, it's Nick."

"How are things, my boy? Any new information?"

"I'm afraid my cover has been broken. The publican, Harry Dalton, knows that I'm not a journalist." Nick tried to keep his voice low, as the Post Office Clerk was hovering close to the counter. "I might have been too zealous with my questioning, although I've told him not to say anything just yet."

"He agreed?"

"Yes."

"Who have you spoken to?"

"I've spoken to the DuBois's, but I'm afraid the good doctor was suspicious of my motives, and his wife does not want to talk about past incidents."

"That's too bad. Anybody else?"

"Yes. I had a conversation with young Maitland, and he indicated to me that neither he nor your person of interest know where the young lady went."

"I see." There was a pause. "Any chance of talking to the person of interest?"

"Possibly, but I need to be careful and lie low for a day or two – become the sightseeing tourist."

"Are you extending?" a female voice enquired brightly.

"Yes," said Nick curtly as he wondered how much of his conversation was being overheard at the exchange. He knew that it happened.

"I haven't heard from Amelia," said Joe, "but I do know that she was going to check on births, deaths and marriages. That could take a few days."

"Yes it will. If she turns up here, well, we'll have to play that one by ear."

"Of course."

"Joe, can you do something for me?"

"What."

"Find out what you can about Doctor DuBois's sister, whom I believe spent many years in a Convent. Bonner-Smythe should know something about her."

"Is this relevant to our case, Nick?"

"No, but I've met her and I'm curious."

"Alright. Another story for your casefile, eh Nick?"

Nick laughed. "Possibly, or a diversion."

"Goodbye, Nick. Keep me informed, eh?"

"Will do." Nick replaced the receiver and delved in his pocket for money.

Looking up, he caught the eye of the Clerk, who shifted his gaze immediately. He had obviously heard half the conversation but smiled as Nick sauntered across to the counter.

"Thank-you, sir," he said pleasantly.

Nick felt eyes on his back as he pulled open the heavy door and stepped outside. It was time to find a nice quiet place to have some lunch.

*

After having posted her letter to Sister Miriam at the Convent of the sisters of Mercy in Sydney, Charlotte DuBois made her way back across the busy intersection of Charing Cross, and stepped up on to the footpath. She smiled to herself as she made her way to the nearest pharmacy. Had she succeeded in throwing up a smoke screen to divert Mr. Armitage's attention from her brother and sister-in-law? She had certainly confused him.

Beau had related their conversation with him, the night they returned from the dinner party, and all had agreed that Mr. Armitage was not what he seemed. Beau had expressed an uneasy feeling about the young man, and she, Charlotte, trusted his judgement. What Nick was really after was unclear to them, but he would get no more information from them, unless he explained his motives.

Charlotte made her purchase of a box of headache powders and headed up the main shopping street and over the bridge that spanned the railway line. She had been living with Beau and Jess for some months now, and her fear of the unaccustomed freedom had begun to subside. Relaxation was something that still tinged her with guilt, and often she would say to Jess, as they sat quietly in the lounge at the end of the day, "Is this what people do every night?"

Jess had laughed at her and told her that she would get used to it, and to not feel guilty about it. It was in preparation for the work that would need to be done the following day. Charlotte's quiet time had always been on her knees on a hard floor, with her head bowed in prayer. She still allowed herself that small part of her former life, when she prepared for bed every night. It was a habit that she would find hard to break.

As she crested the hill, she saw Jess still seated on the verandah, her eyes closed as she gently rocked her sleeping child. Charlotte tried to open the gate quietly, but the ominous creak brought Jess's eyes wide open.

"Oh, it's you, Charlotte." Her tone was tinged with relief.

"Of course it's me!" Charlotte sat on the bench beside Jess and touched the baby's smooth cheek. "She's very beautiful, Jess." Their eyes met and held.

"She has the same eyes and Beau and you," said Jess softly.

Charlotte's expression became hard. "Our mother had the grey eyes, so little Lottie is fortunate there." The smile returned. "Have you had lunch, Jess?"

"No."

Charlotte stood up. "I'll get us some, shall I?" She turned towards the door.

"Before you do," said Jess quickly, "tell me, how was your walk with Mr. Armitage?"

"Oh!" Charlotte resumed her seat. "I think I succeeded in flummoxing him, Jess." She giggled. "I certainly out-paced him."

"Did he question you?"

"He didn't have a chance, Jess, but I did leave him wondering."

"Wondering what?"

"Wondering what my story could be."

"Charlotte, you didn't?"

"He can guess all he likes, and if he's not a journalist, then it really doesn't matter."

"But if he is?"

Charlotte laughed. "I don't think he is, Jess. He's certainly nosey and I think he has ulterior motives, but from what I can gather, his concern is not so much with us as with someone you're related to."

"You mean Sid O'Connor?"

"If that's the name of your woodman, yes."

Jess sighed. "None of it makes any sense. If he's after information about Sid, why doesn't he just say so?"

"I really don't know, Jess." Charlotte stood once more. "Come on, it's time for lunch. I presume Grace is with Freya?" It was a statement rather than a question.

Jess nodded. "Her second home," she murmured.

*

Nick bought a sandwich from a small cafe on the main street and running the gauntlet once more to cross the busy road, he found his way back to the Cascades. Sitting on the grass, he opened the brown paper bag and wrapped his hands around the thick egg sandwich. The park was busy with pedestrian traffic, as people strolled through the gardens, or like him, relaxed in shady nooks. He let the soft buzz of conversations wash over him as he enjoyed the peace and serenity of his surrounds.

Thinking about his time in this town, and the people he'd met, Nick concluded that town folk were vastly different from city folk. There was a lack of sophistication in them that he found endearing, and which made his encounter with the DuBois's more intriguing. They had been instantly suspicious of his motives, and he doubted whether either would give an inch. He would have to think of other ways to engage them and win their confidence.

There was a reticence to Jess DuBois, that Nick felt sure was stemming from the fact that her husband didn't trust his motives. If he could get her to open up, then he felt sure that facts about Sid O'Connor would eventually emerge. He smiled to himself as he thought of Izzy Dalton. She was as innocent with her comments as anyone he'd ever met, but she had not lived in the town for long, so could not speak from her own experience.

Nick screwed up the paper bag, tucked it in his pocket, and lay back on the grass, placing his hat across his face. The warmth of the sun and the rhythmic sound of the cascading water soon sent him into a deep sleep.

Amelia

Harry looked up as the door to the bar opened, and a young woman appeared. She was possibly in her late twenties, with dark hair tucked beneath a bright red beret. Blue eyes smiled at him across the room, as she approached the bar.

"Can I help you?" Harry was taken by surprise as she placed her suitcase on the floor and propped herself on a bar stool.

"Yes," she said with a heavy sigh. "You can get me a gin and tonic please, and you can tell me where I can find Mr. Nick Armitage. I believe he is staying here?"

Harry blinked and took a moment to compose himself. "First of all, Miss - er -"

"Amelia Hudson," was the quick reply.

"First of all, Miss Hudson, I am not supposed to serve you at the bar." Harry saw her nose wrinkle. "If you'd like to move into the Ladies' Lounge, I will attend to you there."

The young woman pulled off her beret, pushed it into the pocket of her coat, and ran her fingers through her dark hair. "It's all so archaic, don't you agree?" Her blue eyes challenged Harry.

"That may be so, Miss Hudson, but it is the rule, and..."

"And you don't wish to be caught breaking it." She slipped off the stool, picked up her case and headed back towards the door. "I shall go meekly."

"Secondly, Miss Hudson," she turned, "Mr. Armitage is staying here, but I have no idea where he is at present."

"In that case, could I please have a room for the night?" She smiled.

"I'll see what I can do."

Harry watched as she stepped out into the passage. His brow creased as he wondered where he was going to put her. Not all the rooms upstairs were ready for guests, and as his family was taking up two of them, there was only one other current possibility. He moved swiftly to the door.

"Isobel!" he called into the empty passage.

Izzy appeared from the direction of the kitchen. "Yes, Harry." He beckoned to her and waited until she was standing directly in front of him. "What is it, Harry?"

"We need to prepare a room for tonight," he said softly.

"Do we have another guest?"

"Yes." He waved his hands to indicate that Izzy lower her voice.

"Who?" Izzy stared at him. "Stop waving your hands at me, Harry!" she said crossly. "Unless it's the King himself, I don't see the need for all this secrecy."

"There's a young woman in the Ladies' Lounge, and she knows Nick. Her name is Amelia Hudson."

"And she needs a room, does she?"

"Yes. Where can we put her, Isobel?"

"Not next door to Nick, obviously." Izzy grinned mischievously. "Leave it with me, Harry. I'll make up Freya's room. She'll have to come in with us."

Harry grimaced. "If that's the only solution, then go ahead." As Izzy turned to retrace her steps, Harry stopped her. "Where's Jean? She hasn't been in the bar all morning, and now here we are halfway through the afternoon."

Izzy shrugged. "I don't know, Harry. This business with Rodney turning up unannounced, has given her the jitters. Maybe she went to see the Solicitor."

"Maybe. Anyway, if you see her, tell her I could do with a hand before the after-work mob arrive."

"Alright, Harry." Izzy headed back to the kitchen. "There's no need to get into such a flap."

"Humph! It's alright for you!" Harry retreated into the bar, where he reached for a bottle of gin.

"She was a looker, eh Harry?"

Harry turned to see one of his regulars, Eric Liddle, grinning at him from across the bar.

"What?"

"I said 'she was a looker', Harry. Don't tell me ya didn't notice?"

Harry sighed as he prepared the gin and tonic. "You mean the young woman who was just in here, Eric?"

"That's the one, Harry." Eric was grinning foolishly, exposing a mouth full of empty spaces.

"To tell the truth, I didn't notice." Harry pushed a slice of lemon on to the rim of the glass and wiped the base with a damp cloth. "This is for her. Watch the bar for a moment, Eric, please?"

"Sure thing, Harry."

Harry pushed open the bar door and headed across the passage to the ladies Lounge. Miss Amelia Hudson was seated at one of the round tables and was lighting a cigarette. She had removed her black coat, revealing a slim-fitting red dress, buckled at the waist and exposing a deal of slender ankle. Harry placed the drink on a coaster in front of her.

"Your gin and tonic, Miss Hudson."

"Thank-you." She smiled, turning away before she exhaled a waft of smoke.

"Miss Hudson," Harry looked around to make sure nobody was within earshot, "can I ask you something?"

"Go ahead."

"Your association with Mr. Armitage, is it of a professional nature?"

Blue eyes narrowed for an instant, before her face creased into a smile.

"What are you suggesting?"

Harry felt his cheeks flush. "I'm not suggesting anything, Miss Hudson. I merely want to establish whether you are both working on the same case."

There was silence.

"How much do you know, Mr. – er -?"

"Dalton. Harry Dalton."

"How much has Nick told you, Harry?"

"I drew my own conclusions, Miss Hudson. Your friend asked too many leading questions."

"Did he, indeed?" Her blue eyes were dancing merrily. "I'll have to have a word with him."

Harry sat quickly on the chair opposite and leaned forward. "I have talked with Nick, and he asked me to keep it to myself for the time being, as the person in question could do a runner if he gets wind of anything."

"Very sensible, Harry."

"Harry!" A voice sounded from the direction of the bar. "You're wanted!"

Harry rose to his feet. "I must get back to the bar. Oh, before I forget, there will be a room for you, Miss Hudson, but it will take a little while to prepare."

"Thank-you, Harry." She smiled widely. "In the meantime, I'll wait here for Nick."

*

Harry walked back into the bar to find Jean there, serving the regulars. She looked up as Harry entered and scowled at him.

"Where have you been?"

"I could ask you the same question, Jean," Harry retorted. "I haven't seen you since this morning."

"I had things to do," muttered Jean, turning her attention to the empty glasses on the bar.

"If it's to do with Rodney, Jean, I need to know about it."

"I know." Her shoulders slumped. "I – I had to find out where he's staying, and when he plans on returning to Sydney."

"Jean!" Harry was shocked. "And did you find out?"

Jean nodded, as she pushed a beer glass across the bar to a waiting customer. "I did."

"Tell me!" demanded Harry.

Jean opened the till, dropped some coins into it and slammed it shut. "He's staying with friends out at Epsom and has no immediate plans to return to Sydney."

"Who told you this?"

"Seamus Oliver."

Harry was silent for a moment. "Isn't he…?"

"Yes, he's the one who got Rodney into trouble the last time he was here."

"And you went to see him? Jean! What were you thinking?"

"I'm sorry, Harry, but I had to know."

"You put yourself in danger, Jean." Harry tried to keep his voice low. "These are dangerous people, from what you've told me about them. Keep away, Jean! This could lead to all sorts of bad situations."

Conversations at the bar had fallen silent, and Harry frowned as he saw the regulars watching him. Eric Liddle leaned confidentially across the bar.

"'E's a bad one that Seamus Oliver. If ya want my advice, ya'll keep well away from 'im," he whispered loudly, receiving murmurs of consent among his friends.

Harry nodded sharply. "Yes, I know, Eric," he said curtly.

"Don't you be saying anything, Eric Liddle?" Jean pointed a finger at him. "We all know what a tittle tattle you are! This is my business, not yours!"

"OUR business, Jean," cut in Harry.

Eric moved back from the bar, as his friends all grinned at him and nudged each other.

"I'm just warnin' ya, Jean, that's all."

"And I'm just telling you to keep your mouth shut!" Jean's face was flushed, and her eyes glittered as she looked around the grizzled faces on the other side of the bar. "That goes for all of you."

There was a low murmur and a nodding of heads. Jean looked up at Harry, who was frowning intently at her.

"We'll talk about this tonight, Jean. Now is not the time." Harry looked up to see Nick watching from the doorway, his face a study of amusement. How long had he been there, Harry wondered? "Oh, Nick, there's a young lady to see you. She's in the Ladies' Lounge."

"Thank-you, Harry." Nick retreated, and Harry wondered how much of the conversation he had overheard. He was certainly here at the right time, thought Harry wryly.

*

Nick headed for the Ladies' Lounge. He knew who would be waiting for him there, and he had to admit that he was looking forward to seeing Miss Amelia Hudson again.

She was seated at one of the small round tables, holding a glass in one hand and a cigarette in the other, while she stared absently out through the window.

"Hello Amelia."

The voice startled her and she spun around, splashing gin and tonic on the table.

"Nick!" Her smile was wide. "So, you turn up at last?"

Nick slid on to the seat opposite, pulling off his hat and placing it on the table. "Did you find anything useful in your search, Amelia?"

She leaned forward, her blue eyes gleaming. "Before we go into that, Nick, I have been talking with your friendly publican, and he tells me that he knows of your little deception." Amelia sat back.

Nick shrugged. "Yes, well I suppose that couldn't be helped. He won't tell anyone."

"He tells me," continued Amelia, as she butted her cigarette into the glass ashtray, "and I quote, 'your friend asked too many leading questions'." Her blue eyes narrowed.

"I got a little zealous, I must admit, but they all know the person in question."

"Hm!" Amelia surveyed him over the top of her glass. "How can I trust you with the information I have gathered from the births, deaths and marriages registry?"

Two women walked into the Ladies' Lounge, moving past them to a table in the far corner of the room. They smiled as they passed and received a quick return smile from Nick. Amelia was busy drawing some paper out of her red handbag. After mopping up the gin and tonic spill with a clean handkerchief, she spread the paper on the table, smoothing it with her long fingers, before looking up at Nick.

"I didn't find much, but it left a few questions that we need to find answers to, and then maybe we'll find out what happened to Miss Powell." She kept her voice low.

Nick leaned forward eagerly. "So what did you find?"

"Phyllis Powell was born here in Bendigo in 1898, which means she was nineteen in 1917 when she was last seen around here. Her mother died when she was seven, and her father obviously couldn't take care of her. Consequently, she was put into an orphanage, where she stayed until she was seventeen."

"An orphanage? Where?"

"Here in Bendigo. It's still in operation and is run by nuns."

Nick was impressed. "You have been busy, haven't you? How did you come by your information?"

Amelia tapped the side of her nose. "Sometimes it pays to have friends in high places, Nick." She smiled benignly. "Would you like to hear my theory on the disappearance of Miss Phyllis Powell?"

Nick spread his hands wide. "Go ahead, I'm all ears."

Amelia glanced across at the two women who were deep in conversation. "I think our Miss Powell, when she knew she was pregnant, and couldn't decide who the father was, took her own way out of the situation, and scurried back to the orphanage, where she had grown up, and where she knew she would, at the very least, be fed and housed. Does that sound reasonable,

Nick?"

Nick scowled. "So, you're saying that our person of interest, may not be guilty of anything other than being the possible father of the child?"

"That's what I'm saying, Nick."

"So where does that leave us? Do we need to check out this orphanage?"

Amelia leaned forward. "Definitely. I was told, too, that it is run on the strictest of conditions and children and mothers alike are sometimes subjected to – shall I say – corporal punishment."

"You say 'mothers' – does that mean they live there too?"

"This particular establishment runs a commercial laundry, operated by young women and single mothers, who are not looked on favourably, Nick, in case you hadn't noticed."

"I've never really thought about it." Nick whistled through his teeth as he sat back on the chair.

"Of course you haven't. You were born with a silver spoon in your mouth, Nick. How could you possibly know what goes on in the wider world."

"Silver spoon? I wasn't…"

"It's just a figure of speech, Nick." Amelia gave him her most beguiling smile, as she laid a hand across his.

"Well, does this call for a celebration, or is it just an interesting little diversion?"

"I don't know, but we can celebrate anyway."

Nick pulled his hand away, aware of the unexpected warm feeling her touch had triggered. "We'll have to call Joe and let him know your 'theory'. I'm sure he'll be interested…"

"Excuse me, Nick!" Izzy's face had appeared at the door. "Are you staying in for tea tonight?" Her glance took in the woman sitting opposite him.

Nick looked across at Amelia, who shook her head discreetly. He smiled at Izzy. "I think we might be dining out tonight, thanks all the same, Izzy."

"That's alright, Nick." Izzy shifted her gaze to Amelia. "By the way, Miss Hudson, your room is ready if you want to take your case upstairs." She held out a key. "Room three."

With a quick look in Nick's direction, Izzy hurried away.

*

The Ladies' Lounge was quiet as Jean, Harry, Izzy and Freya sat eating their tea. Only the clatter of cutlery broke the silence. Harry was biding his time to question Jean about her meeting with Seamus Oliver, and Izzy was impatient to hear the story behind Miss Amelia Hudson's visit to Bendigo.

Harry sat back after finishing his apple pie and custard, wiped a serviette across his mouth, and fixed his gaze on Jean, who sat opposite him. She pushed away her bowl and met his gaze.

"It's time for some explanation, Jean, and I want to hear it all."

Izzy turned enquiring eyes in his direction. "Explanation of what, Harry?" She looked at Jean. "What's going on that I don't know about?"

Jean frowned. "I've disobeyed the rules, apparently, and gone out on my own."

"What do you mean, Jean? Gone where?"

"I had to find out what Rodney is up to, and I risked going to see one of his gambling associates." Jean glanced in Harry's direction. "Harry was not pleased, were you, Harry?"

"I was not. It was a very dangerous and reckless thing to do, Jean, as I told you before." Harry leaned back on his chair. "Nevertheless, you did go, and now I want to know what he had to say."

Jean began stacking the dessert bowls. "I told you, Harry, he said that Rodney was staying with another friend out at Epsom, and that he wasn't planning on going back to Sydney any time soon."

"Was he aggressive towards you?"

"No, he was extremely polite."

"Do you know this other friend that Rodney has supposedly moved in with?"

"Seamus called him Al. I don't think I've heard Rodney speak of him."

"Hm." Harry rubbed a hand across his whiskers. "Perhaps we all need to pay the solicitor a visit to make sure nothing can come unstuck. In the meantime, Jean, please don't undertake any of these ventures on your own." Jean glared at him. "I mean it. We are all in this together."

Izzy, who had been trying to listen while helping Freya with her dessert, suddenly looked up. "You don't think they'll attempt another robbery, do you?"

Harry shook his head. "No. Rodney wants one thing and that's this hotel. He won't jeopardize his chances by using petty thief tactics."

"Don't be too sure of that," muttered Jean as she shuffled towards the door. "Rodney is capable of many things."

Harry and Izzy watched her carry the dirty dishes from the room, before looking at each other. Izzy's eyes were wide with alarm.

"Perhaps it would pay us to be vigilant at night, Harry," she whispered.

"What! Stay up all night, in case something happens?" Harry laughed. "I'll deal with Rodney if he returns, but I'm not losing sleep over what he might do." He pushed back his chair. "Besides, the hotel has guests, so there will be plenty of ears to hear anything that goes bump in the night."

"Don't joke, Harry! This is serious."

"If you want to stay up all night, Isobel, then be my guest." Harry made a move towards the door. "I'd better check the till and wash the last of the glasses."

"Harry! Before you go, can you answer a question I have?"

Harry sighed. "And what is that Isobel?"

"What is Miss Hudson doing here, and what connection does she have to Nick?"

Harry's brow puckered. He didn't want to have to explain to Isobel what the connection was, but he also knew that she wouldn't rest until she found out. He moved back to the table and resumed his seat, pulling the chair in close, and resting his arms on the table.

"Isobel," he said quietly, "I want your solemn promise that you will not say a word about this to anybody, do you understand, not even your sister?"

Izzy's eyes opened wide with surprise. "What are you talking about, Harry?"

"Nick is a private investigator, here to look into the mysterious disappearance of a young woman from here in 1917."

"1917? That's three years ago."

"I know, but she hasn't been sighted since."

"And what does all this have to do with us?"

"Well, it's like this, Isobel." Harry went on to explain what Nick had told him and what he had deduced from Nick's conversation with Billy Maitland.

Izzy listened, her eyes wide.

"But what about Miss Hudson? What has she to do with all this?"

"All I know, Isobel, is that she is helping him in some way. Specifically?" He shrugged. "I don't know, but we need to mind our own business, and let them get on with whatever they do in these situations." Harry stood once more. "No talking to Jess, Isobel. Is that clear?"

Isobel nodded absently. "Alright, Harry."

"Promise?"

"Yes, of course."

Harry moved away, with a feeling that Izzy had no intention of keeping a promise like that.

Nick and Amelia

Nick placed a telephone call to Joe, as he and Amelia stood in the deserted Post Office. The Clerk was watching them covertly as he sorted letters. Nick whispered to Amelia that private conversations were anything but private, and that she would have to keep her voice down as she explained to Joe what she had found.

Amelia looked quickly across at the Clerk, giving him her most beguiling smile. He looked away quickly, closed the drawer, and hurried into a back room.

When Joe finally came on the line, Nick handed the receiver to Amelia, and she quickly explained to him what she had discovered. He was doubtful about it leading anywhere but suggested that they go and check out the orphanage anyway.

Amelia told him that she had every intention of doing just that, and Nick smiled as he heard the explosion of laughter at the other end of the line. Amelia was used to doing exactly what she wanted to do, with or without her father's consent.

She replaced the receiver as Nick delved into his pocket for money. He placed some coins on the unattended counter, and together with Amelia, headed for the door. Behind them the Clerk had silently appeared, his face pensive as he scooped up the coins.

Nick and Amelia hurried down the steps, across the footpath and into the traffic. Nick took her hand as they picked their way between carriages and motorcars, horns blaring and drivers shouting. Reaching the other side unscathed, Nick quickly released Amelia's hand as they stepped up on to the footpath.

"Well, that was fun!" exclaimed Amelia, breathing hard from the exertion.

"Not quite like Sydney traffic, is it?"

"Definitely not!" laughed Amelia. "Where to now, Nick?"

"I think we'll find something to eat, and then I want to show you something, over in the park." He swung an arm in the direction of the town gardens.

"You mean we have to cross the road again?"

"Er – yes. Sorry about that."

"Never mind." Amelia looked up at the town clock. It was about to chime five o'clock. "It's time they were all home anyway."

With that the air began to vibrate with the sound of the five o'clock chime. Amelia placed her hands over her ears until the final dong had died away.

Nick grinned at her. "How about some fish and chips?"

For a fleeting second a frown creased her smooth brow, but it was quickly replaced with a smile. "That sounds just fine."

They found a fish-and-chips shop still open, and within a very short space of time, were scurrying back across the busy intersection, the smell of their purchase tickling their nostrils. Nick was anxious to show Amelia the Cascades, so he grabbed her hand and hurried her through the park. Amelia, who was wearing high-heeled shoes, protested loudly.

"Nick! Slow down, please! These shoes are killing my feet."

Nick merely grinned and kept pulling her along the path. "It's not far, and I assure you that what I'm about to show you will be worth the pain."

Amelia was not convinced, but she had no choice. Nick's grip on her hand was secure; there was no way she could slip free.

"There! Isn't that a sight to behold?"

Nick had finally stopped, and Amelia halted beside him, her temper a little frayed, and her feet throbbing. Scowling, she looked up at what Nick was gazing at. Water danced down the hillside over a series of steps, finishing up at an elaborate wrought-iron fountain. She gasped as water droplets settled on her face, cooling her temperature and her mood immediately.

"It's beautiful, Nick!" she exclaimed, all thoughts of chastising him, gone from her head.

"This is where we are going to eat our fish and chips." Nick pulled her hand as he stepped on to the grass and led her up the hillside. "Here will do."

They sat on the grass, far enough away from the water to avoid becoming wet, and as Nick unwrapped the newspaper containing their meal, Amelia slipped her feet out of her shoes. Her toes were red, and she rubbed them tentatively. Nick grimaced as he saw them.

"Sorry," was all he said.

"Next time we head out on safari, Nick, you had better warn me, so that I can lace my boots on."

Nick couldn't imagine those dainty feet encased in boots, so he merely smiled, and dived his hand into the steaming chips.

"It was worth it, though, wasn't it?" he said through a mouthful.

"I suppose so." Amelia picked at the chips, reluctantly admitting to herself that they were delicious.

Nick lay back on the grass, and with his hands behind his head, gave a sigh of satisfaction. "It's so good to get out of the city, don't you agree?"

Amelia merely shrugged.

They continued eating until the paper was empty. Nick screwed it up into a ball, wiped a hand across his mouth and then resumed his reclining position. Amelia, seated beside him, leaned back on her hands and stretched her bare feet out in front of her. They were silent for a few moments as they each listened to the sound of the running water and contemplated the real reason they were here in this magical place.

"So, Miss Hudson," Nick broke the silence, "are you after my job?"

Amelia swivelled around to stare at him. "Why would I want your job?"

"I don't know." Nick shrugged absently. "You tell me."

Amelia pulled her knees up and turned towards him. "I don't want your job, Nick." She laughed. "Can you imagine me working with Joe?"

"He's thinking of retiring."

"What? He told you that?"

"He did."

Amelia was silent, as she pulled at a blade of grass. "We've never got on, Joe and me, and this little ploy of mine was simply to prove to him that I can be just as dogmatic as he is. If I follow the clues, they will lead to a result."

"Not always, Amelia. It's not as straightforward as that."

"Leave no stone unturned, Joe always said, so I try not to."

Nick was silent for a moment. "You know, if your theory turns out to be correct, there will be no case to answer, because there will be no culprit. You and I, my dear Amelia, will probably not get a penny." He glanced up at her. "Does that bother you?"

"Not in the least. We will have done our job, as far as the law requires. If we find her, in whatever circumstance, we will still be entitled to the reward money. The police can then close their file on missing person, Phyllis Powell, because she will no longer be missing." Amelia reached for her shoes. "It's time we were thinking about moving from here. It will soon be dark, and we don't want to be locked out of our accommodation."

Nick laughed. "That won't happen. We're not in the city now, Amelia."

"No. Nevertheless, I'm getting cool, and that water is not helping matters. Come on, help me up."

Nick scrambled to his feet and held out a hand. "I promise I won't walk as fast on the way home."

"You'd better not." Amelia winced as her toes felt the pressure of her shoes. "You might have to carry me."

"Fireman's lift?" Nick bent his shoulders and made as if to lift her, but she pushed him away.

"I was only joking!"

They both laughed as they headed down the grassy slope. Twilight was beginning to spread a rosy hue across the skyline, and a breeze had begun to rustle the trees. The roadway, when they reached it, was almost deserted, and so they strolled past the fountain and across to the other side without any incidents. The street was also deserted, and they walked in silence until they reached the bridge that spanned the railway line.

"I hope you know where you're going, Nick." Amelia grabbed his arm.

"Of course." Nick stared down at her, walking close beside him, and he experienced a sudden feeling of protectiveness - wanting her to be always within reach. It was absurd of course, for Amelia Hudson was not a shrinking violet, and he almost laughed at his own stupidity.

Amelia saw the smile that flicked across his features. "What are you smiling at?"

Nick shrugged. "I was just being whimsical."

"Whimsical?" She laughed. "You mean something took your fancy? Please indulge me, Nick?"

"And embarrass myself? No."

Amelia took his arm. "Then I'm going to embarrass myself and tell you that I really enjoy your company, Nick, and whatever turns up in this investigation, I hope it is not the end for us."

Nick was silent as their footsteps echoed on the asphalt. Those had been his thoughts exactly. He cleared his throat. "It doesn't have to be."

"Good! Whimsical or not, that's settled."

*

As they entered the side door of the Grey Goose, Harry appeared at the bar to meet them.

"Can I trouble you to step in here for a minute?" he said quietly, as he looked quickly along the passage. It was deserted. "I need to talk to you both."

"Certainly, Harry." Nick ushered Amelia ahead of him as they all entered the bar. Harry hurried to the furthest table and pulled out a chair for Amelia. They all sat, Harry facing his two guests.

"Nick, I have an apology to make to you," Harry began. "Isobel is aware that something is going on. I have told her not to breathe a word to her sister, but I have a feeling that your cover is shortly going to be blown."

A short silence followed while Nick leaned his elbows on the table and studied Harry thoughtfully.

"Maybe that's not a bad thing." He paused. "Perhaps I should explain myself to all those I've had contact with, and…"

"Can that wait, Nick," interrupted Amelia, "until we've checked out the possible lead that I have?"

"Possible lead?" Harry sat upright.

Amelia looked enquiringly at Nick. He nodded.

"I have discovered," said Amelia quietly, "that Phyllis Powell spent many years in the orphanage here, as a child and as a young woman, and I suspect that, if she had nowhere else to go, then maybe she returned to the place that had given her shelter? It seems a logical explanation, as nobody has seen or heard anything of her for three years."

Harry whistled through his teeth. "Yes, I suppose that's a possibility, and you want to check it out, I gather?"

"Yes." Amelia turned to Nick. "I would like us to go there tomorrow, Nick, if you agree?"

"I'm happy to do that." He smiled at her quizzical expression.

"I'm surprised the police haven't checked that one out," said Harry, scratching his head. "It makes you wonder just how diligently they've been looking."

"That's why we have jobs, Harry. No stone unturned, and all that." Nick grinned at Harry.

"Can I pass that on to Isobel, please? I'll threaten her with dire consequences if she dares to breathe a word to Jess."

They both laughed.

"Certainly, Harry," said Nick, "but there's no need to threaten her. I'm sure Izzy has enough sense to see the seriousness of this."

"I wouldn't go that far, Nick. Isobel will stop at nothing if her sister is involved."

"Her sister is not involved, and if our theory is correct, then Mr. O'Connor is not involved either."

"No? You haven't spoken to him yet?"

"Haven't laid eyes on him, and hopefully that will remain the case."

"Well!" Harry stood up. "What if we invite your 'persons of interest' for tea tomorrow night, after you've been to the orphanage, and you can clear the air with them?"

"It's not a fait accompli, Harry. We might still be back where we started."

"True, but it could also mean that you get everyone on side."

Nick nodded thoughtfully. "What about Maitland? Are you going to invite him too?"

Harry paused for a second. "Why not. He might have something to add to the mix."

"Yes, he could."

"Good! That's settled."

The Institution on the Hill

Nick and Amelia stood on the gravel road that ran past the imposing red and cream three storey brick building that stared out over the township like an avenging angel. Many chimneys reached up into the cloudless blue sky. Amelia shivered, not from the cold, but from a sense that all was not well within the grounds that lay beyond the high brick fence. Wrought iron gates barred their way, and a heavy silence lay over the whole area.

"Who did you say runs this place?" asked Nick cautiously, feeling intimidated by the size of the place with its many wings and sprawling outbuilding.

"I didn't," replied Amelia, still staring ahead of her. "It's run by the sisters of the Good Shepherd."

"Nuns? Then why do I get the feeling that this is not a refuge?"

"I don't know," whispered Amelia, afraid that someone might be listening, "but I have the same feeling. Maybe this is not a good idea, Nick." She turned as if to leave, but Nick took her arm.

"No, we have to follow this through. No stone unturned, remember?" He lifted the heavy latch on the gate, and it creaked open. "Come on. We'll either find out something about Phyllis or we won't."

Together they stepped through the gate, and Nick pushed it closed behind them. Their footsteps crunched on the gravel as they walked towards what looked like the main door of the building. As they passed a garden bed to their right, a young girl materialised beside them. She wore a grey serge dress, over which was a white pinafore, stained with grass and dirt. Her hair was restrained with a white scarf and her feet were encased in sturdy boots. She squinted at the two who had halted beside her, and Amelia noticed that her hands, twisting at her waist, were red and calloused. Amelia estimated that her age was probably about sixteen.

"Can I help you?" the girl enquired slowly.

"We'd like to speak with whoever is in charge," said Nick carefully.

"That would be Reverend Mother."

"Er – where can we find her?"

"In there." Her head jerked towards the door.

As they stepped towards the entrance, her next words made them both stop in their tracks.

"Are you here to adopt a baby?"

Amelia turned slowly to face the girl. "No," she said softly.

The girl nodded her head and stepped back into the garden. "That's alright then."

Amelia stared at Nick; her mouth dry. This was something she had not anticipated, and her heart wrenched. The girl probably had a child although she was little more than a child herself. Did she spend her life in fear that the next strangers to appear, were going to take her child? Another thought suddenly occurred to her, and she felt sick inside. If Phyllis was here, and it was highly likely, then perhaps she was here for a reason – to protect her child. The reporter in Amelia longed to run with the story and the headline rushed through her brain – Missing girl found at sanctuary on a hill – but the woman in her balked at the idea of possibly destroying two people's lives. She grabbed Nick by the arm.

"Nick," she whispered, "I'm beginning to think that this is not a good idea."

He stared at her, noticing that her face had paled. "Why not? What's wrong?"

Amelia steered him away from the entrance and along the gravel path, out of earshot.

"We can't suddenly expose Phyllis, if she is here," she whispered. "What if she's here to protect her child from the likes of Sid O'Connor? She won't thank us for that."

"Amelia, we're not here to take her child away from her."

"I know, but if she's been hiding here for three years, we can't just walk in and turn her life upside down. We need to reconsider our options here."

Nick stared at her. "We're here to do a job, Amelia, but if you're getting cold feet, then I will have to continue alone. At this stage we don't know that she is here. Until we find that out, then we're simply whistling in the dark."

"I still don't like it, Nick."

"Fine!" Nick was becoming angry. "You stay out here, and I'll go and find the Reverend Mother."

Amelia looked back at the girl in the garden. "She has a child," she whispered, "and she's terrified that somebody is going to come and take it away."

"How do you know that?" Nick's tone was scornful.

"Because it happens all the time, Nick." Amelia smiled at his puzzled expression. "Alright." She sighed heavily. "I'll come with you, but if I feel uncomfortable, I'm walking away."

Nick shrugged. "You led us here, Amelia."

"I know, and that's what troubles me the most." She frowned. "Who did you say reported her missing?"

"I didn't say. That information was not forthcoming."

"Anonymous?"

"Could be."

The girl in the garden was watching them, and as Amelia turned in her direction, she quickly resumed her weeding.

"She doesn't like us being here," she mused, half to herself.

"Perhaps she knows Phyllis." The words were out before Nick could stop them.

"Perhaps, but we're not going to question her, Nick."

"I thought you had a sense of adventure, Amelia. What's changed?"

"Perhaps I have," murmured Amelia, gazing up at the building overshadowing them. "Look at this place, Nick. Behind these walls are young women and children, who through no fault of their own have nowhere else to go to feel safe."

"I didn't know you had a soft side, Amelia." Nick took her by the arm and steered her towards the main door. "Come on, we're wasting time."

"I like to think I have," muttered Amelia, as she was guided through the massive door and into a foyer that smelled of phenyl. She coughed as it caught in her throat.

They had to sidestep a young girl who was on her knees, scrubbing the linoleum with a wire brush. She looked up as they passed, and sat back on her haunches, staring mutely at them from under a fringe of untidy dark hair. She was dressed in similar attire to the girl outside, and Amelia noted that her hands were red and calloused. These girls worked hard it seemed. Amelia tucked her well-manicured hands into the pocket of her light blue wool jacket and smiled at the girl.

"Where can we find the Reverend Mother?" she enquired softly.

The girl pointed along the wide corridor. "Down there on the left," she said bluntly, before resuming her scrubbing.

"Thank-you."

Their footsteps echoed in the empty corridor as they headed towards a door with OFFICE emblazoned in brass lettering. After knocking loudly, Nick stood back as they waited for a response from within.

Finally, they heard a muffled "Enter!" and Nick pushed on the solid oak door.

They stepped into a large room, warmed by a crackling open fire, and overflowing with shelves of books and manila folders. Cardboard boxes were piled against the far wall, and it was from that direction they heard a voice say, "Mr. and Mrs. Brown?"

Nick and Amelia looked quickly at one another, and Nick answered hastily, "No."

A black clad figure materialised from the assortment of boxes and walked towards them. She was tall with a thin face protruding from a white wimple. Round-rimmed spectacles sat on the end of her hawklike nose, and she stared at her visitors as she brushed dust from her black habit.

"So if you're not Mr. and Mrs. Brown," she said with an imperious tone, "then who are you and what are you doing here?"

"I'm Nicholas Armitage," said Nick quickly, "and this is Miss Amelia Hudson."

The Reverend Mother peered at them in the soft light of the room, and her expression changed from mild curiosity to disapproval.

"You're not here to adopt?" Her eyes flicked over Amelia.

"No," said Nick firmly, realising at once what the Reverend Mother was thinking. "And neither is Miss Hudson pregnant."

Amelia sucked in her breath as she heard Nick mutter these words, and if he hadn't grabbed her arm, she would have turned and stalked from the room.

"Then what are you here for?"

"We're here seeking information on a young woman by the name of Phyllis Powell," said Nick as he released Amelia's arm. "We have reason to believe that she could be living here."

"Have you now?" The tight expression changed back to curiosity. "May I ask why?"

"Is that a correct assumption?" Nick ignored the question.

"That depends on who you are, and why you want to find her."

"So, she is here?" Amelia's eyes gleamed as she looked at Nick.

"My dear," said the Reverend Mother softly, as she leaned towards Amelia, "there are a lot of young women here who would prefer to stay here within our care than face the consequences out there." She nodded towards the one window that Amelia noticed was heavily barred.

"And is Phyllis Powell one of them?" Amelia met her gaze steadily.

"Phyllis is here, yes. She was here as a child and returned to us in her hour of need."

"So you did take her in?" Nick persisted.

"Young man I have already said that." The hawklike gaze switched to Nick.

"Can we see her?" asked Amelia.

"I still don't know who you are. You're not relatives because Phyllis doesn't have any."

"No, we're not relatives," said Nick slowly. "Somebody reported her missing to the police."

"You're the police?" Her eyes bored into Nick.

"No." He shook his head. "I am a private investigator, and Miss Hudson is a reporter with the Sydney Herald."

"Sydney?" Her eyes widened.

"We're both from Sydney actually," said Amelia tightly. "We're doing the job the police here should be doing."

"May I ask who's looking for her?"

"We don't know," said Nick. "That information was kept from us."

The Reverend Mother frowned as she rubbed her forehead thoughtfully. "What are your intentions, if I allow you to see her?"

"We simply want to make sure she's alright and make a report that she's happy to remain here."

"You have no intention of removing her?"

"No," cut in Amelia, "but we would like to hear her story."

"I'm sure you would, young lady." There was cynicism in her tone. "Very well." The Reverend Mother moved towards the door. "I'll see if she wants to see you." Opening the door, she called out, "Mavis! Come here, child."

Nick and Amelia turned to see the young girl they had encountered in the corridor.

"Yes, Reverend Mother." She bobbed her head.

"Go to the laundry and tell Phyllis that I wish to speak with her, please?"

"Yes, Reverend Mother." Another bob of the head and the girl scurried away.

"Is there somewhere we can talk privately?" Nick asked, looking around the cluttered room.

"As you can see, young man," said the Reverend Mother dryly, "I am very busy in here." She thought for a moment. "You can use my private room, which is through there." She pointed beyond the boxes to a closed door. "Of course, you realise that if Phyllis has no wish to talk to you, then there's nothing I can do about that." The smile didn't quite reach her eyes.

"We understand," said Nick, glancing at Amelia's tight face.

"Phyllis is one of my best workers." There was that half smile again. "I would hate to lose her."

Amelia looked squarely at the Reverend Mother. "Do your girls receive payment for their hard work? I understand you run a commercial laundry, and that must keep the girls very busy."

"It does," came the chilly reply. "We provide a roof over their heads; we take care of their children. They don't expect anything in return. They would be on the street if we weren't here to provide for them." She pointed to the boxes. "As you can see, we receive donations of clothing all the time."

"I see."

"They are well cared for."

The sentence hung in the air for several moments, until the creak of the door made them all turn.

"You sent for me, Reverend Mother?"

"Yes, Phyllis." She turned to her visitors. "Mr. Armitage and Miss Hudson wish to speak with you, if you agree."

The young woman swung around, her eyes wide. "What about?" she demanded.

Nick stepped forward, holding out his hand. "We're not here to cause you any trouble, Phyllis," he said quietly. "We simply wish to speak with you about your decision to return here."

The girl blinked, ignoring Nick's hand. She was dressed in similar attire to the two girls they had already encountered. Her brown hair was tucked up beneath a white cap, and damp tendrils fell across her flushed face. Her hands, also red and calloused, clenched and unclenched at her waist.

"Why do you wanna know about me? You're not 'ere to take my Hope away, are ya?"

Nick glanced at the Reverend Mother. "Hope is her daughter," she said briskly.

"No, Phyllis, we're not here to take your child away from you."

Phyllis relaxed visibly. "That's alright then."

The Reverend Mother pushed open the door to her private chambers. "You can talk in here." She looked at Phyllis over the top of her spectacles. "I'll leave the door open," she added, and her meaning was very clear.

They made their way into the adjoining sitting room, and Nick was surprised at the comforts they saw there. A large armchair was pulled up to an open fire, which was now reduced to glowing embers. Colourful crocheted rugs were thrown across the chair. Beside it stood a small table on which was an open book and a pair of spectacles. A single bed stood against the far wall, and it also was covered with crocheted rugs. On the walls Nick saw the usual framed pictures of the blessed Mary and her crucified son. A large bronze cross was hung above the fireplace and in one corner stood a writing bureau and cushion covered stool. The Reverend Mother had comfortable living quarters, which was contrary to what he had read about the numerous orders of Nuns and Sisters.

Phyllis interrupted his thoughts. "Well? What do ya wanna know about me?" She was standing with her back to the fireplace.

Amelia had seated herself on the edge of the bed, a notebook and pencil in her hands.

Nick looked at Phyllis and saw for the first time the uncertainty in her large hazel eyes. He smiled, reassuringly he hoped.

"You've been here three years?"

Phyllis nodded, eyeing the notebook in Amelia's hands. "Are you takin' down what I say?" She asked accusingly, jerking her head at Amelia.

"Yes," said Amelia calmly. "I don't want to make any mistakes."

"Why did you come here, Phyllis?"

Phyllis swung her gaze back to Nick. "Because I'd lived 'ere for most of me life, an' I knew the sisters would look after me an' Hope."

"What about Hope's father? Did he know about this?"

Her chin jutted defiantly. "None of 'is business!"

"Who is Hope's father, Phyllis?" The question came from Amelia.

"Is it Billy Maitland or Sid O'Connor?" Nick watched her jaw working. "I've met Billy, Phyllis. However, I haven't met Sid."

Her eyes blazed suddenly. "Keep away from Sid. 'E's…"

"He's what, Phyllis?" Nick kept his voice steady.

"'E's dangerous, that's what 'e is!" Her voice quivered. "I don't want 'im finding out where I am."

A loud cough was heard coming from the outer room, and the Reverend Mother appeared in the doorway, her expression tight.

"I think that's enough," she snapped. "Phyllis, you have work to do. I suggest you go and do it!"

"Yes, Reverend Mother." Phyllis scurried past them all, pausing briefly at the door. "Don't tell Sid I'm 'ere, please?" Then she was gone.

The Reverend Mother turned to Nick. "And just what did that achieve?" Her tone was bitter. "These girls are here to escape the likes of Sid O'Connor, and you have no right to compromise their situation – no right at all!"

"I'm sorry," said Nick, feeling the weight of his own words, "but I will have to report that Phyllis has been located. However…" He heard the Reverend Mother suck in her breath. "However, I promise it will go no further."

"How can you promise that?" The Reverend Mother stalked back into the outer room. "I have betrayed that girl by allowing you to speak with her, and that is not what we're here for. We're here to protect them. Please go! You have no idea what damage you have just caused."

Nick and Amelia did not speak as they walked along the corridor to the front door. Once outside, Nick took a deep breath, and glancing up, saw the girl who was working in the garden, staring at him. He dropped his gaze.

"I think we've just made a terrible mistake," he said miserably.

"Nick, we weren't to know how this was going to play out." Amelia squeezed his arm. "We'll have to tell Joe and hear what he has to say."

Nick nodded. "Come on, let's get out of this place." He looked behind him. "They might be here to protect those girls, but I have an uneasy feeling about this place."

"Did you notice that all the windows are barred?" Amelia whispered as they walked quickly along the gravel path to the gate.

"Yes, I did, but the gate isn't locked."

"There is a padlock. Perhaps it's locked at night."

Nick turned to look at Amelia. "A bit like a prison?"

"Yes." Amelia clung to his arm as they headed down the hill towards the town. "Maybe the lesser of two evils." She shrugged as Nick gave her a quizzical look. "Work hard for the Nuns or be a slave to a man? Drudgery comes in many forms."

"Don't tar all men with that brush, Amelia." Nick laughed suddenly. "We're not all brutes."

"I know that, but these girls don't."

"Hm. What do we do now?"

"We contact Joe and hear what he has to say."

"Harry has visitors coming for tea tonight to hear us explain ourselves,"

Nick reminded her soberly.

Amelia sighed. "Yes, I know." She paused. "Let's talk to Joe first."

Telling the Truth

Joe was suitably impressed when they talked to him a little later, in the busy confines of the Post Office. Nick tried to keep his voice low, which caused Joe to grumble loudly.

"Speak up, boy! I can't hear you!"

"I'm sorry, Joe, but it's very public here at the Post Office, and we don't want everyone hearing what's going on."

"Alright, so let me get this straight. The young woman in question has been located, at an orphanage, and does not wish anyone to know?"

"That's correct."

"We'll have to let the police know. After all, there is a reward for information."

"Have you any idea who started the search?"

"No."

"So our job here is finished?"

"Not until you've informed the local constabulary."

Nick took a deep breath. "We owe it to her, Joe, to keep the location secret. She seems happy where she is and wants to keep her child safe."

"Very well. That can be arranged, I'm sure. Good work, you two. You achieved a result in a matter of days. Have a few days rest before you come home." Joe laughed.

"You have Amelia to thank for the quick result, Joe. She traced the records and feminine intuition did the rest."

Amelia gave Nick a quick shove. "Feminine intuition?"

They both heard Joe's loud guffaw. "You two are getting on alright then?"

"Yes, certainly." Nick held the receiver away from Amelia, who was trying to grab it. "I'll talk to you later, Joe. Let me know how you get on. Telephone me at the hotel. I should be able to take your call by then. Goodbye, Joe!" He hung up the receiver and smiled wickedly at Amelia.

"Nick!" Amelia was cross, and her blue eyes flickered dangerously. "I wanted to speak to him!"

"Later. Come on, we have some explaining to do to Harry and Izzy."

"What about the Maitland chap?" Amelia was suddenly serious. "If he's the child's father, then…"

"We don't know that he is, Amelia, and anyway, we are not at liberty to tell him anything."

Amelia frowned. "But it's O'Connor she's afraid of."

"Yes, I know." Nick looked up to see the Post Office Clerk staring at him. He grabbed Amelia by the arm. "Come on, let's get out of here. That man behind the counter is making me nervous."

Nick placed some coins on the counter, smiled briefly at the Clerk and headed out the door with Amelia in tow. At the foot of the steps, she dragged her arm from his grasp.

"You can let me go now, Nick." She rubbed her arm. "I think you've made your point."

He smiled sheepishly. "Sorry. Are you hungry?"

"Well, yes, but…"

"Fish and chips at the Cascades?"

"No, Nick! We had fish and chips yesterday. Besides, I thought you had some explaining to do."

"Yes, you're right." Nick was suddenly serious. "We'll have sandwiches at the Grey Goose." He looked at his watch just as the Post Office clock thundered out its one o'clock chimes. "One o'clock. There should be some sandwiches left. Come on."

Twenty minutes later they walked into the hotel. Jean looked up from behind the bar as Nick approached and smiled at him.

"Successful morning?" she asked sweetly, seeing Amelia's flushed face.

"You could say that Jean." Nick leaned over the bar. "We need to speak with Harry and Izzy. Are they available?"

"They're both in the kitchen."

"Good. Any sandwiches left, Jean?"

"You might be lucky. Ask Izzy."

"Thanks, Jean."

Jean watched them walk out into the passage, her face thoughtful. *What are they here for?* She wondered absently, as she wiped the counter.

*

Nick found Harry and Izzy in the kitchen, both busy chopping up vegetables. They looked up, somewhat surprised as he entered. Amelia had excused herself, saying that she was going upstairs to freshen up and change her shoes.

"Hello, Nick!" Harry said cheerfully. "What can we do for you?"

"Firstly, I'd like some sandwiches, if it's not too much trouble," replied Nick. "Secondly, can you both spare a few minutes. Amelia and I have something to tell you."

Harry and Izzy looked at each other.

"I'll make you some sandwiches," said Izzy quickly, "and if you go to the Ladies' Lounge, we can spare you a few minutes, can't we, Harry?"

"Er – yes." Harry put down the knife he was using. "You have news, obviously?"

"Yes, we do."

"Very well." Harry frowned. "It might be best if we use Jean's sitting room, which is directly opposite the Ladies' Lounge. Go in there, and Izzy and I will join you shortly." Harry looked around for Amelia. "Where is Miss Hudson?"

"She's gone upstairs to freshen up. I'll wait for her in the passage. Thanks, Harry." Nick turned at the door and smiled at Izzy. "Thanks, Izzy."

Amelia appeared several minutes later, and they let themselves into Jean's sitting room. It was a comfortable room with a fireplace, two well-used armchairs, a settee with scattered rugs and a small round table on which they saw two empty glasses and a glass ashtray with two butts in it. They seated themselves on the armchairs and waited. A clock above the fireplace ticked loudly in the silence. It was half-past one.

"No wonder we're hungry," whispered Nick. "Look at the time?"

Amelia settled herself into one of the armchairs. "It's been a long morning." She yawned as she rested her head on the back of the chair. "I might just go to sleep if I stay here."

"How are we going to do this, Amelia? Straight down the line?"

"Hm," murmured Amelia, her eyes closed. "That would be best, Nick."

Izzy bustled into the room, followed closely by Harry. She placed a plate of sandwiches on the table and scooped up the empty glasses and ashtray.

"Harry?" Izzy frowned at him. "Have you been smoking?"

"Just a couple, my love." Harry looked sheepish as he sat on the settee.

"Hm." Izzy threw him a loaded scowl before turning to Nick and Amelia. "Drinks?"

"A beer thanks, Izzy," said Nick.

"Miss Hudson?"

Amelia's eyes shot open. "Oh! I'll have a lemonade please, Mrs. Dalton."

"Call me Izzy, and don't start your story until I get back." Izzy moved to the door. "You can start the sandwiches though." Then she was gone.

Harry sighed. "I shouldn't leave the evidence for Isobel to find."

"No, you shouldn't." Amelia reached for a sandwich.

They ate quietly as the clock ticked noisily above the fireplace. Izzy returned shortly, handed Nick and Amelia their drinks, and sat beside Harry.

"You can begin now," she said breathlessly. "What have you discovered?"

Amelia looked at Nick as she brushed crumbs from her blue line dress. "Do you want me to start, Nick?" He nodded, as his mouth was full. "Very well." She turned her focus on Izzy and Harry. "We have found Miss Powell." It was a blunt statement.

There was a moment of silence, broken only by the sound of the clock.

Finally, Izzy found her voice. "Found her already?" she squeaked. "At the orphanage?"

"Yes. She's spent the past three years living there."

Izzy stared incredulously at Harry. "You do mean that big place up on the hill?"

"The very one." Amelia smiled.

"Why?"

"Because apparently, she grew up there, from the age of seven, after her mother died, and she stayed there until she was seventeen. It's the only place she feels safe."

"Blimey!" Harry sat back, scratching his head. "So, she's been there all the time?"

"She has," said Nick, "and now she doesn't want it known, particularly to Mr. O'Connor."

"We didn't get a very warm reception," said Amelia as she took another sandwich. "In fact, the Reverend Mother was quite scathing of our attempts to question the young woman."

"I got the impression that they work very hard there." Nick helped himself to the last sandwich. "The nuns run a commercial laundry, worked by the young mothers." He smiled to himself. "The funny thing is, the Reverend Mother thought we were there to adopt a child."

"OR that I was pregnant." Amelia glared pointedly at Nick.

"Yes, well it is the place young girls run to when they're in trouble." Nick's face had suffused with colour.

"So what do you do now?" The query came from Izzy.

"I've spoken with my boss," said Nick, "and I'll wait to hear back from him. In the meantime, I must inform the police here, and try to make it understood that the young woman in question wants to remain where she is."

"We have guests coming for tea tonight," Izzy reminded them, "and I'm sure they'll be very interested in what you have to say."

"I'm sure they will." Nick frowned as he looked at Izzy. "Is Billy Maitland on the guest list?"

"He was," said Harry, "but he has to work."

"Perhaps that's just as well," said Nick. "He's a mate of O'Connor's, isn't he?"

"I suppose you could say that." Izzy picked up the empty sandwich plate and glasses. "I think Billy simply tolerates Sid. There's not a lot of love lost between them." Izzy headed for the door.

"Isobel!" Harry's voice stopped her in her tracks. She turned at the door.

"Yes, Harry?"

"You are not to speak of this to anybody, do you understand?"

Izzy pouted. "Yes, Harry, of course."

As Izzy flounced out of the room, Harry turned to his guests with a sigh. "My wife does love to talk, as you've probably noticed, and she's not always appropriate." Harry stood up. "I'd better get back to the bar before Jean starts calling for me."

"Certainly, Harry." Nick rose to his feet. "I think I'll go and find a quiet spot to write some notes. Tea is at six-thirty, I presume?"

"Er – yes," said Harry. "Or thereabouts." He grinned before disappearing into the passage.

Amelia stretched and then eased herself gracefully out of the armchair. "I suppose that means I too will have to find a quiet spot to meditate."

"Go out the back of the hotel and check out Izzy's murals," suggested Nick. "You will be amazed."

"I might just do that." As they stepped into the passage, Amelia caught Nick's arm. "I have enjoyed our time together, Nick." She paused. "I'm catching the morning train to Melbourne tomorrow, to see my mother before heading back to Sydney."

"Joe suggested a few more days," said Nick hopefully.

Amelia smiled. "No. I'll leave you to finish up things here. Besides, I've interfered enough."

"Interfered?" Nick laughed. "Without you none of this would have happened. I'd have probably thrashed around in circles, upsetting everybody needlessly, and not drawing any conclusion."

"Female intuition, Nick – you said so yourself."

Nick placed his right hand dramatically across his heart. "Well, whatever it was, from the bottom of my heart I thank you, Amelia."

"You still have to face the DuBois's," Amelia reminded him.

"Yes, and some sort of explanation to Billy Maitland might not go amiss, either."

"I don't know that I'd go that far, Nick. He's too close to O'Connor."

"Maybe." Nick headed for the stairs.

"I'll see you at tea." Amelia called after him.

*

The sound of laughter reached Nick's ears as he walked into the Ladies' Lounge. The large dining table was laid with a crisp damask cloth and gleaming silver cutlery. Crystal glasses had been placed at each setting, and folded cream napkins had been placed across each bread-and-butter plate. Eucalyptus foliage adorned the centre of the table, along with deep red bottlebrush sprigs. Nick was impressed. Izzy had gone out of her way to make this meal as inviting as possible. He was still admiring the effect when he heard footsteps behind him, and Izzy appeared at his elbow.

"What do you think, Nick?" She laughed. "Do we know how to do things in the bush?"

"My mother would be very impressed, Izzy, as am I." Nick gave a slight bow. "You have excelled yourself. It looks marvellous."

"I am so glad you approve, Nick." Izzy's gaze swept across the room to where Jess, Beau and Amelia were sharing a joke. "It looks as though they're getting along." She took Nick's arm. "Come on, let's join them. I have a few minutes before I need to check on the food."

As Nick felt himself propelled across the room, the laughter came to a sudden halt. The DuBois's looked at him with a certain reservation, and only Amelia smiled at him.

"Hello, Nick," she said cheerily, unaware of the coolness emanating from her companions.

Nick returned her smile. "Hello, Amelia. I must say you look very elegant tonight."

Amelia was wearing a slim-fitting black dress with a low neckline that showed off her creamy shoulders. A string of pearls sat at her throat, and her dark hair had been brushed into a bob that framed her elfin face. A flush spread across her cheeks, accentuating the sprinkle of freckles.

"You've scrubbed up rather well yourself, Mr. Armitage," was her coy response.

Nick, who had changed his shirt for a fresh open-necked white one, gave a mock bow.

"Alright! That's enough, you two!" Izzy laughed. "I hope you can put us all out of our misery tonight. I'm dying to find out what you've discovered while you've been prowling around our town."

"All is not as it seems, Izzy," said Nick mysteriously, receiving a frown from Doctor DuBois.

"Well then," said Izzy, "I'd better hurry up with the meal. Find yourselves a seat, and I shall return shortly." She glanced at the wall clock. "Jean and Harry should be with us shortly. Freya is safely out of the way tonight." She smiled at Beau. "Charlotte has agreed to look after her, for which I am extremely grateful."

"We promised Charlotte we wouldn't be late," said Jess quietly.

"And neither you shall, sister dear." Izzy hurried towards the door. "I'll be as quick as I can."

They all enjoyed a sumptuous meal of roast lamb and baked vegetables, and nobody spoke during the meal. When all the plates were clean, Izzy began to stack them on to a tray. She paused before heading out to the kitchen, and all eyes turned in her direction.

"I think we'll listen to what Nick has to say, before I serve the dessert," she said quickly. There were nods of agreement. "So don't start until I've got rid of these dirty plates."

"We wouldn't dream of it, Isobel," said Harry dryly. "Don't be too long."

Izzy hurried from the room, leaving them all staring silently at each other. The clock above the mural on the far wall ticked loudly in the silence. Jean cleared her throat.

"I hope you don't have too many surprises for us, Nick," she said into the silence.

Nick glanced sideways at Amelia. "I hope we can answer the questions you all must have for us at this point."

"So do we," said Beau tightly.

Jess placed her hand hurriedly over his, as it lay clenched on the table. Izzy returned at that moment and took her place beside Harry.

"Are you ready, Nick?" Izzy smiled at him across the table.

Nick took a deep breath. "First of all, I owe you good people an apology. I am not a journalist, as I led you to believe. I am a Private Investigator, and I was sent here to gather information on a young woman who went missing from this area in 1917. Her name is Phyllis Powell."

"Phyllis Powell?" Jess stared at him in disbelief. "I had no idea she'd been missing."

"So why the deception?" Beau's eyes narrowed. "Why not tell us that in the first place?"

Nick brushed a hand across his eyes and then fixed his gaze on Beau. "Because I am employed by Joe Hudson, the Investigator who came looking for you, Dr. DuBois, in 1917."

Beau sat back on his chair and stared at Nick. "And you think the two incidents are linked?"

"No, absolutely not!" Nick held up his hands. "The only connection is your association with Sidney O'Connor, the main person of interest in this case."

"Sid!" Jean groaned. "Why am I not surprised?" Her brow furrowed. "Do you suspect foul play?"

"You'd better explain it all, Nick." Amelia spoke for the first time.

"Amelia Hudson." Beau spoke quietly as he looked in her direction. "You're a relative of Joe's?"

"Yes." Amelia met his gaze. "I'm his daughter."

Beau gave a short laugh. "And you're also a Private Investigator?"

"No." Amelia shook her head. "I'm a reporter for the Sydney Herald."

Beau made as if to rise from his chair, but Jess placed her hand over his once more. "We need to hear what they have to say, Beau."

"Do we?" he replied harshly.

"Yes."

"Very well." Beau turned his gaze on Nick. "We're listening."

Nick cleared his throat. "It was Joe's idea that I come here as a journalist looking for a post-war human-interest story. He felt that people would be less inclined to talk to me if they knew what I was really here for."

"And you, Miss Hudson, where do you fit into this?" Beau was staring at Amelia.

"Nick and I met on the train, coming down from Sydney."

Beau frowned. "You didn't know each other before that?"

"No." Amelia smiled. "As it happened, I was looking for some challenging work, and contacted Joe. He sent me to keep an eye on Nick." She laughed softly. "I tried my deception skills on him, but he soon worked out who I was, and I've been able to help him locate the missing young woman."

"You've located Phyllis?" This came from Jess.

"We have." Amelia looked at Nick. "Tell them, Nick."

"Before I do," Nick said solemnly, "I need you to understand that Miss Powell wishes to remain where she is, and on no account must Mr. O'Connor find out."

"So where is she?" prompted Jean.

"She's at the orphanage."

There was silence in the room.

"Has she been there all this time?" The question came from Jess.

"I believe so." Nick gazed around the faces staring at him. "I don't know what you all know about Miss Powell, but she grew up in that orphanage, from the age of seven until she was seventeen."

"No, I didn't know that." Jess looked across at Jean. "Did you know, Jean?"

"Yes, I did actually, but I had forgotten." Jean's brow was furrowed. "Her mother died in very poor circumstances, and I'm not sure where her father was at that time." She paused. "I remember there being some fuss as to who could look after the child, and the next thing I do remember is that she was whisked away to that place on the hill. It was a long time ago." She nodded thoughtfully. "So she's back there, is she?"

"Yes," said Nick, "with her daughter."

"Ah!" Jean looked up quickly. "There was some confusion about who that child belonged to." She peered at Nick. "Do you know?"

"No, I don't, but I do know that she's afraid of Mr. O'Connor, and I would hate to be responsible for him finding out where she is."

"What about Billy Maitland?" asked Jess, her brow furrowed. "She was his girl before he joined the Army and went off to the war."

Nick shrugged. "I got the impression that it's only O'Connor she's afraid of."

"But they are friends, Billy and Sid." Jess was still frowning.

"I think Billy could be persuaded to keep the secret from Sid," said Jean sagely. "Are you planning on talking to him, Nick?"

Nick looked quickly at Amelia, who raised her eyebrows at him. "Yes, I will talk to Billy."

"Be very careful, Nick," warned Amelia.

"I don't think Billy is as close to Sid as Sid thinks he is." Jean rose to her feet. "Are we ready for dessert?" The subject was closed as far as she was concerned.

Izzy rose, too. "I'll help you, Jean."

The two women left the room.

"I suppose this means you will be returning to Sydney?" Beau glanced from Nick to Amelia.

"Yes," replied Amelia. "I'm heading to Melbourne tomorrow to spend some time with my mother before I go back to Sydney." She looked at Nick. "I'm not sure what Nick's plans are."

Nick looked squarely at Beau. "Firstly, I'll have to visit the Police Station here, and if it's alright with Harry and Izzy, I might stick around for a few days. I rather like this country living." He laughed. "I could easily get used to it."

"So Sid is unaware of Phyllis's whereabouts?" Beau hadn't finished with him.

"Yes, and it must stay that way."

"I take it that you know of our problems with Sid?"

Nick nodded. "I do. It has not been my dubious pleasure to meet the man, but he sounds like someone to be avoided at all costs."

"His upbringing left a lot to be desired, too." Jean had entered the room with a tray of desserts. "Not everybody has the luxury of a good and decent family, Nick." There was silence as she and Izzy distributed the bowls of steaming bread-and-butter pudding and hot custard. Her glance fell quickly on Beau, but his eyes were averted. "Let's enjoy this and forget about the likes of Sid O'Connor and Rodney, and anyone else who has left dirty stains on our lives." Beau lifted his gaze then to meet hers, and a slight tremor touched his mouth.

"A good idea, Jean," he said softly.

*

The meal finished amidst the hum of general conversation, and as Beau and Jess rose to take their leave, Nick held out his hand to Beau.

"I'm very sorry, Beau, to have caused you such angst. Please accept my apologies."

Beau looked at the outstretched hand for a moment before taking it. The grip was firm.

"I accept your apology, Nick," he said as he looked at Jess, "but only on behalf of my wife."

Nick pursed his lips. "I deserved that. I am deeply sorry, Jess." He bowed slightly. "My parents brought me up to be better than this, and I feel sure that, had my mother witnessed my recent behaviour, she would not have let me get away with it."

"It's alright, Nick. I understand that you were only doing your job." Jess glanced quickly at Beau. "Enjoy your few days of rest." Beau had taken her arm.

"I shall." As they began to leave, he added, "Can I take you all out to the Shamrock for a meal?"

Beau turned, a frown on his face. "Thank-you all the same, Nick," he said tightly, "but I don't think that would be a very good idea."

"As you wish."

*

As they reached their own gate, Jess pulled Beau to a halt. They had walked the whole way in silence, and she needed to clear the tension in the air.

"Nick was offering you an olive branch, Beau, and you refused to take it. Why?"

Beau looked up towards the front door as he spoke. "I feel uncomfortable with the man, Jess. Joe Hudson had no doubt told him all about me, and even though he denied it, the thought would have crossed both their minds that maybe I was involved."

"I don't believe that Beau. He was simply being cautious."

Beau smiled thinly in the darkness. "That's the difference between us, Jess. You believe the best in everyone." He touched her face gently. "I'm not so generous."

"That's not true, Beau." Jess placed her hand over his. "I think it's just Mr. Armitage who has found himself on the wrong side of you." She sighed. "Well, anyway the incident is over now, and we can forget about it."

"I don't think it is, Jess. It won't be long before Sid finds out that Phyllis Powell has been hiding right under his nose for three years. I think we both know Sid well enough to know that he won't take that lightly."

"How will he find out? We're the only ones who know."

"Secrets tend to slip out, Jess, deliberately or otherwise."

"Well, it certainly won't come from us." She squeezed his hand. "Come on. Charlotte is getting more than her fair share of child-minding at present, and Lottie is overdue for her feed."

*

Nick and Amelia were standing quietly together in the garden at the rear of the hotel. Nick was deep in thought, while Amelia drew on a last cigarette for the night. Harry and Jean were preparing the bar for the morning, and Izzy was in the kitchen, doing the dishes. She had shooed them away when they offered to help, saying that it wouldn't take her long, and that they should enjoy the mildness of the evening.

Nick was troubled by the reaction of Beau DuBois and wondered what he could do to rectify the situation. He didn't want to leave town before he had made amends. Jess seemed to accept his apology without any hesitation, but Beau...

Amelia interrupted his thoughts. "I don't think Doctor DuBois is going to let you off the hook, Nick." She blew a film of smoke into the clear, starlit night, before crushing her cigarette butt beneath the heel of her shoe.

"No, probably not, and I wouldn't leave that there if I were you."

"What?"

"Your cigarette butt – don't leave it in the grass, of you'll have Jean on your back."

"Oh, yes." Amelia laughed as she bent to retrieve the incriminating evidence. "What will I do with it now?" She held the offending remnant on her open palm.

Nick shook his head as he gingerly picked it up and tucked it into his pocket.

Amelia stared at him aghast. "Nick! What are you doing?"

"It's alright." He shrugged. "I'll find an ashtray for it when I go back inside."

"Well, don't forget." Amelia tucked an arm in his. "Now, where were we?"

"We were talking about Doctor DuBois." Nick turned to face her.

"Ah, yes we were, and I said…"

"I know what you said, Amelia." His face was very close to hers in the darkness. "It doesn't matter right now, because I have the irresistible urge to kiss you, Miss Hudson."

"Do you now?" she whispered. "What's stopping you?"

Nick glanced from side to side. "Nothing at all."

Amelia moved into his embrace and their lips softly explored each other, hesitant at first and increasing in pressure. Finally, Nick pulled away.

"Phew!" he gasped. "That took me by surprise."

Amelia laughed softly. "Did it now?"

"Shall we try that again?"

Amelia placed her hands against his chest and smiled up at him in the darkness. "Perhaps we'd better leave it for a later date, Nick." She sighed softly. "I promised Joe that I was here to work with you, not to sleep with you."

"You what?" Nick threw back his head and laughed.

"Well, I didn't exactly promise, but he suggested that it might be a good idea. Besides, I've decided to leave on the early train tomorrow, so I'll probably be gone before you're awake." Amelia stepped away from him and began heading towards the spill of light from the rear door of the hotel. "We can continue this in Sydney, Nick, where we'll both be in familiar territory. Goodnight, and don't forget that cigarette butt in your pocket."

Nick watched as she walked slowly through the door and disappeared from his sight. He stood for a few moments, listening to the silence and thinking about the last few heady moments. A smile touched his lips. His mother's face slid before his mind's eye, and he could hear her sniff of disapproval. Joe Hudson was not one of her favourite people. His father, on the other hand, would probably applaud the fact that his son was finally making a move.

Nick felt a tug on his trouser leg, and looking down, saw the terrier wagging his tail and looking up at him. Nick bent to stroke his rough head.

"Want a game do you, boy?" The dog gave a sharp yap as Nick straightened up. "Sorry old fella, but it's a bit late for that. Maybe tomorrow. I'll have plenty of time tomorrow."

Chief Constable Whitley

When Nick came down for breakfast the following morning, it was to an empty room. He was obviously the last to arrive, as dirty bowls were stacked on a tray, and the porridge serving pot was almost empty. Nick lifted the lids of the other pots and found both the tomatoes and eggs to be sorely depleted. He glanced up at the clock on the wall. It was eight-thirty. He grimaced. Yes, he'd well and truly slept in. No doubt Amelia was halfway to Melbourne by now.

Nick helped himself to the remains of the porridge, poured a little milk on it, and seated himself at the table. Footsteps sounded in the passage, and Izzy appeared at the door.

"Ah, Nick! You're up!"

"Somewhat late, I gather," replied Nick apologetically.

"That's alright." Izzy scooped up the tray of dirty dishes. "By the way, Miss Hudson has gone. She said to tell you that she'll see you in Sydney."

"What time did she leave?"

"Oh, she's been gone since seven." Izzy laughed. "She also said that she peaked into your room before she left and you were sleeping so soundly, she hadn't the heart to disturb you."

Nick shook his head. "Did she now?" He felt his cheeks flush.

"Is there anything else I can get you?"

"No," said Nick quickly. "I'll finish off the eggs and tomatoes." He turned to smile at Izzy. "Thank-you, Izzy. I'll bring my plates to the kitchen when I've finished."

Izzy headed for the door. "Very well."

"By the way Izzy." She turned. "I need to see Billy Maitland today. Any chance he'll be in for a pint?"

"I expect he'll be in for his sandwiches at lunchtime."

"Good. I'll try to catch him then. In the meantime, I'd better get myself across to the police station and report my findings to Chief Constable Whitley."

Izzy flashed him a smile and then was gone.

*

Nick sat in the empty waiting room, while the young Constable went to search the building for Chief Constable Whitley. He had assured Nick that Whitley was not far away, but the minutes ticked by, and there was no sign of either of them. Nick could hear raised voices coming from a room behind the main reception area, and the occasional thump of something hitting the wall. Somebody was getting a grilling, he presumed, and coming off second best.

Eventually a door swung open and two burly policemen appeared, a bloodied man between them. Behind strode another officer, rubbing at his hand and shaking it wildly. Nick observed that there was blood on his knuckles.

"Take him to the lock-up!" he yelled. "He can sober up before he's formally interviewed."

"Yes, sir!"

The two policemen managed to drag the protesting man out through the screen door, which slammed shut behind them. The remaining officer swung his angry glare on Nick.

"Well?" he barked. "What can I do for you?"

"I'm looking for Chief Constable Whitley," said Nick hesitantly.

"You've found him," he answered, as he dug in his pocket for a handkerchief. This he wrapped around his damaged knuckles. "What's this about?"

"It's about a missing woman, sir."

Whitley stared at Nick for a long moment. "What missing woman?"

"Miss Phyllis Powell, sir."

"Ah, yes, I remember." He squinted at Nick. "Have you found her?"

"I have, sir."

"Then you'd better come into my office and tell me all about it. *Constable Downey!*" His voice reverberated through the waiting room.

The young constable appeared as if from nowhere. "Yes, sir!"

"Mind the desk, Downey." Whitley turned to Nick. "Follow me."

Nick followed Whitley along a dark passageway until finally he opened a door and ushered Nick into a small room. It was sparsely furnished, with a desk and two chairs. Beside the desk was a small table on which Nick saw various liquor bottles, and glasses. Whitley poured himself a whisky, downed it straight away, and with a sigh turned to Nick.

"Drink?"

Nick shook his head. "Not for me, thank-you."

Whitley sank on to the chair behind the desk and pulled a sheet of paper from a drawer. "I'm sorry you had to witness that little fracas," he said as he rummaged in the drawer for a pencil. "Sit down, Mr... er..."

"Nick Armitage, sir."

"Mr. Armitage." Whitley squinted at the blunt end of the pencil he had found. He licked it and began to write. "Now, tell me all, Mr. Armitage."

Nick cleared his throat. "Do you recollect meeting a Private Investigator called Joe Hudson, sir?"

The thickset Whitley stretched his bull neck, and his wide brow furrowed. "I do," he muttered. "So you're the young man he was sending down here from Sydney?"

"I am, sir."

"Where's the young woman you were sent here to find?"

"She is safe, sir, and wishes to remain where she is."

Whitley placed his pencil carefully on the desk and hmphed loudly. "Let me get this straight – you have located her but she wishes to remain – where?"

"She wishes to remain at the orphanage where she has been hiding these past three years."

"Hiding from what?"

"Hiding from a certain Mr. Sidney O'Connor. I believe you know him."

Whitley rocked back on the chair, and Nick was afraid the buttons on his jacket would burst as he threw his arms wide. "O'Connor?" he roared. "She's been hiding from O'Connor?" The chair landed back on its four legs with a thump.

"Yes, sir, she has." Nick was puzzled by this reaction.

Whitley now leaned forward. "That man who has just been escorted to the lock-up is no other than Mr. Sidney O'Connor. Yes, I do know him, Mr. Armitage. He is a thorn in my side!"

"Oh!" Nick moved back from Whitley's whisky-laden breath.

"Oh, indeed! Why has she been hiding from O'Connor?" He paused. "No, don't answer that. I can probably guess."

"Maybe not, sir. The young woman has a child and is most anxious that O'Connor doesn't find out her whereabouts."

"I see." Whitley scratched his balding head. "I will have to check your story, young man, and see for myself that the young woman in question is alright." He squinted at Nick from beneath thick eyebrows. "She's at the orphanage, you say?"

"Yes, the orphanage run by the sisters of the Good Shepherd. It's on the hill…"

"I know where it is, my boy." Whitley waved his arms.

"I need to be certain that Mr. O'Connor does not find out where she is."

"She has a child, you say? O'Connor's?"

"I don't know. She didn't enlighten me."

"Hm!" Whitley was thoughtful. "She's been under our noses all this time, and nobody thought to look for her up there on the hill."

"Apparently not."

"What made *you* look there?"

"My assistant discovered that she had been raised there as a child, and so it was a good starting-point in our search. She went back to where she felt safe."

"Safe, eh? Very well, Mr. Armitage, I will hand your information on to my Senior Sergeant, and hopefully we can clear the matter up."

"Thank-you." Nick rose from the chair. "Incidentally, what has Mr. O'Connor done?"

Whitley gave a mirthless laugh. "He was drunk and disorderly in a public place, amongst other things that I can't disclose. It's nothing new for Mr.

O'Connor. We deal with him on a regular basis."

"I see." Nick opened the door. "Good day to you, sir."

Whitley grunted a response and Nick closed the door quietly behind him. He had a slightly uneasy feeling about all this. With the information out there now, the young woman would not be as safe as she thought she was. He might have just thrown Miss Phyllis Powell to the wolves.

*

Whitley picked up the paper he had been scribbling on and lifted his bulk from the chair.

"Well, Mr. O'Connor," he muttered. "We'll see what we can do with this information."

He strode to the door, swung it open and headed along the passage to a room marked: Senior Sergeant Morrow. Knocking loudly, he waited for the cue to enter.

"Yes! What is it?"

Whitley entered the room where Senior Sergeant Morrow was seated behind his more elaborate desk. He looked up as Whitley entered, and a frown creased his high brow.

"What is it, Whitley?" he barked. "You look like the cat that swallowed the cream."

"Oh, I am, sir. I have some information that will interest you."

"Well, stop grinning like a fool and tell me, man!" Whitley handed the paper across the desk to his Senior Sergeant. "What's this?"

"Miss Phyllis Powell has been located, sir, and living at the orphanage. It seems she has been there the past three years."

"And who gave you this information, Whitley?" Morrow's thin face jutted forward.

"The Private Detective from Sydney, sir. You remember Joe Hudson who…"

"Yes! Yes! It was Hudson, was it?"

"No sir. It was his offsider, a Mr. Nick Armitage."

"I see." Morrow sat back on his large leather chair and flapped the paper at Whitley. "What am I supposed to do about it?"

"Well sir," said Whitley conspiratorially, "as we have Mr. O'Connor in the lock-up at present, I thought it might draw some information out of him if we say we have the lowdown on his girlfriend."

"Very good, Whitley."

"Mind you…" Whitley hesitated. "Miss Powell doesn't want O'Connor to know where she is."

"Doesn't she now?" Morrow laughed. "Riffraff, both of them, so I don't think we need worry too much about that, do you?"

"Er… no sir."

"Have O'Connor brought to the interview room. This could be a very interesting discussion indeed." Morrow folded the paper and placed it in his breast pocket. "We'll see what O'Connor makes of this little gem. It might loosen his tongue."

Whitley fidgeted. "He's been taken to the lock-up to sober up, sir."

"Well, hurry up the process, man! I want to see him in the next half hour."

"Yes, sir!"

*

Sid O'Connor was pushed unceremoniously on to a straight-backed wooden chair by the two burly police Constables, who then stood, arms akimbo, at either side of him. Senior Sergeant Morrow gazed at the dishevelled figure across the table from him, and a smirk spread across his thin features.

"Mr. O'Connor," he purred. "Fancy seeing you again so soon."

"Whatd'ya want with me now?" Sid stared balefully at the Sergeant.

"What do I want?" Morrow sat back on his wooden chair. "I'm hoping that what I'm about to tell you, will make you change your mind about keeping information from us."

Sid's bloodshot eyes blinked rapidly. "Whatd'ya mean?"

"Do you know where your girlfriend is, Sid?"

Sid tried to leap off the chair, but two strong arms held him fast. "'Course not!"

"I do." Morrow laughed. "I know exactly where she is."

"Mongrel!" muttered Sid through his yellow teeth.

"Now, now! That won't get you anywhere, Sid." Morrow leaned across the table. "You tell us what we want to know, and I *could* let slip where she's been hiding these past three years."

"I don't know nothin'!" snarled Sid.

"Of course you do," said Morrow smoothly. "Give me some names connected to the robberies that have been taking place recently, and I'll let you go."

"I told ya, I don't know nothin'!" muttered Sid belligerently.

"I don't believe you, Sid." Morrow glanced up at the constables. "Do you want the constables to rough you up again?" he grinned. "You're itching to have a go, aren't you, boys?"

They flexed their knuckles.

"I can't tell ya what I don't know," whined Sid, as he stared up at the constables.

Morrow rapped his fingers on the table. "Don't make this difficult, Sid."

Sid was silent for a moment before he spoke. "Where is she? Where's Phyllis?"

"I can't tell you that, Sid, until you give me some names."

"I had nothin' t'do with them robberies."

"All I'm asking for is a name, or maybe two. I already have my suspicions - I just need clarification from you, Sid."

Sid slumped. "Seamus Oliver and Al Williams," he muttered.

Morrow expelled a loud breath. "That wasn't so hard, was it, Sid?"

"Now where's Phyllis?"

"I'm sorry, Sid, but that's for me to know, and you to find out."

Sid leapt to his feet, restrained by the constables. "You bastard, Morrow! You 'ad no intention o'tellin' me, did ya?"

"It's not quite like that, Sid. Phyllis apparently doesn't want you to know where she is." Morrow shrugged expansively. "So you see, I am not at liberty to tell you."

"But you said…"

Morrow waved his hands. "Take him out of here and put him back in the lockup until he cools down. Then he can go." Morrow bent forward. "I don't want to see your ugly face back here again, do you understand?"

"I won't forget this, Morrow!" hissed Sid, jabbing a tobacco-stained finger at the Sergeant.

"Get him out of here!"

Morrow watched as the protesting Sid was led away. He smiled smugly.

"Seamus Oliver and Al Williams," he muttered to himself. "I thought as much."

Billy Maitland

Nick wandered into the Grey Goose, in time to see Izzy distributing sandwiches amongst the regulars. She spotted Nick and headed in his direction.

"You're just in time, Nick." She smiled broadly. "Find a seat, and I'll send Harry over with a beer."

"Thanks, Izzy." Nick found an empty table and dropped on to the hard wooden chair. "You haven't seen Billy Maitland by any chance?"

Izzy glanced around the busy bar area. "No, I haven't, Nick, but he should be here soon. It's just after twelve." She placed a plate of sandwiches in front of him. "I'll send him over to you when he comes." She stepped closer. "How did you get on with the police?" she whispered.

Nick shrugged. "I hope I haven't thrown the young woman to the wolves, Izzy."

Izzy's face registered horror. "I hope our police force have more integrity than that, Nick."

"I wouldn't bet on it, Izzy."

Izzy shook her head as she moved away. Nick glanced around the crowded, smoke-filled bar, and his eyes came to rest on Billy Maitland, who had just walked through the door. Nick saw Izzy approach him, say something to him, and then point in his direction. Billy nodded, took a plate of sandwiches and threaded his way through the crowd towards Nick.

"You wanna see me, Mr. Armitage?" He grinned at Nick as he pulled out a chair and sat down.

"Yes, Billy, I do, and please call me Nick."

Billy took a bite out of his cheese sandwich, as Harry appeared beside them, two beers in his hands.

"Here you are, fellas," he said cheerfully, placing the glasses on the table.

"Thanks, Harry." Nick smiled at his host, as Billy nodded, his mouth too full to speak.

Harry moved away, and Nick looked intently at Billy. "I have a confession to make to you, Billy."

"A confession?" Billy wiped a grease-stained hand across his mouth. "What sort of confession?"

"I'm not really a journalist, Billy, and I'm not here to write a human-interest story."

Billy stared blankly at him. "Then what *are* you here for?"

Nick leaned forward on his elbows. "I'm a Private Investigator, Billy, and I was sent here to look for Miss Phyllis Powell."

Billy continued staring at him. "You're looking for Phyllis?"

"I am, Billy."

"Blimey!" He scratched his head. "I 'aven't seen Phyllis since before the war."

"I know that, Billy."

"You need t'talk t'Sid O'Connor." Billy sat back on the chair, and his thin features were grim.

"I don't want to do that, Billy." Nick paused. "Miss Powell has been located."

Billy frowned as he processed the information just given to him. "You've found 'er?"

"Yes, Billy." Nick waited once more. "You're friends with this Sid O'Connor, right?"

Billy snorted. "Yeah, sort of!" he muttered.

"I want to tell you something, Billy, and I am deadly serious. Phyllis does *not* want Sid O'Connor to know where she is."

Billy's pale eyes narrowed. "I can't blame 'er for that," he said slowly. He studied Nick for a long moment. "Where is she?"

"If I tell you, Billy, I want your solemn promise that the information will not reach Mr. O'Connor. Can you promise me that?"

Billy's lips pursed. "Has she got the child with 'er?"

"Yes, Billy, she has, and that's the reason she doesn't want Mr. O'Connor to find out where she is."

Billy was silent for a full minute, before he shifted his gaze up to meet Nick's. "I stopped carin' f'Phyllis a long time ago, Nick. She made a fool o'me, an' t'this day I don't know if the child is mine."

"I can't tell you that either, Billy, but I do know that she's afraid of Mr. O'Connor."

"*Mr.* O'Connor!" Billy spat the words out. "He don't deserve a full title." He leaned forward. "So where has Phyllis been hidin' all this time?"

Nick glanced around the bar. Everyone was preoccupied – not looking in his direction. "She's at the orphanage," he whispered.

"What!" Nick tried to quieten him with a hand movement. "Are you sure?"

"Yes, I've seen her."

Billy whistled through his teeth. "All this time, eh?" He shook his head. "I wondered where she'd got to. She grew up there, ya know?"

"Yes, I know, Billy." Nick threaded his fingers on the table. "I don't know what you intend to do with this information, Billy, but I'm trusting you to do the right thing. I had to inform the police, so I'm hoping they do the right thing, too."

Billy laughed. "Don't depend on the coppers, Nick. They'll do what suits 'em."

"That's what I'm afraid of."

Billy ran his fingers through his thinning hair. "You've fair flummoxed me, Nick." He looked up at the clock before downing the last of his beer and picking up the remaining sandwich. "I gotta go back t'work. How long are you stickin' around 'ere, Nick?"

"Around Bendigo?"

"Yeah."

"A few more days, Billy."

"I'll see ya again then." He leaned over the back of the chair. "D'ya think Phyllis'd wanna t'see me?"

Nick smiled at his serious face. "I couldn't say, Billy."

"Nah! Prob'ly not."

"I'll go with you if you like."

Billy stared at Nick. "Would ya?"

"Yes, of course." Nick smiled at the memory of his reception at the orphanage. "I'm sure the Reverend Mother will be *very* pleased to see me again."

"Alright. I'm not workin' t'morrow."

"Tomorrow it is, Billy. Morning or afternoon?"

"Mornin'. I'll meet ya here at ten."

"Very well." Nick held out his hand, which was taken enthusiastically.

"Now I really gotta go. See ya, Nick."

Nick watched as Billy threaded his way to the bar, gave some money to Harry and headed for the door. As he disappeared, Nick sat back on his chair and folded his arms across his chest. That was a strange reaction and no mistake. He thought Billy might have been relieved that the girl had been found, but to actually want to see her? That was something Nick had not expected. Maybe he thought more of her than he had previously let on? One thing was certain, and that was another trip to the orphanage was imminent. That did not thrill Nick, but he had a sense of the place now, and would handle things differently. He downed the last of his beer and stood up. Izzy appeared at his side.

"How did it go, Nick?" she whispered as she picked up the two empty glasses.

"Better than I expected. He wants to see her."

Izzy's eyes rounded with surprise. "He does?"

"Yes. I'm going over there with him tomorrow morning."

"Well, I never! He must still have feelings for her."

"That's my guess, Izzy."

"He won't tell Sid, will he?"

Nick shook his head. "I wouldn't think so. I'm more worried about the police telling Sid."

"Why would they do that?" Izzy frowned.

"Because Mr. O'Connor is in their custody at present."

Izzy gasped. "For what reason?"

"I don't know, but they were roughing him up while I was there earlier."

"That man has no idea how to stay out of trouble." Izzy picked up the sandwich plates. "Well, at least you know where he is."

"That's true." Nick pushed in the chair. "You must excuse me, Izzy. I should telephone Joe Hudson and let him know what's been happening."

"Use the telephone here, Nick. There's no need to go traipsing off to the post Office."

"Thank-you, Izzy, I'll do that."

Izzy smiled and moved off, collecting more glasses as she made her way towards the bar.

*

After his conversation with Joe, Nick felt his anxiety increase slightly. Joe had assured him that the Melbourne Metropolitan Police were now happy to take Phyllis Powell off the 'MISSING' list, and were happy to leave the situation to the Bendigo Force. Nick was not so sure, and told Joe that he would be staying in Bendigo for a while longer, to make sure things didn't get out of hand. He felt responsible for the girl's welfare, which made Joe snort.

"Your job's done, Nick," he laughed. "You're not responsible for what happens to these people now."

Nevertheless, Nick had made up his mind, and he told Joe that he was planning another visit to the orphanage with Billy Maitland.

"That's a very foolish idea, Nick, but I'm presuming I can't talk you out of it?"

"No." Nick was definite.

Joe did not know these people, and therefore could not understand Nick's feelings of responsibility, having walked into their lives and shaken the ground on which they all walked. He had to stay and see it through to a satisfactory conclusion. If that meant a confrontation with Sid O'Connor, then he was prepared for that, too. He certainly hoped it wouldn't come to that.

The last thing he had asked Joe was whether he knew who had reported the girl missing. Joe could still shed no light on this matter, and it had to be assumed that it was anonymous. The girl had no living relatives to speak of, and it would hardly have been Sid O'Connor. Nick had to be content with that. The only other person was Billy, and Nick had already ruled him out.

Billy and Phyllis

Nick rapped on the brass knocker and stood back. He glanced at his companion and was pleased to note that Billy had gone to some trouble with his appearance. His unruly fair hair had been tamed with water, and he was wearing a dark blue suit. It was too large for his thin frame, and somewhat frayed at the cuffs, but nevertheless he had tried to look respectable.

"How are you feeling?" asked Nick.

"Nervous." Billy pulled at the collar of his white shirt, and flashed Nick an apprehensive smile.

Nick patted his shoulder reassuringly. "Don't be," he said with a grin. "There are only two things that are likely to happen."

"Yeah! An' what are they?"

"The Reverend Mother will let us in, or she won't. Put on your best smile, Billy, and charm the socks off her."

Billy smiled ruefully and at that moment the door creaked open. A face appeared, and Nick recognised one of the young women he'd encountered previously. He removed his hat and smiled.

"Good morning," he said cheerfully. "I'm Nicholas Armitage and I have with me my friend, Billy Maitland. Can we speak with the Reverend Mother, please?"

"You were here the other day," said the young woman, opening the door a fraction more.

"Yes, I was."

"I'll see if the Reverend Mother wants to speak to you."

"Thank-you."

The young woman disappeared, and the two men waited for what seemed like a long time, before they heard the swish of skirts on the floor, and the door swung open. Nick recognised the sharp features of the Reverend Mother and inclined his head respectfully.

"Good morning, Reverend Mother."

"Mr. Armitage, isn't it? What are you doing here again?" was her tight reply.

"Mr. Maitland here is a friend of Phyllis Powell's, and he would very much like to speak with her."

The Reverend Mother cast her eyes over Billy and the frown on her brow deepened. "I can't let you do that," she said irritably. "Phyllis has had enough disruption to her life, and she wishes to be left alone." With that she tried to shut the door, but Nick put his foot in the way.

"Mr. Maitland has waited three years to find out what happened to Phyllis, and I feel sure he is not going to give up now." Nick looked at Billy. "Are you, Billy?"

Billy cleared his throat, not sure how to respond. "Phyllis an' me were close once, an' then I went away to war, an' I didn't see 'er."

The Reverend Mother was glaring at them from behind the half-open door. "I'm sorry about that, young man, but these girls are my responsibility, and I won't have them harassed. Now would you please leave, both of you?" She pushed hard on the door, and Nick winced. "Go! Please!"

Nick eased his foot out and stepped aside. "You are making a mistake, Reverend Mother," he said between clenched teeth. "Mr. Maitland is not a threat to Phyllis; I can assure you."

"That may well be, Mr. Armitage, but I'm taking no risks. Good day to you!"

The door slammed in their faces. Billy slumped.

"Well, that's that, I suppose," he muttered as he began to head back towards the gate.

"Not so fast, Billy." Nick caught him up and grabbed his arm. "I'm not giving up that easily. Come on, we'll see if we can find the laundry. Phyllis may be there, if we're lucky."

Nick walked quickly, pulling Billy along with him. They skirted the front of the main building and headed around the corner. Their footsteps crunched on the gravel as they walked the length of the north-facing wall. Nick spied an outbuilding with a corrugated iron roof. Steam was issuing from vents, and it was towards this building that Nick propelled Billy.

"That is the laundry if I am not mistaken," he said excitedly.

As they neared the building, a group of young women appeared, all dressed in grey uniforms with white aprons. They were laughing together as they peeled off the white caps that covered their hair. Billy came to a sudden halt, jerking Nick to a stop beside him.

"There she is!" he whispered hoarsely. "There's Phyllis!"

Nick squinted as he searched the faces of the young women. Sure enough, there she was. Billy was rooted to the spot, as he stared in her direction. One of the girls spotted them standing not far off and nudged her companion. Soon they were all looking in the direction of the two men, and the laughter died. Nick saw Phyllis clutch at her breast, and a sob escaped her. She took a step forward but was restrained by the girl closest to her.

"What are you doin' Phyllis?" the two men heard her hiss. "They shouldn't be here! Somebody go and get the Reverend Mother!" Nobody moved.

Phyllis shook herself free and walked unsteadily towards them. She stopped several feet away and Nick heard her draw a ragged breath.

"Billy! What are you doin' here?"

Billy took a hesitant step forward. "I came t'see you, Phyllis," he said awkwardly.

"Why?"

"I dunno really." He shrugged. "Nick here said he'd found ya' an' I wanted t'see for meself."

"Sid don't know I'm here?" she asked cautiously.

"No." Billy shook his head.

A tall redhead stepped forward; her face flushed as she pointed an accusing finger at the two men. "'Ere! You two shouldn't be 'ere." She turned to Phyllis. "You'll get what for if the Reverend Mother finds out ya had a man 'ere!" She glared at the two men. "I don't suppose the Reverend Mother knows you're 'ere?"

"Actually, she does," said Nick with feigned confidence.

The redhead squinted at him. "She does?"

"Yes." Nick glanced at Billy, whose eyes were large and fearful.

"But I betcha she didn't send ya around 'ere."

"What makes you say that?"

"'Cos she wouldn't, that's why. Men are not 'er favourite things."

"So I gathered," said Nick under his breath. "Billy, what else did you have to say to Phyllis?"

Billy shrugged, suddenly tongue-tied. "I dunno," he muttered.

"Yes, you do. Billy. What about the child?"

"Oh yeah!" He looked at Phyllis. "How's the little'n, Phyllis? Proper growed by now, I'd say."

"Yeah." For a moment a sweet expression touched Phyllis's plain features. "She's nearly four."

"What's she like?"

"She's sweet, Billy."

"So she's not like Sid?"

Phyllis's hazel eyes blazed as she jerked out of her reverie. "No!" she cried. "She's not like you either, Billy!"

"Who *does* she look like, Phyllis?" Billy was exasperated. "She must look like somebody."

"Like 'erself, Billy. Hope looks like 'erself." Nick noticed Phyllis's bottom lip tremble.

"Can I see 'er?"

"No. She's in the nursery at present."

"When can I see 'er?" There was a pleading tone in Billy's voice.

"When I..."

Phyllis got no further. The girls were all staring at the apparition in black striding towards them across the grass. Nick and Billy turned to see the Reverend Mother descending on them, her black veil flapping in the wind and reminding Nick of a crow about to descend on its prey.

"What is the meaning of this?" she snapped as she stopped within a yard of them. "I told you two to leave the premises. Why didn't you?"

Nick held up his hands. "This is all my fault, Reverend Mother. Billy deserved a chance to see Phyllis, and I suspected that we would find her at the laundry."

"Did you now?" The Reverend Mother was scowling ferociously. "Well, he's seen her, so now you can both clear off, and don't you *ever* pull a stunt like that again."

Nick turned to Phyllis. "I'm sorry, Phyllis. I hope you're not in trouble over this." He switched his gaze back to the Reverend Mother. "Phyllis had nothing to do with this, Reverend Mother, and you would do well to remember that." Nick took Billy by the arm. "Come on, Billy. We'd best be out of here before we cause any more trouble."

Billy looked back at Phyllis. "I'll figure out a way t'see you and the little'n, I promise."

"I don't think so, young man," retorted the Reverend Mother. "I don't want you darkening this place again, do you hear me?"

Billy ignored her outburst. "That's a promise, Phyllis."

Audrey's Admission

Nick and Billy made their silent way down the hill towards the town. Their thoughts were both sombre, as each tried to justify what had been done, and wondered desperately how they could have improved the situation. Billy was astounded by his renewed feelings for Phyllis. He thought they had died a long time ago. Now he had made a promise to the girl that he would see her again. He had to honour that promise, in spite of the difficulties it would bring, and the ever-present knowledge that Sid was bound to find out.

Nick, on the other hand, was annoyed with himself for bungling the whole thing. The Reverend Mother was a force to be reckoned with, and obviously did not want to lose any of her girls. They were protected from the world of men and were also a valuable commodity to the orphanage. That's how they would stay until their children were old enough for them to want to move on. Phyllis's little girl was only four, and still there was no indication of whom she belonged to. Nick knew that Billy was anxious to find out, and perhaps seeing the child might be just the right trigger.

He looked down at Billy's scowling face and knew for certain that the matter was not closed as far as he was concerned.

"What are you thinking, Billy?"

Billy stopped walking. "I dunno, Nick. I'm confused."

Nick stopped beside him. "Confused over what? Your feelings?"

"Yeah." Billy sighed. "Three years ago, I thought Phyllis was a tramp when she —when she threw me over for Sid, while I was away at the trainin' camp. Now I don't know what I think." He looked searchingly at Nick. "Is it possible for feelin's t'change?"

"Of course it is, Billy." Nick slapped him good-naturedly on the back.

"I promised I'd find a way t'see 'er."

"And you will, Billy. You might have to organise a clandestine meeting," Nick said half-jokingly.

"A what?" Billy peered up at Nick, not sure what his friend was on about.

"A clandestine meeting, Billy – one arranged secretly."

"Oh!" Billy shrugged. "That Reverend Mother was somethin' else, wasn't she?"

"She's just looking out for her own, Billy, like a protective mother hen."

"I can think of another name for it," muttered Billy, as they began to walk again.

"So can I, Billy," laughed Nick, "but I'll try to keep my thoughts nice."

They walked on in silence, until they were nearing the Grey Goose, and then Billy touched Nick on the arm.

"Would ya like t'come an' meet me mum, Nick? We live just along this street."

Nick looked at his watch, mainly from habit. It was eleven-thirty. "Yes,

I'd like to do that, Billy." He grinned. "Who knows, but I might get my human-interest story yet, if I stick around here much longer."

"Yeah, well mum's seen a lot in 'er day."

"I'm sure she has, Billy."

They walked along a narrow street, lined with single-fronted wooden miners' cottages, until Billy stopped.

"This one's ours," he said proudly, pointing to the cottage with flowers blooming in the small front yard. "Mum likes 'er garden."

He pushed open the wooden gate, and Nick followed him along a narrow path that ran the length of the cottage and around to a rear door. Nick noticed that the cottage was badly in need of a fresh coat of paint, but the yard was neat and tidy, and the back lean-to porch was swept of dirt and leaves.

Billy pushed open the screen door.

"Are you there, mum?" he called out, as Nick followed him into a small kitchen.

In the centre of the room Nick saw a scrubbed pine table, surrounded by four chairs. Along the wall to his right was a sideboard displaying cream china plates with dark green borders. A fireplace took up the opposite wall, with a black-lead stove on which a large black kettle was singing merrily. A sink occupied the rear wall, but no taps were visible, leading Nick to assume the cottage had no running water.

A door opened opposite him, and a woman appeared. Her grey hair was covered with a floral scarf and around her slight frame she wore a matching pinafore. She smiled at Billy, and Nick could see the resemblance between the two, although her face was care-worn. Her eyes focused on Nick and widened with surprise. He had seen her once or twice at the Grey Goose.

"Oh!" she exclaimed. "You're the young man who's staying at the hotel, aren't you?"

"Yes, I'm Nick Armitage," said Nick, removing his hat. "I'm pleased to meet you, Mrs. Maitland."

"Mum does the cleanin' there when Mrs. O'Malley needs 'er," said Billy hurriedly.

Audrey Maitland wiped her hands on her pinafore and gestured for Nick to sit at the table. He did so, and Billy sat beside him.

"Would you like a cup of tea, Mr. Armitage?"

"That would be lovely, thank-you, and please call me Nick."

Audrey nodded and smiled again, before busying herself with the tea caddy that she took from the mantel above the stove.

"Nick an' me have been to the orphanage, mum," said Billy.

Her eyes widened with surprise. "The orphanage? Whatever for, Billy?"

Billy looked quickly at Nick. "Nick's a Private Investigator, mum, and 'e's here t'look for Phyllis."

Boiling water splashed on the stove as Audrey's arm jerked suddenly, and Billy leapt to his feet. "What's the matter, mum?" He took the kettle from her shaking hand. "Sit down, mum. I'll do it."

Audrey sat opposite Nick, and her hands fluttered around her face. "You're looking for Phyllis?"

"I am," replied Nick, a little puzzled by the reaction. "I'm pleased to say that I found her."

"You found her?" parroted Audrey. "At the orphanage?"

"Yes, Mrs. Maitland. She's at the orphanage."

Tears welled in Audrey's eyes, and she brushed at them hurriedly. "That's good."

Nick's brow furrowed as he glanced up at Billy, who had poured the tea, and was pushing a cup in his direction. "Mrs. Maitland," he said slowly, "was it you who reported Phyllis missing?"

Audrey gazed from Nick to Billy. "Yes," she stammered.

Billy stared at his mother, open-mouthed. "I didn't know that, mum." He sat heavily. "Why'd ya do that an' not tell me?"

"I wanted to know where the little one was, Billy. She could be my granddaughter."

Billy shook his head. "Ya shoulda told me, mum."

Audrey reached across the table and clutched her son's hands. "Did you see the little one?"

"No, mum!" said Billy sharply. "We didn't!" He sat back on the chair. "I can't believe you did that and not a word to anyone."

"Look," said Nick quietly, "it's a good discovery from my point of view. I can put another piece in the puzzle. Phyllis wouldn't have been discovered otherwise."

"So she's been at the orphanage all this time?" Audrey smiled tremulously at her son.

"Yes mum, she has," sighed Billy.

"Why would she do that?"

"To escape Sid O'Connor, that's why!" Billy thumped his fist on the table, causing the cups to rattle.

"What about the little one, Billy?"

"What about 'er, mum? I can't do anythin' when I don't even know if she's mine."

"She's yours, Billy, I'm certain of that."

"That's the thing, mum. We *can't* be certain," said Billy miserably.

"Well, in any case, Billy, that child needs a family, and we're the closest she's got."

Billy took a sip of his tea. "I promised Phyllis I'd see 'er again." He looked searchingly at his mother.

"That's good, Billy." Audrey was smiling. "I'll come with you."

"It might not be as easy as that, Mrs. Maitland," interrupted Nick. "We didn't exactly get a good reception, did we, Billy?"

"Nah!"

"From Phyllis?"

"No, from the Reverend Mother, who runs the place."

"Well," said Audrey calmly, "I might have to use some feminine intuition to get on her right side."

"Good luck with that," laughed Nick. "She rules with a rod of iron."

"We'll see." Audrey sipped her tea. "Anyway, I want to thank you, Mr. Armitage. You've eased my mind somewhat. I was worried that Sid might have done her some harm."

Nick was reminded of Sid's current situation. "Speaking of Mr. O'Connor, I saw him at the Police Station yesterday. They were hauling him to the lock-up."

Billy put down his cup. "What's 'e been up to now?"

"According to Senior Constable Whitley, and I quote, 'being drunk and disorderly in a public place, amongst other things that could not be disclosed.' End of quote."

"That sounds like Sid," muttered Billy. "Well at least 'e's out of the way."

"Yes, for the time being."

*

Nick and Billy stood at the gate of Audrey's cottage, and silently reviewed the past half hour. Billy had been shocked by his mother's admission and was at a loss as to what to do next. Nick, on the other hand, was pleased that the mystery had been cleared up, and was anxious to relay the information to Joe. He wished that Amelia had not left in such a hurry. Her journalistic skills could certainly be put to the test here in this town where everyone had secrets it seemed.

"I dunno what possessed mum t'do that, Nick." Billy was shaking his head. "I didn't know she cared so much about Phyllis's child."

"Well now you know, Billy, and as long as you can keep Mr. O'Connor out of the picture, you might stand a chance, with your mum's support. Good luck with it all, and I will be keen to know what happens."

"When are ya leavin'?"

"I'm not in a hurry, Billy. I'll stick around a bit longer." He grinned at his companion. "Besides, this town keeps spitting out stories of interest." Nick patted Billy on the shoulder. "Now I must go. I need to contact my boss with this latest revelation."

"How am I gunna do this, Nick?"

"I'd be letting your mum lead the way, Billy. She could be right where it comes to female intuition. Trust me, it does work." Nick tapped the side of his nose. "It was female intuition that guided me to the orphanage in the first place." Billy stared at him blankly. "The female intuition wasn't mine, Billy!" He laughed. "I had a female assistant who has since left the scene."

"Oh!" Billy was obviously none the wiser.

"Never mind, Billy. Trust your mum." Nick jammed his hat on his head. "Now I really must go. Best of luck, Billy." He held out his hand.

Billy shook it and then watched as Nick strode off along the street. He had no idea how all this was going to play out, but he needed to have a long discussion with his mother. Billy turned and headed back inside.

"Mum!" he called out. "We need to 'ave a talk."

A Good Deed Gone Wrong

Nick made his way back towards the Grey Goose. His good feeling about the outcome of this story was only hampered by the niggling concern about Sid O'Connor. He had not actually met the man, except to see him dragged by two burly policemen, but he was obviously a very troubled soul, who caused problems for a lot of people. If Billy was serious about his reunion with Phyllis, then Nick felt sure he would handle any interference from O'Connor with care. After all, they had known each other a long time, and obviously had history, although Nick was unaware of the details.

His steps slowed as he headed along Oleander Street, and he squinted as he saw a figure running wildly towards him. It was Jess DuBois. Sensing that something was wrong, Nick hurried towards her.

"Jess!" he called out. "What's happened?"

Jess stopped in front of him, out of breath, and clutching at her chest.

"It's Charlotte!" she gasped. "I'm afraid she's had an accident. My telephone's not working, so I'm going to the hotel to call Beau."

"Where is she?" Nick gripped her shoulders.

"She's in the back yard. I told her not to go up the ladder, but she insisted, and…"

"I'll go and see what I can do."

Jess nodded weakly. "Thank-you."

Nick took off at a run, while Jess continued on to the Grey Goose. He reached the front gate, flung it open and headed along the side of the house to what he presumed was the back yard. Seeing immediately what had happened, Nick ran towards the fallen ladder and the victim lying beneath it.

He pulled the ladder away, and Charlotte groaned as she clutched her ankle. She looked up at him and a smile twisted her mouth.

"Mr. Armitage to the rescue!" she muttered faintly. "I've twisted my ankle."

Nick knew a little first-aid and began unbuttoning her boot. "Let's have a look, shall we?"

"I'd rather leave it until Beau gets here." She tried to resist his assistance.

"He'll probably be a little while," said Nick brusquely. "In the meantime, we need to get that boot off and have a look at the damage."

"You're not a doctor!" she gasped as pain shot through her ankle.

"I know, but I have a little knowledge." He pulled the boot carefully away from Charlotte's foot. "I'm going to carry you inside, and we'll find something cold to put on that foot." He could see the swelling starting to take place.

Charlotte tried to resist, but Nick ignored her protests. Instead, he carried her across the verandah and into the kitchen. There he sat her on a chair and headed back out to the verandah, where he had seen an ice-chest. An ice pick sat on top of the chest, so he quickly used this to chip away a large chunk of ice. He needed something to wrap it in. There was nothing that he could see, so he delved into his trousers pocket and retrieved his handkerchief. It was clean, so he wrapped the piece of ice in it, and strode back into the kitchen. Charlotte was sitting quietly. Her face was deathly pale, and Nick suspected that she was in severe pain.

"Here," he said as he lifted her foot. "Let's see if this helps." He pulled out another chair, lifted Charlotte's swollen foot on to it, and placed the ice pack beneath it. Her eyes were tightly closed.

Nick pulled out another chair and flopped on to it. From there he watched his patient as her face muscles tightened with pain. At one point she opened her eyes and stared at him, but then the grey eyes clouded, and she squeezed them shut.

"Thank-you, Mr. Armitage," she panted weakly. "I should be alright to wait for Beau now."

"I'm not leaving here until he arrives," said Nick firmly, as he re-adjusted the ice pack.

"As you wish." Charlotte's eyes were still closed.

Nick looked at her for a few moments before saying what was on his mind.

"Just as a matter of interest, Miss DuBois, what were you doing up the ladder?"

She laughed. "The boys had thrown a ball on to the roof yesterday. I was retrieving it."

"Shouldn't you have left that for your brother to do?"

"Possibly, but I'm no stranger to climbing ladders, Mr. Armitage."

Nick was silent.

"At the Convent, you mean?" he said finally.

Charlotte's eyes flew open, and she stared at him. "Yes," she said sharply. "We had no men to do the physical tasks required." Her chin quivered, whether from pain or memories, Nick could not be sure.

"I have to ask you, Miss DuBois," he said quietly, "and this is strictly on a personal level, what made you take the veil?"

Once again, the grey eyes stared at him, unblinking. "I can't tell you that, Mr. Armitage," she replied stiffly.

"Then let's take the other end of the scale." Nick rubbed a finger along the dent above his chin. "What changed your mind and made you return to the real world?"

"The real world?" Her face went through a range of expressions as Nick waited for her answer. "I let my brother down, many years ago, Mr. Armitage, and that preyed on my mind for most of my life. I left him at the mercy of one who knew nothing about love." Her eyes filled with tears. "When I finally had the chance to make amends, I decided to leave the safety of the cloister, and I came here to be with Beau and Jess and their family; the 'real world' as you put it."

Neither had heard the arrival of Beau at the door, and they both turned as he entered the kitchen, followed by Jess.

Nick stood up quickly, pushing the chair behind him. He had no idea how much of that conversation Beau had heard, but he was staring at him and his expression was anything but welcoming.

"Mr. Armitage," he said tightly. "We meet again."

"For once I was in the right place at the right time, it seems," said Nick, laughing nervously.

Beau bent over his sister's injured ankle and pressed gently on the swelling. "I need to get you to the hospital for an x-ray, Charlotte, to see if it's broken."

Jess moved quietly to Nick's side and touched his arm. "Thank-you, Nick," she whispered.

"I have Charles's car out the front," Beau was saying. "Let's get you into it."

"Here, let me help." Nick stepped forward.

Beau straightened up. "I can take it from here," he said stiffly.

Charlotte sighed. "For pity's sake, Beau!" Her voice had an edge. "Let the boy help! He's twice your size, and he managed to carry me in here!"

For a long moment there was silence, before Beau stepped aside.

"Alright," he said slowly. "I'll go and start the car."

When he had left the room, Nick placed his arms beneath Charlotte, and lifted her easily from the chair. Jess ran ahead of them to open the front door.

Within moments Charlotte was seated in the back of Charles's car, her legs elevated on the seat, and a rug wrapped around her knees.

Without a word, Beau let out the clutch and the big car moved on to the road. Jess and Nick stood back and watched them drive out of sight. Finally, Jess turned to Nick.

"I must apologise for my husband's rudeness," she said quietly. "He's not usually like this. I don't know what's got into him."

"There's no need to apologise, Jess." Nick followed her back through the gate and up the steps to the verandah. "We started off on the wrong foot, I'm afraid."

"Nevertheless, Beau had no right to treat you like that. He hasn't been the same since…" Her voice trailed off.

"Since what, Jess?"

She smiled at him. "Do you fancy a cup of tea?"

Nick nodded. "Yes, I'll be in that." It was only half an hour since his last cup of tea with Billy and his mother.

"Very well. Come back into the kitchen and I'll tell you a little bit about

Beau and Charlotte. It might explain a few things." Jess turned as they reached the kitchen door. "This is strictly between you and me, Nick."

Nick placed his hand across his heart. "My lips are sealed, Jess."

*

Meanwhile Beau and Charlotte were silent as they headed in the direction of the hospital. Charlotte gritted her teeth as the bumpy road sent pains shooting through her foot. She sensed that her brother was in no mood to be trifled with and guessed that he had heard the last of her conversation with Nick Armitage.

"Beau! Can you slow down, please?" she pleaded. Beau immediately released pressure on the accelerator, but Charlotte noticed how his hands gripped the steering wheel. "What is wrong with you, Beau? Your behaviour is quite out of character."

"I heard you telling that man about us." Beau glanced at Charlotte in the rear-vision mirror. "He doesn't need to know our business!"

"No, he doesn't." Charlotte met his gaze. "But he was curious as to why I was climbing a ladder, when I should have left it to you."

"So you told him…?"

"I told him that I was no stranger to a ladder, as it was one of the regular tasks at the Convent." She dropped her gaze. "He wanted to know why I chose to leave the Convent and come here, so I told him, and that's what you heard."

"You know I don't like him, Charlotte."

"Why, Beau?"

"Because he reminds me of somebody, and I puzzled for a long time over who it could be."

"Who?"

Beau's eyes caught hers in the mirror. "Somebody we both hate, Charlotte."

There was only one person who fitted that image. "He reminds you of father?"

"Yes, as strange as it seems."

"But that's not even possible." Beau had stopped the car at the front of the hospital, and two orderlies appeared with a wheeled stretcher. They manoeuvred Charlotte out of the car and on to the stretcher, and as she was wheeled away, she heard Beau say,

"Isn't it?"

Charlotte shivered in the warm sunshine, and a cold feeling swept through her heart.

Part Two

Within these walls

Sister Miriam

Sister Miriam's footsteps echoed on the flagstones as she hurried along the corridor to the Reverend Mother's office. She had been sent for, and her heart was fluttering because she knew the reason for the summons. What could she say to the Reverend Mother that would allay her concerns?

Her footsteps stopped in front of the heavy door that led to the Reverend Mother's office, and she knocked softly.

"Enter," came the muffled order from inside.

Sister Miriam slowly pushed open the heavy door and stepped into the dim interior. The Reverend Mother looked up from her writings and placed her pen slowly beside the inkwell. Sister Miriam stood before the large desk, her heart now pounding in her ears.

"Sit down, Sister," said the Reverend Mother, not unkindly.

The Irish-born Nun sank on to the hard-backed chair that faced her superior and she waited, eyes cast down. The Reverend Mother stared at her for some moments, concern in her hazel eyes. She took a deep breath.

"Do you know why I have called you here today, Sister?" Her deep voice resonated in the cool air.

Sister Miriam hesitated.

"Yes, Reverend Mother," she whispered uncertainly.

"You have been here a long time, am I right, Sister?"

"Thirty-four years," came the soft reply.

"That *is* a long time." There was a pause. "Perhaps you need a change."

The words hung in the cool air, as Sister Miriam looked up in alarm. "A change, Reverend Mother?"

"That's what I said." There was another pause. "Do you want to know why?" When there was no answer, the Reverend Mother continued. "I have only been here for the past ten years, but I have always found you to be a leader in every respect. You have looked after the novices and attended to their every need. I could rely on you, Sister Miriam. Your sense of humour has lightened many a traumatic time and your service to this Convent has been impeccable. That is why I am troubled by your behaviour over recent months. Can you explain to me why your attitude has taken a sudden turn? I have my suspicions, but I would like to hear it from you, Sister."

Sister Miriam stared at her superior for a long moment, before looking down at her hands that were clasped tightly in her lap. She licked her dry lips, but the words she needed to utter would not come.

"Very well," said the Reverend Mother tightly. "Shall I tell you what I think?" Sister Miriam nodded mutely. "I believe this goes back to the departure of Sister Agnes, (or Charlotte DuBois, as she is now known.) You two had a very close working relationship, and I observed that you were totally distraught when she decided to give up the veil and seek her family in the outside world."

"I didn't think she would ever do that." Sister Miriam had found her tongue. "I have known Sister Agnes for all the thirty-two years she was here. I was here for her when she arrived, so uncertain of her future and that of her unborn child."

"I believe the child died?" There was a pause. "Sister?"

"I took care of it, Reverend Mother."

"Hm. You had a letter from Sister Agnes recently?"

"Yes."

"How is she?"

"She finds the lack of discipline hard to get used to, but she spends a lot of time with her brother's child." Sister Miriam's voice faltered.

"I see." The Reverend Mother tapped her fingers on the desk. "I too had a letter this last week, from a former Sister whom I'd worked with in the Congo some years ago. She is now in Bendigo."

Sister Miriam looked up, startled. "Bendigo?"

"That's what I said. She is now the Reverend Mother, in charge of the orphanage there, and they are sadly lacking in nuns to take care of the children."

Sister Miriam blinked behind her thick spectacles. "What are you saying, Reverend Mother?"

She leaned forward on her elbows. "I am saying that the change might do you good, Sister Miriam, although..." she leaned back on her chair, "I will be sorry to lose you."

"You're getting rid of me?"

"Not exactly, but you're no good to me the way you are, and I thought if you were closer to Sister Agnes, then who knows?" She shrugged. "Your demeanour may change."

"I can't leave here Reverend Mother."

"Why not?"

Sister Miriam was wringing her hands in her lap. "I just can't," she hiccoughed.

"I want you to go to your cell, Sister Miriam, and spend some time there, thinking about all I have said." The Reverend Mother's round face was puckered with concern. "I want you to pray for guidance, and then, when you have the answer you need, come back and see me. I will not push you out, if it is your wish to stay, but I strongly believe that your time here is at an end. You may go now." She picked up her pen.

Sister Miriam stood and hurried from the room, her mind in turmoil. This was not supposed to happen, just as Sister Agnes was not supposed to leave the Order. She fled along the empty corridor towards her cell, and pulling open the door, stumbled inside. The door closed with a bang behind her.

On trembling legs, she knelt beside her cot and folded her hands in prayer. For too long she had carried her burden of guilt, knowing that at some point it would all come crashing around her, and what she had done would be revealed. That time was getting closer, and she needed to address it, knowing that the consequences would shame her forever. She would be banished from the life she loved, and worse still, would be shunned by all those she held dear. There was only one thing she *could* do, and that would take all her courage, but she had no choice. Maybe God would forgive her, even if nobody else could. She pressed her rosary beads to her mouth as she murmured, "God forgive me."

She remained in that crouched position for some time, contemplating her time in this sanctuary, and reluctant to tear herself from its protection. The Reverend Mother, she feared, knew more than she was revealing, and was relying on her to do the right thing.

Finally, stiff from kneeling on the cold floor, Sister Miriam stood, and brushing down her habit, walked on unsteady legs to the door. The corridor seemed endless as she made her slow way back to the Reverend Mother's office, but finally she stood before the massive door, her heart hammering loudly in her chest. She knocked.

"Enter."

She found herself standing before the oak desk, the Reverend Mother staring intently at her.

"I need to see Father Thomas," she stammered.

"For confession?"

"Yes." It was just a whisper.

Nick

Nick walked towards the Grey Goose Hotel, his head reeling. He had spent an explosive half hour with Jess, listening to her tell of Beau's recent disappearance after discovering that his sister had been abused by their father during her adolescence. He learnt that she had fled to a Convent to escape, and there had given birth to a child that had consequently died. Convinced that her brother was safely away at boarding school, she had remained at the Convent, which was only a short distance from their family home. Nick, who had grown up in an orderly household, with strict rules and tight boundaries, found it all so hard to believe, but he could now understand Beau's reluctance to become involved in any more intrigue. Having also lived through the war, and having suffered mental trauma, Nick had to agree with Jess that Beau was entitled to be left alone with his family.

Shaking his head as he walked, Nick thought about the woman who had fallen from a ladder, and who had stoically tried to brush off his assistance. It seemed that the DuBois siblings were strong, independent people, and he had to admire them for that.

Nick pushed open the side door to the hotel and stepped into the cool passageway. The hum of voices reached his ears as he headed for the bar. Harry caught his eye as he stepped into the lunchtime crowd and raised a hand in greeting.

"Beer, Nick?" he shouted over the noise.

"Thanks, Harry." Nick made his way towards an empty seat and sat heavily.

Izzy, who was passing around the sandwich tray, made her way towards him. She sat opposite and lifting a round of sandwiches on to a plate, slid it across the table in Nick's direction.

"How did it go?" she asked eagerly.

Nick rubbed his hands through his thick dark hair. "I have had a very interesting morning, Izzy." He cast his eyes around the crowded bar. "Has Billy been in?"

"No, not today." Izzy's blue eyes were shining. "Well?"

Nick spotted Harry weaving his way towards them, so he waited. Harry placed the beer before him, wiped his hands on his apron, and looked at his wife.

"More sandwiches are needed, Isobel," he said dryly.

"They can wait, Harry." Izzy replied quickly, brushing her hand in the air. "I want to hear what Nick has to say."

"No, the sandwiches can't wait, Isobel." Harry's jaw was set firmly.

Izzy raised her eyes heavenward but slid obediently from the seat. "Very well, Harry." She pointed a finger at Nick. "Don't go anywhere, Nick. I'll be as quick as I can."

As she disappeared into the crowd, Harry sighed and shook his head. "This is our busiest time of the day, Nick, but Isobel doesn't understand the business side of things."

"Don't be too hard on her, Harry. She has a natural curiosity for things out of the ordinary." Nick laughed as he picked up a sandwich. "You *do* know why this is your busiest time of the day, Harry?"

Harry grimaced. "The free sandwiches? Jean was doing this long before we arrived on the scene."

"It wouldn't happen in the city, Harry." Nick chewed on the egg and lettuce sandwich. "Still, it's a very nice gesture, and one that is appreciated, I have no doubt."

"No doubt." Harry moved off towards the crowded bar, where Jean, flush-faced, was dealing with the surge of workmen.

Nick turned his attention back to his lunch and waited for Izzy to return.

*

The last of the workmen had trickled out the door when Izzy returned to her seat opposite Nick.

"Well?" Her eyes were shining.

"Should we wait for Harry?"

Izzy glanced towards the bar, where Harry was deep in conversation with Jean. "Harry!" She called out. Harry looked up as Izzy beckoned to him. "We're waiting!"

Harry frowned. "I'll be there in a minute, Isobel." He turned his attention back to Jean.

Izzy shrugged. "It looks serious," she whispered to Nick. "Maybe Rodney's causing more trouble."

"Does he cause her trouble often?" Nick was observing Jean's heated responses to Harry.

"No, but when he does, they *are* serious."

Nick watched as Harry laid a hand on Jean's arm in an effort to calm her. It was brushed off as Jean flung down the towel she was holding and stalked off in the direction of her sitting room. Harry looked in Nick and Izzy's direction before shrugging, and leaving the bar unattended, he came towards them.

"I'd better follow her," he muttered. "Keep an eye on the bar, Isobel. Fortunately, it's quiet at the moment. I'd better make sure Jean is alright."

Izzy grabbed his arm. "Is it Rodney?"

"Naturally," said Harry. "It seems he's been caught up in a robbery, and he wants his mother to bail him out of gaol."

"She's not going to, is she?" Izzy's tone was anxious.

"No, but we all know *that* could change." Harry moved off.

Izzy gave an expansive sigh and turned back to Nick. "Well, there's nothing we can do about Rodney, so you'd better fill me in on what's been happening with you, Nick."

"Is there always something going on here, or do you have quiet times, Izzy?" Nick's handsome features were crinkled into a frown.

Izzy laughed. "No, it's not always like this, Nick. You've brought your fair share of intrigue to this town; I must remind you."

"True." Nick's face relaxed as he sat back.

"Now tell me what happened this morning, before I die from curiosity!"

Nick folded his arms as he related his morning's adventures to Izzy. She sat, wide-eyed, as he told of Billy's encounter with Phyllis, and gasped when he mentioned Audrey's admission.

"So it was Audrey who reported her missing?"

"Yes, it was. I don't think she could stand not knowing what had happened to her grandchild, if indeed she *is* her grandchild."

"Well, I never!" Izzy stared at Nick. "So, Billy plans on trying to see Phyllis again?"

"With Audrey's help, yes."

"You did have an exciting morning, didn't you?" Izzy laughed wickedly. "Then of course you got caught up in Charlotte's unfortunate mishap. How did Beau take your appearance there?"

"Not well," said Nick slowly, "but after he had taken his sister to the hospital, Jess told me some of the things that had happened to him over the years."

"Did she now?"

"Yes, and I can now understand why he behaved the way he did. Though why he's taken it out on me, specifically, I have no idea."

"I think perhaps you opened the old wounds with your questions." Izzy stood and picked up the empty sandwich plate. "It's time for me to get back to work, seeing as Jean and Harry have both disappeared. Thanks for telling me, Nick. We can share it with Harry this evening." She made to move away. "You are in for tea this evening, I presume?"

"Yes." Nick replied. "With Amelia gone, I have no reason to go out."

Izzy smiled at his downcast expression. "You'll have a lot to tell her now."

"And a lot to tell my boss," said Nick, rising to his feet. "I'd better do that now, before I forget."

"Do it while there's not many about, Nick." Izzy flashed him one last smile and then was gone.

Beau's Reaction

As Jess prepared the evening meal for the family, the house seemed strangely empty. Charlotte's energy was missing even from such simple tasks as peeling the vegetables for the stew. The silence was heavy, and Jess suddenly realised that while Charlotte's presence increased the workload of the household, there was a definite hole with her absence.

Lottie began to whimper from the confines of her cot in the corner of the kitchen, and as Jess turned from the sink to attend to her, she thought of the times when Charlotte had been the first to rush to the baby's aid.

Jess wiped her hands on her apron, and after grabbing a clean napkin from the pile on the kitchen dresser, she leaned over the cot. Baby Lottie gurgled up at her, grey eyes wide and bubbles forming on her tiny rosebud mouth. Jess smiled, and Lottie held out her arms, in the hope of being picked up.

"No," said Jess gently. "You can wait, little missy. Aunt Charlotte isn't here to spoil you, and I have to get tea ready for your father." The tiny face crinkled. "Your brothers will be home soon, and they can entertain you." Jess hooked the safety pin into her apron as she removed the sodden napkin. "My goodness! You are a wet girl."

With the napkin changed and the wet cot sheet removed, Jess headed for the washhouse. As she did, she heard the screen door slam, and the two boys rushed into the kitchen, calling out as they went.

"Where are you, ma?"

"I'm in the washhouse," she replied, as she plunged the wet napkin and sheet into the trough.

Ben appeared at the door. "Oh, there you are. Where are Grace and Aunt Charlotte?"

Jess left the washing to soak and followed Ben into the kitchen. Edward was leaning over the cot, and Lottie was chuckling as he tickled her tummy. It was a heart-warming sound, and Jess smiled to herself as she went back to the task of peeling carrots. Edward had a way with his baby sister, whereas Ben could not see what all the fuss was about. He had objected to the idea of another sibling, right from the start, and had told Beau in no uncertain terms...

Ben's voice broke through her thoughts now. "Ma! *Where* are Grace and Aunt Charlotte?"

He sounded cross, and his brown eyes were hooded as he looked at his mother.

"I'm sorry, Ben." Jess slid the carrots off the chopping-board and into the saucepan. "Sit at the table and I'll tell you. Edward, come over here please."

"I'm hungry," grumbled eight-year-old Edward, who was growing at an alarming rate, out-stripping his older brother by inches.

"I'll get you something shortly," said Jess calmly. "In the meantime, I want you to sit at the table and listen to what I have to say."

"Has something happened?" asked Ben, always the perceptive one.

"Yes, Ben." Jess sat beside him, while Edward flopped on to the chair opposite his brother.

"What?" Edward leaned forward, eager to learn if it was something ghoulish.

"Aunt Charlotte had an accident today."

"What sort of accident?" Edward asked eagerly.

"She fell off the ladder while retrieving the ball that *you* threw up on the roof yesterday, Edward."

"Was she hurt?" Ben was glaring at his brother.

"Yes, she was. Beau has taken her to the hospital to see whether she's broken any bones."

"She shouldn't have climbed the ladder," said Ben, leaning back on his chair and folding his arms.

"I know, Ben," said Jess gravely, "but Aunt Charlotte is used to doing things like that."

"At the Convent?"

"Yes, Ben. Anyway, the young man who is staying at the Grey Goose at present, just happened to be in the neighbourhood, and he helped lift Aunt Charlotte into the house, for which I was very thankful."

"Will she be alright?"

"I'm sure she will, Edward. It was her foot that was a concern." Jess clapped her hands. "So, now that we've cleared that up, I want you two to put your schoolbags in your room, change your clothes, and get your chores done." She stood up, pushing in the chair. "While you're doing that, I will get you some afternoon tea."

"I suppose Grace is down with Freya?" said Ben as he pushed back on his chair.

"Yes, she is."

"She's always there," grumbled Edward, as he picked up his schoolbag from the floor. "She doesn't have to do chores, like we do."

"She will when she's older, now off you go. Ben, I've had the chooks roaming in the garden today, so you'd better look around for eggs. They could be anywhere."

Ben sighed and rolled his eyes. His shoulders slumped and Jess knew that he wouldn't be pleased. He never was, when she let the chooks out to free range. She hid a smile as she turned to the stove.

*

The front door slammed, and Jess heard Beau's footsteps in the passage. She heard him go into the bedroom, and then several moments later, he appeared at the kitchen door.

"How is Charlotte?" asked Jess as she crossed the kitchen to give him a kiss as she always did when he came home from work.

"Her ankle is broken." Beau folded his arms around her. "She'll be out of action for several weeks."

"Poor Charlotte." Jess took his arm. "Come and sit down, my love. You look done in. Tea will be ready shortly. The boys are just finishing their chores." She smiled. "They'll have to do a little more now that Aunt Charlotte is unable to help them."

Beau sat in his usual place at the table. "I've left her at the hospital for tonight. Tomorrow she'll have to practise walking with crutches and a plaster cast." He ran his fingers through his greying hair.

"Oh dear!" murmured Jess. "She *will* be handicapped. She's not going to like that."

"No, she certainly won't."

Jess pushed the kettle across the stove to boil as she contemplated telling Beau what had transpired between her and Nick Armitage after Charlotte had been taken to the hospital. However, her nerve failed her, so she remained silent as she made Beau a cup of tea.

"I hope Mr. Armitage didn't hang around after I'd gone, Jess." Beau's grey eyes were studying her as she placed the cup of tea on the table in front of him.

Had he read her mind? Jess blinked, avoiding his stare. "I made him a cup of tea, Beau," she said tersely. "It was the least I could do."

"I don't want him in this house, Jess." Something in his tone made Jess quake as she stared at him.

"Don't you think you're being unreasonable, Beau?" she ventured to say. "He seems quite a nice young man, and anyway…"

"I will not have him in our house, Jess, whether you think I'm being unreasonable or not!" His voice rose dangerously as he struck the table with his fist.

"Knock, knock!" came a tentative voice from the doorway. "Is this a bad time?"

They both looked up to see Izzy standing uncomfortably at the kitchen door, Grace by her side.

Jess looked quickly at Beau, who had now picked up his teacup.

"No," she said quietly. "Come in, Izzy."

"I thought you might be missing someone." Izzy was trying to make light of an awkward moment. "So I've returned her." She sent Jess a smile that said: *Is everything alright?*

"Thank-you, Izzy." Jess smiled down at Grace. "Tea will be ready soon."

"I –er- I won't stay." Izzy wiped her hands down her blue skirt. "I have to prepare tea, too. I'll see you tomorrow, Gracie?" Grace looked up at her aunt and nodded solemnly. "How is Charlotte?" Izzy added, not as an afterthought, but because she needed to know.

"Her ankle is broken," said Jess tightly.

"Oh dear, that's no good." Izzy tut-tutted.

The uncomfortable silence continued while Beau drank his tea. Izzy looked from him to Jess and back again, unable to comprehend what was happening with these two who never had angry words.

"I'll go," she said finally. "I'll talk to you soon, Jess."

Jess nodded mutely.

Izzy turned reluctantly and they heard her footsteps in the passage, and then the closing of the front door. Jess looked down at Beau, and her eyes were brimming.

"I don't know what's got into you, Beau." She stumbled over the words, "But you need to explain to me why you are so hostile."

Beau looked up at her as he placed his empty cup on the table. "I will, Jess, but not right now." His eyes had that haunted expression that she had seen in them at other times, and it frightened her.

He rose slowly. "Let me know when tea's ready." His shoulders were slumped as he headed for the outside door, and Jess noticed how he rumpled Grace's hair as he passed her. It was almost as an apology. Jess felt the tears well.

The wire door slammed after him and as Jess stood, unable to move, she heard the sound of the axe chopping into wood. Beau was releasing the tension that had built up inside him.

"Ma?" Jess felt Grace tugging at her skirt.

"Yes, Grace?"

"Is Beau angry with me?"

"No, darling!" Jess knelt beside her daughter, hugging her to her breast. "He's not angry with you."

As Jess buried her face in Grace's golden curls, she realised that Beau had not even acknowledged baby Lottie. He always scooped her out of the cot when he came home from work.

"How's my girl, today?" he would say and then he would grin at Jess. "How are my girls?" he would correct himself.

Something was terribly wrong, and she needed to find out what it was, very quickly.

*

Tea was eaten in silence, and the boys, as though sensing something was wrong, refrained from their usual banter. They glanced surreptitiously from their mother to Beau, but no smiles were forthcoming. Once they had eaten, they excused themselves and left the table. Grace stared miserably at her mother, before following the boys.

"It's bath night!" called Jess after their retreating backs. "Ben, could you light the chip heater, please?"

"Yes, ma."

Jess looked across the table at Beau as the children disappeared, but he was looking down at his empty plate. Lottie stirred in her cot, so Jess rose to attend to her.

"When the children are bathed and in bed, Jess," she heard Beau's husky voice saying, "I have something to show you."

She turned to look at him. "Will it answer my questions, Beau?"

"Possibly." He pushed back his chair. "I'll go and help the boys get the bath ready."

As Jess turned back to her youngest child, she had a hollow feeling in the pit of her stomach. Secrets were still coming out. What was she going to hear this time?

Startling Revelations

Jess hurried through the task of getting the three older children to bed, and for once had to forego story-time. This was met with much opposition from the two boys. Their mother had never neglected their story-time, and Edward pouted sullenly. Jess rubbed a hand through his unruly blonde hair and promised him double time the following night. He had to be content with that.

Once the lights were out, and peace reigned in the bedrooms, she went in search of Beau. He was on the front verandah, butting out his last cigarette for the day. She grabbed a shawl from the bedroom, threw it around her shoulders and stepped out into the night. Standing close beside him at the verandah rail, she slid an arm around his middle, and waited in the silence that followed. He turned to look at her in the semi darkness. They stared miserably at each other for some moments. Finally Beau broke their gaze when he reached down to pick up his crushed cigarette butt from the floor. Placing it in a small cigarette tin, he slipped it in the pocket of his trousers.

"Come into the lounge, Jess," he said quietly. "I have something to show you."

Jess followed him into the lounge, where he motioned her to sit on the old brown couch. He sat beside her, and Jess could see that he was struggling with whatever it was he had to say to her. She patted his knee.

"We haven't done this for a while," she said as an opener. "It was always my favourite time of the day, sitting here with you, Beau, listening as you told me about your day."

He nodded as he reached into his jacket pocket and pulled out a piece of paper. Unfolding it carefully, he handed it to Jess.

"What's this?" Jess peered down at the newspaper article that was obviously very old. The print was faint, and a photograph above the print was grainy and rubbed where the paper had been folded.

The headline was still readable: **Prominent Doctor Denies Allegations of Misconduct.**

Jess sucked in her breath and gazed frantically at Beau.

"What *is* this?" she demanded this time. "What misconduct? Beau? Tell me this isn't about you?"

"No, Jess, it's not about me." He paused, swallowing hard. "It was my father."

Jess was relieved that it wasn't about Beau, but she was terrified of what she was about to hear.

"Tell me what it's about, Beau," she said gently. "It's obviously something that happened a long time ago." Her eyes scanned the paper, but it was almost illegible. "What misconduct?" In her heart she knew what the answer was going to be.

Beau rubbed his hands together in a nervous gesture as he looked sadly at Jess.

"My father" he began slowly, "always had trouble with young girls – patients – which is a frightful admission from one who knows the rules and respects them to the utmost degree." His voice rose, almost as though he was defending himself. "This was a case where the young woman in question decided that he was not going to get away with abusing his position as a doctor."

"So she took him to court?"

"Her family did." Beau shrugged. "My father denied it, of course, and ultimately won the case." He took the newspaper article and pointed to a line. His finger was trembling. "This is the bit that I wanted to show you, Jess."

Jess peered at where his trembling finger lay, and she gasped. "His defence lawyer was a Hugh Armitage?" She stared at Beau. "Hugh Armitage?" she repeated the name slowly.

"Yes. Now look at the picture, Jess. What do you see?"

Jess looked at the grainy picture of a dark-haired man and frowned. "Who is it?"

"That's my father." Beau paused. "Does he remind you of anyone?"

Jess looked closely, but the image was faint. She frowned, suddenly feeling perturbed. "Who, Beau?"

"Does he remind you of Nick?"

Jess looked up quickly. "Why should he remind me of Nick?" The words froze on her mouth, and she glanced once more at the photograph. "What are you saying, Beau?"

"I don't know what I am saying, Jess." Beau rubbed at his forehead in a gesture of frustration. "But to me the resemblance is uncanny."

"When did all this happen?"

"This incident? It was about twenty-five years ago."

"But Nick is older than that, Beau."

"Yes, I know." He shrugged helplessly. "When Nick arrived here, I had a funny feeling about him, but I didn't know why. I didn't know whether it was his expression, his voice or his gestures. I only knew that they were familiar."

"How long have you had this newspaper article?"

"A long time."

"Why did you keep it, and why have you not shared this with me before now?"

"Over the years I'd forgotten I had it, but I think I kept it to remind myself that in my job there is no room for that kind of behaviour." He took her hands. "Like a lot of things to do with my father, I blocked them out, Jess. I didn't want to know."

"And your mother? Was she alive when this incident occurred?"

"No. She died many years before that. As I've told you, I was just a child when she died." He rubbed her fingers gently. "Poor mother, I think she knew what he was like, and that sent her to an early grave."

They sat in silence, their hands entwined tightly. Finally, Jess broke the silence.

"It could all just be coincidence, Beau. We don't know whether Hugh Armitage has any connection to Nick."

"No, we don't, but I don't like coincidences, Jess, and this is an enormous one."

"Maybe you should ask him, straight out. They could be forty-second cousins or…"

"Or father and son, Jess."

"Well, he's sticking around town for a few more days, to see if Billy has any luck with Phyllis, so you're sure to run into him."

"Part of me wants to see him gone, Jess, and the other part of me wants to know."

"You've opened this can of worms, Beau, so you are the only one who can empty the can, so to speak."

Jess released her hands and slipped her arms around Beau, holding him tight.

"I don't want to ever have words like we had earlier, Beau," she murmured in his ear. "I love you and I don't want you to keep things from me, even if they are terrible things."

"I'm sorry, Jess. I shouldn't have bawled you out like that. Please forgive me."

"You're forgiven."

Beau sought her mouth as they clung together on the couch, and Jess's insecurity melted under his touch. There was still so much about Beau that she didn't know, but at this moment, none of it mattered except their love for each other.

*

At the grey Goose, the evening meal was about to get underway. Izzy had returned from Jess's place, feeling very concerned about what she had witnessed. Beau never got angry, or so she thought. What could have possibly caused him to snap at Jess like that? Was it something to do with Nick? She would have to get her sister alone and find out.

The clatter of dishes brought her back to the present moment, and she smiled at Harry, who was watching her quizzically.

"What?" She asked, fearing that she had missed something that Harry had said.

"You looked far away then, Izzy," said Harry, as he helped himself to the dish of boiled potatoes.

"Did I?" Izzy buttered a slice of bread for Freya. "I was thinking about Jess, that's all."

"How's the situation with Charlotte?" Nick was also buttering bread.

"She has a broken ankle," said Izzy, "and that's all I can tell you."

"Is she still at the hospital?" Nick persisted.

Izzy shrugged. "I suppose so. She wasn't at the house."

"You're a little offhand with this news, Izzy," interrupted Jean. "Was everything alright?"

Izzy sat, toying with her fork. How much should she say? "I arrived at a bad time," she said. "Jess didn't have time to talk to me, so I delivered Grace and left." She punctured a potato with her fork.

"What? No conversation?" Jean's tone was sceptical. "That's unusual for you two."

"Jess was getting tea ready. She didn't have time to talk." Izzy waved her fork. "Now let's eat before this gets cold." The conversation had ended.

Tea was finished in silence. At the first opportunity, Nick placed the cutlery across his empty plate, and wiped his mouth with the linen napkin.

"I have news," he said as he deliberately folded the napkin.

"Yes, you do, Nick" said Izzy hurriedly. "You'd better tell Harry and Jean what you told me earlier."

Harry put down his cutlery. "Tell us what?" He looked at Nick.

"Billy has been to see Phyllis, (not without opposition from the Reverend Mother) and he plans on trying to see her again, with her little girl."

"That's wonderful!" Jean was smiling broadly. "The child is his then?"

Nick shook his head. "We still don't know, Jean, but we found out something else today." He stopped.

"Well? What is it? Don't leave us hanging, Nick," said Jean impatiently.

"It was Billy's mother, Audrey, who reported her missing." Nick sat back to watch the reactions.

Jean tut-tutted loudly. "I did wonder about that," she said sagely. "Audrey desperately wants that child to be Billy's."

"Yes, she does," replied Nick, "but even if she's not, I think Audrey would be very happy to claim her as her own grandchild."

"How does Billy feel about that?" asked Harry. "I mean it could cause all sorts of problems if Sid O'Connor gets wind of it."

"Don't talk about that man," grumbled Jean. "He's a problem to everybody."

"He shouldn't be a problem to anybody at present," said Nick mildly, "because he's in the lock-up."

"He's where?" Jean sat up straight on her chair. "The police lock-up?"

"That's where I saw him."

Jean slumped. "So is Rodney." She sighed. "He wants me to bail him out."

"Don't be foolish, Jean!" Izzy's tone was sharp.

"What's he there for, Jean?" Nick wanted to hear it from Jean's lips.

"Involvement in a robbery, along with his two friends, Seamus Oliver and Al Williams."

"And Sid O'Connor, I suspect," said Nick.

Jean stared at him. "You think Sid was involved as well?"

"I can't be sure, but the Chief Constable told me he was being held for being drunk and disorderly and involved in 'other things that he couldn't disclose' to me."

"So the four of them have been up to no good?" Jean's eyes glittered with anger. "In that case Rodney can stay there and rot for all I care!" She looked intently at Nick. "What were you doing at the Police Barracks, Nick?"

"I had to report that Phyllis Powell had been found, and that she was safe."

"You reported that to the Chief Constable?"

"Yes."

"Chief Constable Whitley?"

"Yes."

Jean slumped back against her chair. "You know what that means, don't you?" They all shook their heads. "Whitley will have to report it to Senior Sergeant Morrow." She spread her hands. "Those two are as bad as, if not worse than the villains they incarcerate!" Her voice rose as three pairs of eyes stared at her. "Phyllis won't be safe if those two know where she is."

"But they *are* the law," said Nick, puzzled by Jean's reaction. "Surely…"

"That means nothing, Nick!" Jean stood abruptly, pushing back her chair. "Billy needs to find another safe place for Phyllis and that child, if he cares about them at all." She looked directly at Nick. "I'm serious, Nick. They are no longer safe where they are." She picked up several dirty plates and marched resolutely towards the door.

"What do you think she meant by that?" whispered Izzy when Jean had gone.

"I don't know," muttered Harry. "You should be safe enough giving information to the police."

"Hm." Nick's brow was furrowed, as he recalled the bloodied state of Sid O'Connor when he had seen him being frog-marched by the constables. He also recalled the uneasy feeling he had about throwing Phyllis to the wolves. "I'll talk with Billy tomorrow."

"What?" Harry raised his eyebrows in disbelief. "You think Jean could be right?"

"I don't know." Nick's expression was serious. "I do know that when I saw Sid at the Police Barracks, he had obviously received a beating."

"From the police?" Izzy was horrified.

"Most likely. It happens, Izzy." Nick sounded apologetic. "Not all our keepers of the peace are sympathetic towards law-breakers, you know?"

"Well, I'm shocked!" Izzy looked down, suddenly realising that Freya was still seated beside her. "Oh, my goodness! Harry, do you think *someone* understood what we were talking about?"

Harry looked across at Freya, who was playing with the ribbons on her doll's hair and shook his head. "I don't think so, Isobel."

Nick Talks To Billy

The following morning, Nick left the hotel early, in the hope of catching Billy before he went to work. It was only a short walk to the Maitlands' cottage, and Nick stepped it out. The morning was fresh, and a slight breeze stirred the elms along the street. Nick said, "Good morning!" to the milkman who was doing his rounds and received a cheerful "Mornin!'" in reply. Apart from the milkman and his slow-moving Clydesdale, there was nobody else about. It was the perfect morning for a long walk, Nick contemplated, but there was work to do first.

Joe had been pleased that the search was wrapped up so quickly, and he was eagerly waiting for Amelia to arrive, to hear the story in detail. He had given Nick permission to spend as much time as he liked in the town. Laughingly he had suggested that Nick find another story, if he liked the place so much. Nick smiled to himself as he opened the gate at Billy's house. Heading along the narrow path that led to the front door, he knocked loudly and waited.

The door opened slightly, and Audrey's thin face appeared, framed by a white cotton nightcap. She peered at Nick.

"Good morning, Audrey," said Nick cheerfully, raising his hat. "Sorry to disturb you at this hour, but I wondered if I might have a word with Billy before he goes to work."

Audrey opened the door fully. "Oh, it's you, Mr. Armitage. Billy isn't working this morning. He's got the afternoon shift."

"Good!" Nick removed his hat and ran his fingers through his hair.

Audrey, wrapped in a blue chenille dressing gown, stepped aside to let Nick enter the narrow passage. "Go through to the kitchen, and I'll call him," she said quietly.

"No need, mum." Billy appeared in the passage, pulling up his braces. "Good mornin', Nick! You're up early f'r a gentleman!" He was smiling broadly, pleased with his joke.

"Gentleman?" Nick laughed. "Well, I hope I am, Billy, though some may disagree."

"I'll make you some tea." Audrey scurried past the two men and disappeared into the small kitchen. Nick and Billy followed.

"What brings ya here at this hour?" rasped Billy. "Not trouble, I 'ope?"

"I'm not sure, Billy, but I do need to talk to both of you about something that's bothering me."

Chairs scraped on the wooden floor as the two men sat opposite each other at the table. Audrey lifted the singing kettle and poured its scalding contents into the teapot that stood on the hob.

"You want to talk to me too, Mr. Armitage?"

"Yes, Audrey, and *please* call me Nick." He smiled reassuringly at her worried expression.

Nick waited until the tea was poured and set in front of them before he began his account of the conversation the previous night. Audrey sat at the head of the table and listened carefully.

"As you both know," he began, "the discovery of Phyllis's whereabouts has led to me having to report it to the police." They both nodded, looking at each other warily. "As I also told you, I saw Sid O'Connor being taken to the lock-up." Again, they nodded. "I wasn't comfortable at the time with what I'd had to do, but it was proper procedure. Do you understand?"

"Yeah," said Billy slowly, while Audrey bit her lower lip.

"I've learnt a few things since, that lead me to believe that Phyllis may no longer be safe where she is." He took a deep breath. "Billy, if you're serious about helping her, I suggest you do it quickly."

"What 'ave you learnt, Nick?" Billy's thin face was screwed into a frown.

"I've learnt that some of Sid's mates, including Jean's son, Rodney, have been involved in a robbery, and they are all in the lock-up awaiting their time in front of the Magistrate."

"Jeez!" rasped Billy. "So that's what's been goin' on?" he frowned. "Rodney O'Malley's in on it, too? Jean won't be 'appy about that!"

"She's not, Billy, and she's not going to bail him out." Nick leaned forward. "My worry is that Chief Constable Whitley, having Sid in his sights, is not going to keep quiet about Phyllis's whereabouts."

"Whitley, you say? 'E's the one ya spoke to?"

"Yes, and Jean's opinion of both him and Senior Sergeant Morrow was not flattering."

"No, I bet it wasn't." Billy sat back on his chair, cradling his teacup in one hand. "What do ya suggest I do, Nick? The Reverend Mother's not likely t'listen to a story like that."

"She'll have to, Billy."

"I'll go with you, Billy." Audrey spoke for the first time. "If we sound desperate enough, she should listen, even if she only agrees to give Phyllis extra protection at the orphanage."

Billy looked from his mother to Nick. "Whitley knows Phyllis's at the orphanage?"

"Yes, he does. I'm sorry, Billy."

Billy looked up at the clock above the stove. "Right!" he said matter-of-factly. "It's 'alf past eight. Get dressed, mum, an' we'll see what the Reverend Mother 'as t'say." Billy looked at Nick. "You comin', Nick?"

"I certainly am, Billy. I can't leave a job unfinished."

Facing The Reverend Mother

By mid-morning the trio was standing at the massive front door of the orphanage, and Nick knocked loudly. Billy was dressed in his suit once more, and Audrey wore a neat floral dress. Both had passed inspection by Nick's standards, and he smiled encouragingly at them as they stood nervously at his side.

The door swung open, and the Reverend Mother stood there. She stared at them for several moments before pulling herself up to her full height.

"What do you want?" Her expression was cold. "I thought I told you to stay away from here."

Nick removed his hat and stepped forward. "Reverend Mother, it's important that you listen to us. We are genuinely concerned for Phyllis Powell's welfare, and fifteen minutes of your time will not be wasted, I assure you."

"What could you possibly have to say that you haven't said before?" She was staring at Nick.

"Circumstances have changed somewhat."

The Reverend Mother turned her gaze on Audrey. "And who might you be?"

"I'm Audrey Maitland, Reverend Mother." Audrey touched Billy's arm. "I'm Billy's mother, and possibly the little'n's grandmother."

The dark eyebrows were raised imperiously. "Indeed?" This was followed by silence as they waited for an invitation to enter. "You'd better come in, and this had better be worth my while."

The door was opened fully, and the Reverend Mother stood aside, allowing them to enter the large open vestibule. It still smelled of phenyl, and Nick coughed involuntarily.

"Something wrong, Mr. Armitage?"

"Er – no, Reverend Mother. It's just the smell of the phenyl."

"Cleanliness is next to Godliness, Mr. Armitage." The Reverend Mother swept past them as she led the way to her office.

Once they were all seated in the cluttered confines of the office, the Reverend Mother folded her arms and swung her gaze across the three sitting opposite her.

"I'm listening," she said, her eyes resting on Nick.

"Since we were here last..." began Nick.

"Two days ago," interrupted the Reverend Mother.

"Since we were here *two days ago*, I had a visit to the Police Barracks to report that Phyllis had been located. I insisted that she was safe, and that she did not want a certain Sid O'Connor to know where she was."

The Reverend Mother nodded. "I hope that still stands."

"That's the problem, you see. Mr. O'Connor was being locked up at the same time as I was there, for various misdemeanours, including, (we think) taking part in a robbery. We don't know that for sure, but what I do know is that he had received rather a beating from the police. I saw the results with my own eyes."

"And what has this to do with Phyllis's welfare, may I ask?"

"It's called duress, Reverend Mother – the obtaining of information by unacceptable methods."

"I still don't see how that affects Phyllis."

Nick could see that Billy was anxious to speak, so he nodded in his direction. "Go ahead, Billy."

"These coppers are mean, Reverend Mother," began Billy. "I know 'cause I've 'ad dealin's with 'em. If they come 'ere lookin' f'Phyllis, they won't stand on ceremony, if ya know what I mean."

"Why would they come here looking for Phyllis?"

"Because I've reported that she is here," said Nick coldly, "and they will have to check on that information. Also, they might use Phyllis as a means of gaining information from Sid."

"They wouldn't do that, surely?"

"We're not prepared to bet on it, Reverend Mother." Nick leaned forward. "We need your support and a guarantee from you that if they do come here, they will not find Phyllis."

The Reverend Mother gave a short laugh. "Mr. Armitage, you of all people should know how hard it is to get into this place."

"Yes and no." Nick grinned. "However, they are the law, whether we like their methods or not, and you may not have any choice but to let them in."

"I see." The Reverend Mother was silent as she let this sink in. Finally, she looked at Audrey and her expression softened somewhat. "And what do you think, Mrs. Maitland?"

"Well!" Audrey plucked nervously at the sleeve of her dress. "It was me who wanted Phyllis found, so I suppose that makes me responsible for what happens now. I want to see them both safe, her and the little one, and I'm prepared to take them in if that's what it all comes to."

Billy stared at his mother. "But mum, the little'un might not be mine."

"Don't give me that, Billy – of course she is."

"Have you seen 'er?"

"No."

"Then how can ya say that?"

"I just know." Audrey's jaw was set stubbornly.

The Reverend Mother watched the interaction between mother and son, and her lips pursed in what could almost be described as a smile. When they were silent, she folded her arms across her chest.

"I have to say," she began, "that you are very persistent, so in that light, I will see what Phyllis has to say on the matter. If she refuses to see you, I cannot make her. You do understand that?" They all nodded. "From what I can gather, a lot of what you are saying is purely supposition and may or may not occur."

"Granted," said Nick, "but you do not know these people, and what they are all capable of."

"If the police let Sid go, an' he knows Phyllis is 'ere," growled Billy, "'e'll be on your doorstop like a shot, an' 'e won't be polite, I can assure ya."

The Reverend Mother drummed her fingers on the table. "Wait here," she said as she rose from her chair. "I'll see what Phyllis has to say."

"Can I see the little one?" asked Audrey as the Reverend Mother reached the door.

She turned and a frown etched her high brow. "I'll ask," was all she said before exiting swiftly.

The three looked at each other, and Billy let out a big sigh.

"Do ya think Phyllis'll see us, Nick?"

"I don't know, Billy. Let's wait and see, shall we?"

Audrey was looking around the cluttered office, where large cardboard boxes spilled their contents on to the floor.

"Goodness me!" she exclaimed. "There's an awful lot of women's and children's clothing here." She nodded towards the boxes. "There must be a lot of mothers and little ones living here."

"I would say you're right, Audrey, and I suspect that war casualties might have had something to do with the numbers – women with nowhere else to go."

They were all silent after this remark from Nick.

The minutes slowly ticked by, but eventually they heard the sound of footsteps in the corridor and the door opened. The Reverend Mother swept into the room, and behind her, hesitating in the doorway, was Phyllis. A small girl clung to her skirts, and Phyllis gave her a gentle push, forcing them both into the room. Audrey rose to her feet, her eyes on the child, and Billy was looking at Phyllis, a frown on his thin face.

Nick suppressed the gasp that had risen to his throat as he looked from Phyllis down to the child, and all of a sudden, he realised why Phyllis had been so protective. The child had the round, bland features of what was unkindly referred to as 'mongoloid.' She was looking at the three strangers in front of her, and her blue eyes were wide. Suddenly she smiled, and her face lit up.

"I told ya, Billy, that Hope looked like 'erself," said Phyllis, her tone defensive, "an' nobody's takin' her away from me!"

Nick could see that Billy was speechless, unsure of how he should react.

Audrey stood slowly and squatting so that she was at the same height as the child, she held out her arms.

"Come to grandma, Hope," she whispered. "I have waited a long time for this moment."

The awkward silence was broken as the child gave a squeal of delight and ran into Audrey's waiting arms. Audrey looked over her head at Phyllis, who stood silently, tears running down her face.

"She's beautiful, Phyllis," whispered Audrey, her own eyes awash.

"Now you'll understand why they have to remain here," said the Reverend Mother, her voice faltering. "These children are so often abandoned and left in institutions where nobody can see them. Phyllis does not want that for her child."

Billy was nodding slowly. "I wish we'd known, Phyllis," he said, as he watched the reaction between his mother and Hope. "We'll be 'ere for ya, that I will promise." He took a deep breath. "An' if ya wanna stay 'ere, I'll see ya safe." He was blinking rapidly.

"From Sid?" It was just a whisper.

"Especially from Sid." Billy looked gravely at the Reverend Mother. "I must apologise t'you, Reverend Mother. I thought you were keepin' these girls 'ere against their will. I can see now that ya do care for 'em."

"Of course I care for them, young man!" The moment of softness was gone, and once again the Reverend Mother pulled herself up to her full height. "Now tell Phyllis what you told me, so that we can execute a plan." For a moment her eyes glittered with unexpected wickedness. "It will give me great pleasure to enter into battle with the lawmen of this town." She looked at Phyllis. "Not to mention Mr. Sidney O'Connor. Are you ready for this, Phyllis?"

Phyllis nodded.

Nick exchanged glances with Billy. This was not what either of them had expected, and the prickly Reverend Mother they had both encountered before, was obviously a smokescreen thrown up to protect those girls within her charge. They had an ally, and both were relieved.

As for Audrey, she had the grandchild she had craved for so long, and it made no difference that the child had a disability. She was going to love her anyway.

*

Sometime later, Nick, Billy and Audrey were heading down the hill towards the town. Their steps were light, as they were now confident that a plan had been hatched to protect Phyllis and Hope from the likelihood of a visit from the police and from Sid. Billy was smiling to himself as he walked and wished fervently that he could be a fly on the wall when Sid encountered the Reverend Mother.

The police would be granted permission to search the premises for Phyllis and her child, but secret places still existed in the halls whereby she would not be found. The Reverend Mother had brushed aside the fact that the police might think she was deliberately being evasive.

"They wouldn't dare touch a woman of God!" was all she had said, her eyes flashing once again.

"Who'da thought, eh?" said Billy cheerfully. "I never thought we'd get past first base with the Reverend Mother, but I think she's enjoyin' this."

"That child needs protecting at all costs," said Audrey firmly. "I'm pleased that Phyllis has reacted the way she has." There were tears in her eyes. "It shows she really loves her."

Billy took his mother's arm. "An' you'll love 'er too if I'm not mistaken, mum."

"She's very sweet, Billy, and I'll enjoy getting to know her."

"Good onya, mum. She's lucky t'have you on 'er side."

Nick smiled at their enthusiasm. "I think the Reverend Mother had better get used to seeing you two at her door."

"Ya'd better believe it, Nick." Billy gave his mother a squeeze. "One day we might even be able t'persuade Phyllis t'bring Hope t'see us. That won't be until I've sorted Sid out, of course!" He added vehemently.

"That will be a day to remember, Billy. Pity I won't be around to see it."

"You off soon then?"

"Yes, I'll have to leave here soon Billy. I can't hang around forever."

"'Course ya can! This is a great town."

"It is, I agree, Billy, but I have a home in Sydney."

"Yeah." Billy glanced up at Nick. "Well, it's been good gettin' t'know ya, Nick, an' we both thank ya f'what you've done, don't we, mum?"

"Yes, indeed." Audrey's eyes were moist. "It's taken three years, but I think everything will be alright now."

"We're not entirely out o'the woods yet, mum." Billy was scowling as he thought of his next encounter with Sid.

"I think Mr. O'Connor probably has a lot on his mind at present," said Nick.

"I'll be ready for 'im!" Billy was resolute.

"I'm sure you will, Billy," murmured Nick. "I'm sure you will."

The Newspaper Article

Izzy was washing out beer glasses when she looked up to see Beau standing on the other side of the bar. Her blue eyes opened wide with surprise.

"Beau!" she exclaimed. "What are you doing here?" She glanced up at the clock. It was half past eleven. "Shouldn't you be at work?"

"I've given myself some time off, Izzy," Beau replied hastily. "As a matter of fact, I want to speak to Nick if he's here."

"I'm sorry, Beau. Nick went to see Billy."

"Oh!" Beau frowned. "Any idea when he'll be back?"

Izzy shook her head. "No."

Beau drummed his fingers on the bar. "No matter." He smiled at her concerned expression. "I'll pop back at lunchtime." He headed for the door.

"When he comes in, I'll tell him you want to speak to him, Beau!" called Izzy to his retreating back.

Beau raised a hand in acknowledgement as he pulled the door shut behind him. Izzy frowned as she set a tray of clean glasses on the bar. Beau had certainly been acting very strangely, ever since Nick's arrival in their midst. It had to have something to do with Nick's association with the Private Investigator who had come searching for him several years ago, but what? Izzy didn't know enough about Beau's past to put two and two together, and Jess didn't want to discuss it either.

Izzy was still deep in thought when Nick's voice drew her back to the present.

"How about a drink for a thirsty man, Izzy?"

"Oh, Nick! You startled me. Where did you spring from?"

"My room, actually." Nick seated himself on the nearest stool and looked around him. "Where is everybody?" The bar was deserted.

"Don't worry," said Izzy, looking up at the clock. "They'll all be in soon for their sandwiches."

"You're too generous," laughed Nick.

"Yes, I know," sighed Izzy. "By the way, Nick, Beau was in here looking for you. He'll be back, so don't go anywhere."

"Beau was looking for me?" Nick frowned. "Was he in a good mood?"

"It's hard to tell with Beau lately." Izzy pulled a beer for Nick and slid it across the bar.

"Well, I'll make room for the regulars and when he comes back, I'll be sitting over there in the corner." Nick slid off the stool and carrying his beer, headed for the end of the bar where they could talk in private if necessary.

It wasn't long before the regular lunchtime crowd began filtering in, most in overalls or boilersuits. Nick listened to the camaraderie as he sat quietly in the corner, and he couldn't help but compare this lifestyle with the one he had in Sydney. He felt a slight twinge of envy as he watched the men greet each other with such enthusiasm. Their faces were lined and work weary, smudged with grease, dust or both, but they were all comrades, and this was their time to forget how hard they worked, and just enjoy a pint before heading back to the slog.

Nick saw Jean passing around the sandwich tray, laughing and joking with the men as she went. She was a remarkable woman, and when he thought of how her son was taking advantage of her, he shook his head with disgust.

"Nick!" Jean was standing in front of him. "Sandwich?"

"I don't mind if I do." Nick smiled graciously. "Thank-you, Jean."

"My pleasure." She moved on.

As Nick took a bite out of his sandwich, he saw Beau making his way towards him. Nick gestured to the chair opposite. Beau sat and moved the chair closer to the table.

"Hello, Beau." Nick wiped the crumbs from his mouth.

"Hello, Nick." His tone was cool but not hostile.

"What can I do for you?"

Beau seemed to be struggling to find the right words. Finally, he spoke. "Did the name DuBois mean anything to you before you were asked to come down here, Nick?"

"Only what Joe Hudson had told me about you. Why?"

"You hadn't heard it mentioned at home?"

"At home? What do you mean, Beau?"

"Had your parents ever mentioned the name?"

"No, I don't think so." Nick was puzzled. "Why do you ask?"

Beau reached into his jacket pocket and pulled out a folded piece of paper. Carefully unfolding it, with the photograph hidden, he laid it on the table, turning it to face Nick.

"What's this?" Nick peered at the old newspaper cutting before looking across at Beau. "Where did you get this?" He had seen the headline: **Prominent Doctor Denies Allegations of Misconduct.**

"I've had it for a long time, Nick." Beau licked his dry lips. "The doctor at the centre of this case was my father, and his defence lawyer was a Hugh Armitage."

Nick sucked in his breath. "My father!" he stuttered.

"Hugh Armitage was your father?"

"Hugh *is* my father, Beau. He's semi-retired now, but I believe he was very good at his job." Nick scanned down the newspaper article, getting the gist of the faded print. "When was this?"

"Twenty-five years ago, Nick."

"I would have only been seven at the time." Nick sat back on his chair. "Why have you shown me this, Beau?"

"I wanted to establish whether this was your father or not."

Nick nodded slowly. "You must be pleased that your father was exonerated?"

Beau laughed harshly. "I was eighteen at the time, and just starting at Medical School." He looked out the window, unable to meet Nick's gaze. "My father was not a good man, Nick, and where there's smoke there's usually fire," was all he said as he tucked the paper back in his jacket pocket.

Nick frowned. "What do you mean? Are you saying that he *was* guilty of misconduct?"

"He was guilty of many things, Nick. This may or may not have been one of them."

Nick rubbed his chin thoughtfully. "If you like, I can talk to my father when I get home and see if he remembers the case. There are a lot of people…" He stopped. Beau was staring at him. "What's the matter?"

Beau stood quickly, scraping his chair on the floor. "No, I don't think that will be necessary, Nick," he said. "Now if you'll excuse me, I must go."

Nick watched as Beau made his way to the door. What just happened then? He took a deep breath and scratched his head in bewilderment. Izzy, who had been covertly watching the exchange from behind the bar, stepped across to Nick, with the pretence of removing his plate and wiping the table.

"Beau was in a hurry to leave?" she said conversationally.

"Yes, he was, Izzy, and I'm not sure why." He sat back on the chair.

Izzy hesitated. "What was he showing you, Nick?"

He looked up at her, a frown on his face. "A very old newspaper clipping, Izzy." He paused, staring into the space beside her. "May I use your telephone, please Izzy?"

"Yes, of course."

Nick rose, with an apologetic smile, and headed for the alcove where the telephone was located. Izzy watched him go, frowning. Something was going on – something that she was not privy to, and it irked her. Beau's reaction to Nick had been somewhat strained right from the time he arrived, and she had a niggling feeling that the two had some connection. From the part of the conversation she had heard at Jess's just recently, it was painfully obvious that Beau wanted nothing to do with Nick. She would have to sit Jess down at the earliest opportunity and drag the truth out of her. Izzy picked up her cloth, determined to find out what that truth could be.

"Izzy!" Jean's voice carried sharply into her consciousness. "I need you!"

"Coming, Jean!"

*

Nick stood waiting for the exchange to put through his call to Sydney. Eventually he heard a 'click' and then his mother's voice came over loud and clear.

"Beatrice Armitage speaking," he heard above the noise of a group of workmen walking past him into the passage.

"Mother, it's Nick," he replied.

"Oh, is it indeed?" she said sharply. "You've suddenly remembered that you have parents, Nick?"

"I'm sorry, mother, but I have been very busy."

"Found the young woman, did you?"

"Yes, she's been found, but that's not why I'm calling." Nick paused. "Is father there?"

"No, of course not. He's out with the dog." Nick now heard the resignation in her tone. "What do you want to speak to him about?"

Nick wasn't sure whether his mother would know about the DuBois case so many years ago, but there was only one way to find out.

"Mother, do you remember father defending a doctor by the name of DuBois, many years ago?" There was silence at the other end of the line. "Mother? Are you still there?"

"Yes, Nick, I'm here. Why do you want to know?"

"One of the many people I've met here, is a Doctor DuBois, and he is the son of the same Doctor DuBois whom father defended."

"Yes, I remember the case. Your father exonerated him, I believe." Nick heard his mother take a deep breath. "Where is this leading, Nick?"

"I'm not sure, but I need to speak with father about it." Beatrice was silent once more. "Mother?"

"Yes, Nick. I'll get your father to call you when he comes in. Where exactly are you?"

"I'm at the Grey Goose Hotel here in Bendigo. The number is…" Nick searched for the number on the wooden casing. "The number is Bendigo 187."

"Very well."

"Are you extending?" a bright female voice interrupted.

"No," said Nick hurriedly. "Good-bye, mother. I should be home within the next few days."

There was a click, followed by silence. Nick stood pondering the strange situation that was evolving around him. He could still see the look that had passed across Beau's face as he had stared at him before abruptly leaving the hotel. It was almost as though he had seen a ghost. Nick needed to understand, and maybe his father would be able to answer questions for him.

As he replaced the receiver, Nick turned to see Izzy standing in the passage beside the bar door.

"Is everything alright, Nick?" she asked hesitantly.

He smiled. "Yes, Izzy. Everything's fine."

*

Beau hurried home, his mind in a daze. His meeting with Nick had turned up something completely unexpected, and he wasn't sure what he should do about it. He had never believed in coincidence, and this was too blatant to be a coincidence. He had deliberately not shown Nick the photograph of his father, but now he wished he had, even if it was only to see Nick's reaction. His head was spinning as he opened the front gate and sprinted up the steps. The front door was unlocked, so he entered the house and hurried along the passage to the kitchen.

Jess was busy at the table, rolling out pastry. Grace was lying on the floor surrounded by paper and crayons, and he could see baby Lottie kicking her feet as she lay in her cot. Jess looked up as he entered, surprise etched on her face.

"Beau!" She brushed a stray golden hair from her flushed face. "Where have you been?"

Beau rested his hands on the table and looked searchingly at Jess. "I've been to talk to Nick, as you suggested."

"Oh? And what did you learn?"

Beau pulled a chair out and sat heavily. "I showed him the newspaper clipping."

"And the photograph?"

"No, not the photograph." He licked his dry mouth. "Nick knew nothing of the case against my father and has never heard our name mentioned in his household."

"I think you're looking for evidence where there is none, Beau."

"Not quite, Jess. There was something else – something that I've seen before, but not realised the significance of it until now."

"What was that, Beau?" Jess put down her rolling pin and rubbed her fingers together to remove the remains of the pastry.

"It was something Nick did." Jess waited silently. "He rubbed his finger across his chin."

"A lot of people do that, Beau. It seems to help the thinking process."

"I know, but this was different. I had a vision of my father doing the same thing." Beau pressed his hands on the table. "Jess, I believe that Nick has some connection to my father and therefore to me."

"Like a half-brother?" Jess said the words slowly.

"Yes, like a half-brother." Beau thumped the table. "Given my father's reputation, it is entirely possible, Jess."

"But Beau, Nick has parents."

"I know, and one of those parents is a very skilled lawyer."

"Beau, I think you need to leave this alone. It's only going to stir up things that maybe shouldn't be stirred up." Jess reached across the table and gripped his hands. "Please, Beau, tell me you'll forget about all this. Let Nick go home to Sydney. If something happened a long time ago, then let's leave it there."

"I don't think I can, Jess. I have to know."

Jess sighed. Deep inside she knew that Beau would not rest until he found answers. She squeezed his hands. "Does this mean that you're going to have another trip to Sydney?"

"Not yet, but it may be necessary." Beau released his hands and looked up at the clock above the mantel. "I must get back to the surgery. I have Raymond Simmons' car, and I promised I'd be back by lunchtime. It's now one o'clock."

"What's happening with Charlotte? Is she coming home today?"

Beau turned at the door. "No. I'll leave her there until tomorrow." He smiled sheepishly. "You might as well enjoy the rest."

Jess raised her eyebrows. "I know what I said about Charlotte being here, Beau, but I *do* miss her."

"Do you now? Well, she'll be home tomorrow, but I'm afraid she won't be much help for a while."

"She's very good at keeping Lottie entertained." Jess returned to her pastry.

"She should still be able to do that, Jess." Beau grinned. "Now I really must go."

Jess watched him go with a sinking heart. Beau would not rest until he had resolved the issue with Nick. It seemed that although his father had been dead many years, he was still haunting his son, and the injustices that had occurred were not easily erased. She knew he wouldn't listen to her pleas, and that it was simply a matter of time before he headed north to find answers.

Sighing, she reached for the pie dish in which to lay the pastry.

Hugh and Beatrice Armitage

Beatrice paced the length of the verandah, an unlit cigarette between her trembling fingers. The light was fading from the sky, and the cockatoos were causing mayhem in the eucalypts beyond the house. Where was Hugh? He should have been home by now. She opened the screen door and hurried inside. Beneath the telephone was a small wooden cabinet. Beatrice opened the drawer and rummaged amongst the contents until her hand found a box of matches. Opening it, she drew out a match and struck it on the side of the box. It flared instantly. Placing the cigarette in her mouth, she lit it with shaking fingers, before inhaling deeply. How long was it since she had lit up a cigarette? It was a long time ago. She shook the match and dropped it into a glass bowl on the table. Hugh would be angry with her, she was certain, but she needed it. Was it all happening again? It was so long ago that it all seemed like a bad dream.

Beatrice stepped back on to the verandah. If Hugh smelt the cigarette smoke in the house, he would be extremely angry. She began her pacing once more, as the shadows lengthened, and the daylight became a thing of the past. Then she heard a dog barking. A mixture of relief and anxiety filled her, and she dropped the half-smoked cigarette on to the verandah. Crushing it with her heel, she then pushed the remains over into the garden bed below.

Hugh was striding across the lawn towards the house. She could just make his tall figure with the Red Setter, Ralph, loping at his side. They climbed the steps, and Hugh was about to open the screen door when he saw Beatrice standing beside the verandah rail, her arms wrapped tightly around her slender body. He started.

"Beatrice! What the devil…?" he sniffed the air. "Have you been smoking?" he asked sharply.

Beatrice nodded. "I needed it, Hugh," she muttered.

"Needed it? Since when have you needed a cigarette?"

"Nick was on the telephone."

"Nick?" Hugh scowled. "Is something wrong? Is Nick alright?"

"Yes, Nick's alright." Beatrice took a deep breath. "He – he wants to talk to you."

"What about?"

"He wanted to know about the DuBois case."

Hugh turned from the door. "The DuBois case? My God, Beatrice! What's he been unearthing?"

"I don't know, Hugh, but he's met the son." She laughed shakily. "In all the corners of the country that he could have been, he has to meet a DuBois."

"That would be Beauregarde." Hugh slumped and a long sigh escaped his lips. "How many years has it been?"

"Twenty-five."

"What do I say to him, Beatrice?"

Suddenly Hugh looked old and care-worn, and Beatrice stepped closer to him. She touched his face gently.

"It's time we told him the truth, Hugh," she said slowly.

Hugh put his hand up to touch hers, and for a moment their eyes locked. "I had hoped that wouldn't be necessary," he said huskily.

"Well, talk to him first, and see what he wants to know." Beatrice withdrew her hand.

"Perhaps you'd better brief me on what he said exactly." Hugh opened the door and they stepped into the passage, the dog bounding ahead of them. Beatrice flicked a light switch. It sputtered for a moment before giving them enough light to show their way into the sitting room.

"He didn't say much, Hugh – just that he'd met a Doctor DuBois, and you had defended his father many years ago." Beatrice shrugged. "That was all he said."

Hugh scratched his head as he stood in the doorway. "Very well. I'd better get this over with."

"The number is on the table, Hugh."

Hugh groped in the pocket of his jacket for his spectacles before he put through a call to the Bendigo exchange. Finally, a voice answered.

"Harry Dalton! Grey Goose Hotel!"

Hugh cleared his throat. "Good evening," he muttered. "It's Hugh Armitage here. May I speak with my son, Nick, please?"

"Certainly, Mr. Armitage." Harry's voice carried through the line as he called out to Nick. Hugh winced as he held the receiver away from his ear.

"Father? Is that you?" he heard eventually.

"Yes, Nick. It's me. You wanted to speak with me?"

"I did, yes."

"What's this all about, Nick? Your mother tells me that you've met a certain Doctor DuBois?"

"Yes, I have. His name's Beau." Nick stopped.

"And what do you want to ask me exactly?"

"You defended his father many years ago and got him off. Beau showed me a cutting from the newspaper at the time. I was under the impression that he believed his father to be guilty. He was 'not a good man', he told me."

"Nick, that was twenty-five years ago! The man's been dead for over ten years, at least. Why bring it all up now?"

"*Was* he guilty, father?"

"Look, Nick, this is not something I want to discuss over the telephone."

"Did you make a deal with the prosecution?"

"No!" Hugh sucked in his breath. "I did not! Now, I am not going to say anything more, Nick. Please respect my wishes, and I will try to explain when you get home."

"Very well, father. I'll say no more, and I'll see you in a few days' time."

"Yes."

Hugh returned the receiver to its cradle and turned to look at Beatrice. He shrugged resignedly.

"Well Beatrice, it looks as though the past has finally caught up with us." He ran his fingers through his greying hair. "It was only a matter of time, I suppose."

Beatrice nodded bleakly. "It's actually a relief, Hugh, knowing that we've been forced into telling Nick the truth."

"He won't like it, I know he won't."

"We'll cross that bridge when we come to it." Beatrice smiled thinly. "I know he's only been gone a few days, but I miss him, and I'll be glad when he's home again."

Izzy and Jess

Izzy banged on the front door of Jess's house and waited. Freya stood meekly beside her; a rag doll clutched in her arms. It was just after nine and Izzy had made the excuse that the two little girls wanted to play together at Grace's house. She had bundled Freya into her play clothes and whisked her out the door before Jean or Harry could find a job for her. It was important that she speak to Jess, in an attempt to establish what was going on with Beau. She stamped her feet as she waited.

The door opened and Jess stood there in her dressing gown.

"Izzy! You're early. Grace is still having her breakfast." Jess pushed her hair away from her face.

"I thought the girls could play here today, if that's alright with you, Jess."

Jess nodded, opening the door to her sister and niece. "I think I can cope with that, Izzy. Go into the kitchen, where you'll find Grace. I need to get dressed."

Izzy smiled and ushered Freya ahead of her and into the kitchen. "Take your time, Jess. I'm not required at the hotel. Besides, it will give me a chance to see baby Lottie. I don't see her very often."

Izzy marched Freya into the kitchen where Grace was seated at the table, a bowl of porridge in front of her. As Freya entered the kitchen, Grace put her spoon down and made to scramble off the chair, but Izzy was too quick for her.

"Oh no you don't, Gracie!" Grabbing Grace's arm, Izzy hoisted her back on to the chair. "Finish your breakfast first. Freya can wait." Turning to her daughter she added: "Sit quietly, Freya, and let Grace finish her breakfast, and then you can go out and play."

Freya dutifully complied and sat beside Grace. She knew, at her young age, that it was no use arguing with her mother. Izzy smiled at the two sullen faces before turning her attention to Lottie, who was rattling a small toy in the confines of her cot.

"Well, look at you, little miss!" she cooed. "Aren't you growing?"

Izzy scooped up the child and her blanket and hugged her to her breast. Grey eyes stared seriously at her, and Izzy laughed. "You are so like your father," she sighed, before kissing the rosy cheek. "Come on, we'll go outside and leave these two here while Gracie finishes her breakfast."

Izzy pushed open the wire door with her shoulder and stepped out on to the back verandah. The sun was warm, and she hummed softly as she moved away from the verandah, and into the garden. Beau was doing a good job with the vegetable patch, and she picked her way between the rows of beans, peas, lettuces and carrots. Along the perimeter there was a good patch of parsley, and Izzy bent awkwardly to pick some. She didn't have any growing at the hotel, and this would go very nicely with the stew she was planning for tea. Nick had decided that he would return to Sydney the following day, as he felt that his job was finished.

"Raiding my garden?" Jess's voice broke through her thoughts.

"Just a little parsley," said Izzy, smiling at her sister.

"Hm."

Izzy stepped back to the path and placed a quick kiss on Jess's cheek. "I'm making Irish stew for tea, and this will be perfect with it."

"Hm," said Jess again. "Why are you here so early, Izzy?"

Izzy grinned mischievously, as she shifted Lottie on to her other hip. "You know me, sister dear – always curious."

"Yes." Jess sighed. She knew what was coming.

Grace and Freya appeared on the verandah, and Jess faced them, her hands on her hips.

"No playing in the chook pen, girls," she warned, "and no treading on Beau's garden. Are you clear on that?"

"Yes, ma," said Grace meekly.

"Freya?" added Izzy.

"Yes, mummy."

"Good." Jess stepped past them to the back door. "We'll be just inside."

The two girls nodded

Izzy moved into the kitchen and placed Lottie back in her cot, where she immediately began to cry.

"There, there!" chided Izzy. "Be a good girl."

"I'll get her some breakfast," said Jess, placing the kettle over on the stove to boil. "Now, curious sister, what is it you want to know?" Jess opened the firebox and threw in more wood.

"Everything!" replied Izzy, seating herself at the table.

"Everything?" Jess frowned.

"I'm not leaving here until I'm satisfied, Jess."

Jess was silent as she poured Lottie's baby cereal into a bowl. "I don't know that I'm at liberty to tell you everything, Izzy," she said as she poured a little hot water over the mixture and stirred it slowly.

"Then tell me what you can, please Jess! I know there's something going on. I saw Beau and Nick at the hotel, and it looked to me as though Beau was showing him something that affected both of them. What was it, Jess?"

Jess lifted Lottie from the cot, sat down with her, and after blowing on the warm cereal, spooned a little into the baby's open mouth. After Lottie had taken several spoonfuls, Jess looked up at her sister.

"I don't want Beau to know that I've been speaking with you about this, Izzy."

"Very well. I can be silent if I have to be."

"I'm serious, Izzy. This is not something to be thrown around as gossip."

Izzy blinked. "I get your meaning, Jess."

Jess fed Lottie a few more teaspoons of the warm cereal, while Izzy waited.

"Beau was showing Nick a newspaper cutting from many years ago. It was about his father."

"Beau's father?"

"Yes. He was up on a charge of misconduct." Jess paused, her throat working. "He – he was accused of betraying the trust of a female patient."

"You mean he was accused of doing something to her that he shouldn't have?"

Jess nodded. "His defence lawyer was a Hugh Armitage."

Izzy let this sink in. "Any relation to Nick?"

"His father."

"Oh!" Izzy sat back on the chair. "What was the outcome?"

"He was acquitted."

"It still doesn't explain Beau's hostility to Nick, unless…" Izzy stared at Jess. "Unless he *was* guilty."

The two sisters stared at each other.

"That's what Beau believes," whispered Jess.

Izzy expelled a long breath. "Surely it doesn't matter now," she said slowly. "Beau's father is long gone, isn't he?"

"Yes."

"So why has Beau kept such damning information?"

"I think it's to remind himself that he is not his father, and he would never behave the way his father did."

"Fancy Nick coming here, of all places. It's a small world, isn't it?" Izzy pushed back her chair. "I need a cup of tea."

"There's a lot more that I can't tell you, Izzy." Jess looked meaningfully at her sister. "Beau needs time to sort through the mess."

"I see." Izzy emptied the kettle into the teapot and placed the lid on it. "So there's more to the story, eh?" She sighed. "I'll have to be patient, won't I?"

"Yes, you will."

"I'm not good at that, Jessie, as you very well know."

"I know, but this time it is extremely important that you say nothing, not even to Harry."

"Not even to Harry," Izzy repeated solemnly.

Nick Returns To Sydney

Nick came down for breakfast the following morning, his suitcase packed ready for his return trip to Sydney. Izzy greeted him in the Ladies Lounge, as she placed the porridge pot on the table.

"So this is it, Nick?" She smiled brightly. "You're leaving us?"

Nick placed his suitcase beside the door. "I'm afraid so, Izzy. I need to get home." He shrugged. "There's nothing more I can do here, as far as Phyllis is concerned. I think Billy is quite capable now of dealing with Mr. O'Connor." His brow puckered. "It's funny that I didn't actually get to meet the man at the centre of all of this."

"That's just as well, Nick." Izzy shook her head. "He has caused quite a deal of trouble over the years, apparently. It will be interesting to see how Billy deals with him." She gave a little chuckle. "With his fists, I have no doubt. Now come and get some porridge while it's still hot."

Nick sat at the table, and scooped porridge into a bowl. As he poured milk on the top, Harry appeared at the door, with Jean and Freya not far behind.

"Nick!" Harry thumped him on the back. "Going back to the big smoke, eh?"

"Er- yes, Harry." Nick coughed as he was forced to swallow quickly. "I'm afraid so."

"We'll miss you, lad, won't we, family?"

Izzy and Jean nodded as they sat at the table.

"We certainly will," said Jean, as she served a bowl of porridge for Freya. "So your work here is done, Nick?"

"Yes, Jean." He smiled. "Besides, I am looking forward to seeing Amelia again."

Izzy hid her own smile. "Of course you are. Say 'hello' to her for us, Nick?"

"I'll do that."

"What time's your train?" Jean looked up at the wall clock. It was half past eight.

"Ten o'clock."

"Yes, of course," muttered Jean. "I should have known that." She smiled at Nick. "Well, take care of yourself, lad. Maybe we'll see you down here again some time?"

"You never know, Jean. I rather like this town, and its residents, of course." Nick pushed away his bowl. "You take care too, Jean. I hope you can resolve the issues with your son."

Jean snorted. "Yes. It appears he's got himself into very hot water this time, and I don't think any of them will come off lightly. I hope the Magistrate throws the book at the lot of them! The sooner Rodney leaves this town, the better." Jean pushed back her chair. "Cup of tea, Nick?" The subject was closed.

"Yes, thank-you, Jean." Nick turned to Harry. "When I've had my tea, I'll settle my account, Harry. Then I'll pop in on Billy and Audrey on my way to the station."

"Certainly." Harry held out a hand, which was grasped firmly. "You certainly livened the place up, Nick." He laughed loudly. "Never a dull moment, eh?"

"Yes." Nick grimaced as he released his hand. "I hope I haven't caused too much stress along the way." He turned to Izzy. "Say goodbye to Jess and Beau for me, please Izzy?"

"I'll do that, Nick." Izzy's eyes were glistening with unshed tears. "Please come and see us again."

*

Half an hour later, Nick had settled his hotel account and was ready to leave. He picked up his suitcase from just inside the Ladies' Lounge, pushed his hat on his head and headed for the side door of the hotel. Izzy was standing at the door of the bar, a towel in her hands.

"Goodbye, Nick," she said quietly. "Take care of yourself."

Nick raised his hat. "I will, Izzy. I won't forget this place in a hurry."

"You'd better not."

Nick saw that her eyes were swimming, so he quickly made his exit.

Once out on the street, Nick took a deep breath and headed in the direction of Billy's house. It was only a short walk, and in five minutes he was knocking at the door. Audrey appeared and smiled broadly at him. Nick removed his hat.

"Come in, Nick!" She ushered him along the narrow passageway to the kitchen, where she pulled out a chair for him. "Tea?"

"No thanks, Audrey." Nick waved the offer aside. "I've just got up from the breakfast table."

"Oh! Alright." Audrey sat opposite him and smoothed the check tablecloth with nervous fingers. "Billy isn't here," she said finally. "He's on day shift this week."

"That's alright, Audrey. I just popped in to say goodbye and wish you both all the best."

"So you're going home to Sydney?"

"I am." Nick smiled at her crestfallen expression. "I'm sure everything will turn out, Audrey. Billy has you on his side, and now the Reverend Mother, which I must say, surprised me completely."

"That little girl is special, Nick, and she has to be protected." Audrey sat back on her chair. "I don't care whose child she is; I will fight for her welfare." She hesitated. "That Sid O'Connor isn't going to want her anyway."

She looked up at Nick, her eyes welling. "You know what they do with children like her, don't you, Nick?"

Nick shook his head. "No, I don't, but I can guess." He reached across the table and took Audrey's hands. "Hope is very lucky to have you and Phyllis. We can't possibly know what her future will be, but one thing is for sure, she will have plenty of love." Audrey nodded silently. "If you ever need my help, Audrey, I'll leave you a telephone number where you can contact me."

Nick scribbled his home number on a scrap of paper and handed it to Audrey. "This will get me, and even if it's only to talk, I'll be listening." He smiled.

"You're a good man, Nick. I'll tell Billy what you said." Audrey sighed. "I had two sons, Nick. My older son, Frank, was killed in France."

"Billy told me," said Nick, with a twinge of guilt.

"He was always trying to keep Billy out of trouble." Audrey dabbed at her eyes. "He wasn't a hothead like young Billy, but I must say, since he's been back from the war, Billy has more sense."

"Take care of each other, Audrey, and if you ever need me, please don't hesitate to contact me."

"I will, Nick. You take care, too."

Nick pushed back the chair and stood up. "I must go. I don't want to miss my train. Goodbye, Audrey."

Audrey stood slowly and watched as Nick placed his hat on his head and after a quick look in her direction, walked out the door. She sighed heavily.

Nick picked up his suitcase, which he had left just inside the front door, and stepped out into the sunshine. A big part of him was sorry to leave this town, but he had a mystery of his own to solve, and the sooner he got home, the sooner he would find answers. He stepped it out and was soon clattering down the concrete steps to the platform.

*

Nick had a compartment to himself, and after hoisting his case up on to the parcels rack he removed his jacket, closed his eyes and was soon in a deep sleep. Silent figures invaded his dreams and the most prominent vision he had was of Beau's scarred face and his eyes staring at him as though he had seen a ghost. He heard Izzy's voice rising to a crescendo, saying, *don't go, Nick. Stay here and resolve all these awful things that are happening to our family. Please, Nick!*

Nick woke with a start, beads of perspiration on his brow. He looked around, expecting to see Izzy sitting beside him, but of course she wasn't there. Wiping his brow, he sat up straight and tried to concentrate on the landscape rushing by the window. Nothing out there seemed out of place, yet as he thought about the people he had met, and the situations that surrounded that tiny part of the universe, he realised that, without exception, everyone had a story that needed unravelling.

As he sat there, listening to the rattle of the wheels beneath him, he questioned his own ability to begin unravelling what had obviously gone on within his own family, without his knowledge. If what Beau had indicated about his father was true, then where did his own father fit into all of this? Hugh had always assumed an air of nonchalance when it came to the cases he had won, and Nick held him high on a pedestal. Honesty and truth had been drilled into Nick from a young age, but there was a niggling doubt he was experiencing now, and it needed to be addressed. There had to be a logical explanation for what had happened, and the sooner he heard it from his father, the more comfortable he would feel.

Beau had been uneasy in his presence right from the moment they met, and seemed determined not to like him, which Nick thought was strange. He had always had an easy-going nature and responded well to most people. Jess had also put up an invisible barrier, but Nick could see through it now, and felt that it was due to her husband's attitude and not her own feelings. She had a compassionate nature, and after listening to Izzy explain her sister's life, Nick felt the utmost respect for her. It could not have been easy for her.

Then there was Beau's enigmatic sister, Charlotte. Jess had not been very forthcoming about her, except to say that Beau had recently contacted her after some thirty years. She had fled the family home at age eighteen, to escape a dominating father, and had sought refuge in a convent, where she had remained for all those years. Having been reunited with her long-lost brother, she had recently decided to become a part of his family.

Nick thought about this and realised that their father must have been a man to be feared. Maybe Joe could throw some light on this when they eventually had a chance to catch up. The first thing Nick knew he had to do was face his father and see what he had to say for himself. He would telephone his mother when he arrived at Melbourne's Spencer Street station, and make sure she was there at Sydney's Central station to meet him the following afternoon.

He closed his eyes once more and drifted back into a restless sleep. This time it was Amelia who was laughing up at him, setting his pulse racing, before turning away and waving him goodbye.

Nick Faces His Father

Beatrice was at Sydney's Central station the following afternoon, and Nick spotted her tall figure the minute he stepped off the train. She smiled as he planted a kiss on her cheek, but there was strain in her returned smile.

"Hello, mother," said Nick as he took her arm. "It's good to be back home. It seems like much longer than ten days since I left here."

"Yes, it does. I trust you had a successful venture to the south?"

"I did. Most of the loose ends tied up. Now, where is the car parked?"

"On George Street." Beatrice hurried to keep pace with Nick as he steered her through the crowd milling on the platform.

Once down the steps and on to the street, Beatrice pointed to her left.

"The car's just along there, Nick. You can drive."

Nick smiled. His mother was not keen on driving the modern contraption they called a car. Horse riding had always been her passion, but the streets were dangerous these days and competition was fierce between rider and driver.

Nick opened the passenger door of Hugh's dark green Ford sedan, and Beatrice stepped on to the running board. After removing his jacket and then throwing his suitcase on to the rear seat, Nick cranked the engine to life. He jumped into the driver's seat, and after wrestling with the gearstick, pulled out into the traffic. Beatrice shuddered as he swerved to miss a horse and cart, and Nick grinned at her.

"Don't worry, mother, I won't hit the horses."

"I hope not," Beatrice replied stiffly.

They were silent as Nick negotiated his way out of the centre of the city and headed west into the suburbs. Once the roads were clear of traffic, Nick turned to his mother.

"Is father at home?"

"No, but he shouldn't be long. He took the tram in to the city this morning, so that I could collect you." Nick noticed how her hands clasped and unclasped on her lap.

He reached across and patted her hands. "Don't worry, mother," he said softly. "I'm sure whatever father has to tell me isn't all that bad."

Beatrice stared at him for a long moment before turning away. Her voice trembled as she spoke.

"Whatever your father and I have done in the past, Nick, was always for your welfare."

"My welfare?" Nick frowned. "What did it have to do with me?" Beatrice was silent. "Mother?"

"I'll leave your father to explain."

Nick was now completely mystified. His mother wasn't making any sense. He wrestled with the gearstick to change down a gear, as they headed up the last gravel slope towards their house. At the top of the hill he swung around the curved driveway that led to the front door. As he pulled up, Beatrice opened the door and quickly stepped down to the ground. Nick watched as she hurried towards the house. The Red Setter bounded off the wide verandah to greet her. Beatrice gave him a quick pat before disappearing into the house. Nick shook his head as he sat in the car. What was going on that had his cool, calm and collected mother so agitated?

The Red Setter had his front paws on the top of the driver's door and was trying to catch Nick's attention.

"I'm glad to see you too, Ralph," said Nick, stroking the rough head. "It's a pity you can't tell me what's wrong with my mother."

He clambered out of the car, retrieved his suitcase and jacket from the rear seat, and strolled towards the house, the dog leaping excitedly at his side. Together they entered the front door, and Nick headed towards his own room. It was just as he had left it, with clothes scattered on the large bed. Nick threw his case on top of the pile, and stood for a moment, while the dog waited expectantly at his side. He looked at his watch. It was five o'clock. His father would probably walk through the door at ten minutes to six. That was his custom on the days that he went into the city office. Nick would have to endure his mother's silence until then.

He looked down at the dog. "Let's go for a walk, Ralph." The dog wagged his heavy tail in response. "I've had two days sitting on a train, and I need some fresh air. Come on!"

The dog took no second bidding and barked as he bounded for the door. As he opened the front wire door, Nick heard his mother's voice.

"Where are you going, Nick?"

"I'm taking Ralph down to the dam!" he called. "I won't be long."

"Your father will be here at six, you know?"

"Yes, I know."

Nick stepped on to the front verandah and hurried down the steps to the gravel driveway. He would have to put the car away, but that could wait until he got back. The dam was half a mile away from the house, and was reached by a steep bridle path, which Ralph took at great speed. Nick followed, a little more carefully, and when he reached the dam, Ralph was already swimming across its width. Nick stood beside the water and watched as Ralph reached the other side, bounded up on to rocks that prevented seepage from the dam, and there he shook himself vigorously. Nick whistled sharply. Ralph leapt back into the water and swam back towards Nick. The dam was perhaps fifty yards wide, and at this time of the year was almost full. It was used primarily to water the few sheep that Hugh had grazing in the paddocks around it, and Beatrice's two horses.

Nick gazed around him as he waited for the dog. To his right he looked across the hills to where the sprawl of houses was beginning to encroach on the landscape. To his left he looked up and across the paddocks where the sheep and horses grazed, and if he turned a little more, he could just make out the chimneys of their house on the top of the hill. Smoke was curling lazily from one of the smokestacks. It was a peaceful scene, and Nick recalled the summer days of his youth, when he would swim in the dam with his school pals. He tried to think back to when he was seven years old. Was there anything different about his family life then? There was nothing that stood out as being 'out of the ordinary'. In fact, his life had always been very ordinary, to the point of being dull. Routine had never changed within the household. Nick wondered what explanation his father would give him about the DuBois case, now that he was an adult. He whistled the dog.

Ralph leapt out of the water and shook himself all over Nick, who stepped back to lessen the impact. Nonetheless he was drenched and knew that his mother would be less than impressed. He looked up towards the house.

"Come on, boy," he said to the dog. "let's go! We're both going to be in trouble, you know?"

As they made it to the top of the hill, Nick saw his father walking slowly across the gravel drive. He had his jacket slung across his shoulder, and he carried a briefcase. Ralph barked, drawing his attention, and he looked down the hill to where his son was approaching. The dog reached him first, and Hugh managed to stave off his attempts to jump up on him.

"Down, Ralph!" he growled.

Nick stopped as he drew nearer, and the two men stared at each other.

"Hello, father," said Nick finally.

Hugh nodded his head. "Successful trip?" was all he said.

"Yes. I wouldn't say the situation is completely resolved yet, but I did what I had to do, with some help, I might add." Amelia's face swam before him.

"Good." Hugh made a gesture towards his car sitting on the gravel driveway. "You'd better put the car away before you come in."

"I had intended to." He paused. "Father, what went on all those years ago?"

Hugh stopped on his way up the front steps and turned to look at Nick. "We'll talk about it after tea." He stepped up on to the verandah. "Good to have you home, son," he added gruffly.

Nick knew that it was no use pressing his father further, so he headed for the car. Ralph made a rush in the same direction, but Nick stopped him.

"No, Ralph! You cannot get in the car." He lifted his arm in the direction of the verandah. "Bed!"

The dog paused for a moment, before receiving the same command. "Bed!" Then thinking better of it, he slunk up the front steps and along the verandah to his kennel.

*

Tea was eaten in an uncomfortable silence, and it wasn't until Hugh had placed his spoon in his dessert bowl and wiped a white linen napkin across his mouth, that he spoke.

"So you want to know the story, Nick?"

"Yes, father, I do."

Beatrice got up quickly and began stacking the dirty bowls and cutlery.

"Sit down, Beatrice," said Hugh stiffly. "That can wait." Beatrice sat, staring at Nick as she did so. Hugh continued. "First of all, tell me what you know of Beauregarde DuBois."

Nick thought for a moment. What did he know about Beau? "I know he took an instant dislike to me," he said. "I didn't know why, and I still don't know why."

"What did he have to do with your case of the missing young woman?" Nick sensed the lawyer talking as his father spoke.

He shrugged. "Nothing, except that he and his wife had had dealings with our person of interest."

"Would you say he was a man of good character?"

Nick saw his mother watching him intently. "Yes, I would say he was very-well liked. He is a local doctor, after all."

Beatrice sucked in her breath, and Hugh frowned at her.

"What was the newspaper clipping he showed you?" Hugh continued.

"It was from a Sydney paper, I presume. I didn't see all of it - only the bit stating that you were the defending lawyer in a case against his father. The impression I got from Beau was that he believed his father may have been guilty."

"Are those the words he used?"

"No, not exactly. He implied that his father was guilty of many things, as he was not a good man, and that this could have been one of those times."

"So he didn't say categorically that he knew his father was guilty?"

Nick was beginning to feel edgy. "This is not a courtroom, father; I am not under oath here!"

Hugh sat back. "I know, Nick, but I need to know the details from Beauregarde's point of view."

"I can't tell you anymore, father. He left me in rather a hurry after that, and I didn't see him again."

There was a time of silence before Hugh spoke again. "Nick, the case against Doctor DuBois was twenty-five years ago, and the evidence against him was flimsy, to say the least." Nick nodded slowly. "You asked me if I had made a deal with the prosecution?" His eyes met Nick's. "I can tell you honestly that I didn't, although I knew what the man was capable of. He…"

"He was evil, Hugh!" Beatrice had risen quickly to her feet. "We cannot gild the lily here. Samuel DuBois was an evil man!" Nick and Hugh stared at her in stunned silence. "Of course he was guilty! Everyone knew that except you, Hugh! A leopard doesn't change its spots, no matter how hard you scrub at them."

"Have you quite finished, Beatrice?" Hugh finally managed to say.

"Yes." Beatrice resumed her seat. "Now can we please talk about the real issue, Hugh?"

Nick scowled at them. "Does that issue concern me?" he asked.

"Yes, it does." Hugh suddenly looked old and forlorn.

"Well, I would appreciate it if you would stop beating around the bush, and just tell me whatever it is that's eating at both of you." There was silence. "I am a grown man, and I think I can handle most things – some more effectively than others – so I'm not moving from here until you tell me what's on your minds." Nick sat back and folded his arms.

"It's time for the truth, Hugh. It's no good hiding it any longer."

"What truth?" Nick was becoming exasperated.

"The truth about something else that happened a long time ago."

The Altercation

Izzy was behind the bar, drying the last of the previous day's glasses. The hotel was quiet, as the lunchtime crowd had not yet arrived. Izzy sighed. Nick had only been gone one day, and already she missed his presence. He had kept them all on their toes, and that suited Izzy. Harry, she knew, had breathed a sigh of relief to see him gone, but then Harry, for all his loud talk, enjoyed regularity not spontaneity. Izzy smiled to herself.

"What are you smiling at?" She heard Harry come up beside her.

"Oh, nothing," said Izzy, shrugging lazily.

"It didn't look like nothing," persisted Harry.

"Well, if you must know, I was thinking about Nick." Izzy challenged him with her eyes.

"Were you indeed?" Harry glared at her. "The man's only been gone twenty-four hours."

"I know, but you must admit he kept the place alive, Harry."

"Hm. He's too young for you, Isobel."

"Harry! That's absurd! Why did you say that?"

"I did notice how you held on to his every word," muttered Harry.

Izzy laughed suddenly. "Why, Harry Dalton, I do believe you are jealous!"

"Jealous? No, I'm not!" said Harry indignantly. "But I did wonder how long it would be before you made a complete and utter fool of yourself."

Izzy's eyes opened wide, and she was about to speak when the bar door opened, and a familiar figure appeared. They both turned to see Sid O'Connor walking unsteadily towards the bar.

"Good mornin'!" he shouted. "I'm the first, am I?"

"Good morning, Sid," said Harry tersely. "You are the first, but it appears to me that you've already been somewhere else. Who threw you out this time?"

Sid ignored the dig from Harry. Instead, he perched on a stool, and leaning over the bar, breathed his foul breath on Izzy.

"I'm lookin' f'me mate, Billy. 'Aven't seen 'im in a while, 'cos ya know what? I've been in gaol."

"We did hear something about that, Sid," said Harry scathingly. "So they've let you out, have they?"

"Yep. Me mates weren't so lucky. They gotta do time."

"For what?" asked Izzy.

"F'doin' over a toff's place."

"What toff?" Izzy's eyes widened as she looked at Harry.

"'Im what lives in the big 'ouse, up on the 'ill, other side o' the creek." Sid grinned, showing tobacco-stained teeth. "Made a right proper job of it, they did. Only trouble is they got caught."

"Sid O'Connor!" Jean had appeared in the doorway. "You've got a cheek coming in here!"

Sid grinned at Jean. "Sorry about Rodney. 'E got caught in the crossfire, if ya know what I mean."

"No, I don't know what you mean, Sid." Jean stood alongside him, her hands on her ample hips.

"Well, you - you know," stammered Sid, "bein' mates with Seamus an' Al, 'e was bound t'get caught up in shady deals 'n'things."

"Thanks to you, Sid, I don't wonder!"

"I didn't do nothin'," muttered Sid, shrugging his lean shoulders.

"You dobbed them in, that's what you did!" Jean was glaring at him.

"Anyway, I 'eard ya didn't want nothin' more t'do with ya son, Mrs O'Malley," Sid flung back at Jean, his expression smug.

"That's not the point, Sid, and you know it! Rodney wouldn't be in this trouble if it wasn't for you."

"Nah, that's where y'wrong. Gettin' mixed up with Seamus was Rodney's first mistake."

"Be that as it may," sniffed Jean. "I want you to get your sorry self out of my hotel."

"I wanna catch me ole mate, Billy, first. Then I'll be off, an' not before." Sid stood his ground as Jean stepped towards him.

Harry, who could see things getting out of hand, moved around from behind the bar, and stood behind Sid.

"Billy's not here, Sid, as you can see, and we don't know whether he'll be in today. So, if you've got any sense, you'll push off, and wait for him somewhere else."

At that moment a whistle sounded, marking the commencement of the lunch hour for the railway employees. Sid heard it and seated himself resolutely on the nearest barstool.

"I'm not movin' 'til Billy gets 'ere," he said stubbornly. "An' I'll 'ave a beer, *please*, Mrs. Dalton."

Izzy looked at Harry who nodded resignedly.

"I want no trouble, Sid," warned Harry. "The first sign of trouble and you are out of here, preferably on your backside. Is that understood?"

Sid shrugged as Izzy pushed his beer across the bar. "Sure, Harry."

Jean made a noise like a wounded bull and stormed out towards the kitchen. There were sandwiches to make, and men would be streaming through the door within the next few minutes. She didn't want to have to deal with Sid O'Connor, or she might be tempted to swing a punch at him herself. How did he always manage to wriggle out of trouble? *Because he's a snake, that's why!* Jean muttered to herself as she made her way to the kitchen.

Behind the bar, Izzy caught Harry by the arm and steered him out of Sid's earshot.

"Harry," she whispered. "You know why Sid is looking for Billy?"

"No, why?"

"Because he wants to find out about Phyllis, obviously."

"Ah." Harry looked in Sid's direction. "Then if Billy comes in, we'd better keep a close watch on them both."

"Precisely. There could be trouble if Sid's found out that Billy knows where she is."

"How would he have found out? He's been in gaol."

"It's not the most secure place, Harry, and Nick was there to report that she'd been found."

"Of course."

The sound of men's voices broke their conversation, and the lunchtime crowd filtered in. Harry and Izzy scanned the faces for Billy. There he was, laughing and joking with one of his cobbers. Sid spied him too and yelled across the barroom.

"Hey, Billy! 'Ere, mate!"

Harry leaned across the bar. "The warning still stands, Sid," he hissed. "Any nonsense and you're both out of here!"

Sid merely grinned as he made way for Billy to sit beside him.

Soon the bar was crowded with men wanting to quench their thirst. Harry and Izzy found themselves fully occupied, and unable to pay full attention to the two sitting at the centre of the bar. The beer flowed in a constant stream, as did the chatter and laughter. Before too long Jean appeared with the sandwiches, and the tray was lifted over the heads of all those gathered around the bar. Within minutes it was emptied and returned to Jean, who then headed back towards the kitchen.

"Keep an eye on those two," she muttered to Harry, jerking her head in the direction of Billy and Sid.

The two in question were deep in conversation, and they kept their voices low, making it difficult for Izzy to hear what they were saying as she hovered close by.

"Well, Billy, old son, I heard the precious Miss Powell 'as been found. What do ya know about it?" Sid eyed his friend over the top of his beer glass.

Billy shrugged nonchalantly. "Not much, Sid," he rasped.

"You know where she is though, don't ya?" Sid leaned forward.

"Why would I know where she is, Sid?" Billy frowned, before draining his glass.

"She always 'ad a soft spot f' you, Billy," snarled Sid. "Ya shouldn'a gone off t' war an' left 'er."

"I went t' fight for me country, Sid, which is more 'an you did." Billy was becoming angry. "I don't know where she is, an' what's more, I don't care. Now push off an' let me drink in peace."

"Fightin' overseas changed ya, Billy."

"Did it?" Billy placed his glass on the bar and stood up. "I gotta get back t' work, Sid." He looked up at Izzy who was eying them intently. "See ya, Mrs. Dalton."

"'Bye, Billy."

"'Ere! I 'aven't finished yet!" Sid lurched after Billy, but Harry, who had also been observing the two, made a dash for him and grabbed him by the collar. "Someone'll spill the beans, Billy, an' when I find 'er, I might just kill the bitch!"

Harry shook him violently. "That's no way to talk, Sid! Go home and sober up!"

"Do you know where Phyllis is, Mr. Dalton?" slurred Sid, squirming under Harry's firm grip.

"No, and if I did, I wouldn't be telling you, Sid O'Connor. Now get out of here before you make a complete fool of yourself."

"I'll find 'er," muttered Sid belligerently. "Someone'll know where she is." He swivelled towards the bar crowd. "Anyone 'ere know where Phyllis is?" he shouted.

Amid the murmurs and shaking of heads he was marched unceremoniously out the door. All eyes followed his exit.

"He's trouble, that one!" muttered a grey-haired worker.

"Yes, he is," responded Harry, returning to the bar, "and if anyone gets wind of where Phyllis Powell might be, they'd better keep it to themselves. You all heard what he said." A murmur went around the crowd. "Now, I reckon lunch break is nearly over, fellas."

Slowly the crowd dispersed, and within minutes the bar was empty.

"He's bound to find out," said Izzy to Harry, as she collected dirty glasses.

"Yes, I'm sure he will, but we can't worry about that, Isobel. Billy will have to sort that out himself."

Billy and Audrey

Billy thundered through the door of his mother's cottage, pulling his boiler suit off as he went. Sid's drunken words had sent a wave of fear through him, and all afternoon he had agonised over leaving the workshops and heading up to the orphanage to speak once more with the Reverend Mother. Sid had always been one to make threats, and usually he carried them out. This time, Billy had to make sure that his threats could not be carried out.

"Mum!" he called out, as he threw his greasy clothes in the large cane basket that stood in the passage. "Where are ya, mum?"

Audrey appeared at the kitchen door, her face flushed, and her hands covered in flour.

"What is it, Billy?" Her tone showed her annoyance. "You don't have to shout the place down. I wasn't far away."

"Mum, Sid's on the rampage, an' I reckon he's gonna go searchin' f' Phyllis." Billy tugged at his mother's arm. "I have t' get back t'the orphanage an' speak with the Reverend Mother. Phyllis could be in mortal danger."

Audrey's eyes opened wide. "Mortal danger? Why? What's he said?"

"He's threatenin' t' kill 'er!"

Audrey wiped flour-covered hands on her floral apron. "Then we'd both better get up there." She pulled off her apron and hung it across the back of a chair. "The pie'll have to wait. Give me a minute, Billy, to get my hat and jacket, and we'll go together."

With that she bustled out of the kitchen. Billy ran grease-stained hands through his fair hair and groaned loudly. Sid O'Connor was a menace to society and needed to be locked up. Sure, he was drunk when he had thrown that threat at Billy, but serious or not, it was still a threat.

Billy headed for his room, where he pulled off the rest of his clothes and searched in the old wardrobe for clean shirt and trousers. When he was dressed, he dragged a comb through his tousled hair, and dabbed a little cologne on his neck. The mirror on the dressing table revealed that he needed a shave, but there was no time for that.

In the passage he met his mother, dressed in a neat blue jacket over her grey housedress. A straw hat quivered precariously on her silvery hair.

"Come on, son," she said quickly, as she produced a large key from her black handbag. "Let's go!"

*

Forty-five minutes later, Billy was knocking loudly on the solid wooden door of the orphanage. They waited for several minutes before a face appeared. It was a young girl, in the now familiar grey cotton dress, a white scarf tied around her hair. She stared at them with large brown eyes. Audrey was the first to speak.

"Can we see the Reverend Mother, please?" she asked gently.

"Who are you?" the girl said tentatively.

Billy stepped forward. "Tell the Reverend Mother that it's Billy Maitland and his mother…" he began but got no further.

The door swung open, and the Reverend Mother stood before them, a frown etched on her thin face and her mouth pulled tight. When she saw who was at the door, her expression relaxed somewhat.

"Thank-you, Agatha," she said, addressing the young girl, "I'll take it from here." Agatha disappeared from their view. "What brings you here? Not trouble, I hope."

Audrey and Billy stepped into the wide corridor, still reeking of phenyl, and hurried after the swiftly moving nun to her office. She had not waited for an answer. Once inside the cluttered space referred to as an office, she shut the door and turned to them.

"Well?" she said stiffly.

"There could be trouble, Reverend Mother," said Billy, as he ushered his mother on to the only vacant seat in the room. "Sid O'Connor is out of gaol and threatenin' t' kill Phyllis if 'e finds 'er."

"Is he indeed?" The reverend Mother pursed her lips as she gazed at the two before her. "Well, we can't have that, can we?"

"'E was drunk when 'e said it," stuttered Billy, "but Sid's well known f' carryin' out threats."

"Can you guarantee Phyllis's safety?" asked Audrey, blinking away tears that threatened to spill.

"Unfortunately, there are no guarantees in these situations," said the Reverend Mother slowly. "Does he know she's here?"

"Not at this stage," said Billy, "but it's only a matter of time before 'e finds out."

"The police have not been here yet." The Reverend Mother drummed her fingers on the corner of her cluttered desk. "I'm fully expecting them to arrive soon. In fact, I thought it might have been them when you arrived."

"I'm not callin' on them f' protection," Billy said stiffly. "I don't trust 'em."

"That's unfortunate. You should be able to trust them."

"Not the ones we've got at present," growled Billy.

"What about Mr. Armitage?"

"'E's not 'ere. 'E's gone back t' Sydney."

"That's a pity."

The Reverend Mother paced between the boxes scattered about the room. "If Mr. O'Connor does find out she's here, the only thing I can do is to make sure that I'm the one who answers to his knock." She stopped pacing and turned towards the two waiting anxiously for some answers. "The child, Hope, does cause some - shall we say - tense moments here at the orphanage, because of her disability. Unfortunately, there are those who would like to see her gone." She sighed.

"I could take them in," said Audrey quickly.

"Don't be silly, mum!" Billy was aghast. "That's the first place Sid'll look."

"Not necessarily." The Reverend Mother smiled enigmatically.

"What d'ya mean?" Billy stared at her.

"I have an idea that just might work."

"We're listenin'." Billy was doubtful.

"Well, if we can let slip to the newspaper that this is where she has been hiding for the past three years, that will send Mr. O'Connor running in this direction, and when he does, we'll be waiting for him, and Phyllis won't be here. She'll be with you." The Reverend Mother frowned. "Are you sure there's nobody at the Police barracks that you can trust?"

"Certainly not the two in charge." Billy tried to remember the name of the young constable who had attended to Beau's call out, the night Sid threw a brick through their window. "I can find out the name of a constable who should be trustworthy," he said slowly. "Anyway, I don't think Sid can read."

"That doesn't matter," said the Reverend mother briskly. "He'll soon find out." She touched her nose. "It's surprising how quickly word of mouth travels."

"How will we know when all this is about to happen?" asked Audrey fearfully.

"Leave it with me." Her dark eyes twinkled momentarily. "I'm going to enjoy this!"

Billy and Audrey stared at her, nonplussed.

As they made their slow way home, Billy and Audrey pondered on the Reverend Mother's final words before she had shooed them from her office and watched them leave the premises.

"How is this gunna work?" said Billy miserably. "Sid might be a lotta things, but 'e sure as hell is a cunnin' bugger. 'E'll smell a rat."

"We must trust the Reverend Mother, Billy," said Audrey carefully. "She's probably been dealing with Sid's kind for a long time." She patted his arm. "It will be nice to have a child in the house, even if it's only for a short while. Now come on, we have to get ready for visitors."

Chief Constable Whitley Pays a Visit to the Orphanage

The following morning the Reverend Mother had the anticipated visit from the constabulary. She opened the big door to be confronted with the smiling face of Senior Constable Whitley, accompanied by a lowly constable.

"Good morning, Ma'am," said Whitley politely, as he removed his hat.

The Reverend Mother, her thin lips pursed, looked them up and down imperiously. "Who might you be?" she asked sharply as she drew herself up to her formidable height.

"Senior Constable Whitley, and Constable Ogilvy, ma'am, from the Bendigo Constabulary."

"I see." Arms folded across her chest, the Reverend Mother made no move to let them in. "What can I do for you?"

Whitley smiled ingratiatingly. "I think you know why we're here ma'am. We have had word that a missing young woman, by the name of Phyllis Powell, has been hiding here, while the whole town has been looking for her - for the past three years, I might add. Is that a correct assumption?"

"I don't know." Brown eyes were hooded. "Hiding, you say?"

"Yes, ma'am."

"Nobody *hides* here, Senior Constable."

"With all due respect, ma'am, the young woman concerned has been *hiding* somewhere, and now we know she's here, we need to check and make sure she's alright." He smiled briefly. "She *is* here, isn't she?"

The Reverend Mother fixed her intense stare on Whitley. "If I tell you she's here and she's alright, will that suffice?" She paused. "Your presence here will upset a lot of my charges if I let you set foot in this building."

"The Church is not above the law, Reverend Mother," said Whitley smugly. "I will obtain a warrant if necessary. Maybe you have other girls *hiding* here."

"I told you," said the reverend Mother icily, "that nobody *hides* here. They choose to be here and can come and go as they please."

"I need to speak with Miss Powell," said Whitley stiffly. "Please don't make me use force."

"Force?" The Reverend Mother glared at Whitley. "You wouldn't dare!"

The Reverend Mother noticed that the young Constable's face had flushed to a deep crimson, and his eyes were wide with consternation, although he said nothing.

Whitley's tone softened slightly. "I don't want to have to do that, ma'am, but you will leave me no choice, if I don't see for myself that Miss Powell is here."

"Don't call me 'ma'am'!" The words came from between clenched teeth. "I am Reverend Mother."

"My apologies, Reverend Mother," said Whitley meekly, "but you are making things difficult. Is there any reason why the young woman does not wish to be seen? In my book that is tantamount to hiding, and yet you insist that she is not hiding."

The Reverend Mother sighed. "There is only one person that Miss Powell is afraid of, and that is a man by the name of Sid O'Connor. On no account must he know that she is here."

Whitley glanced quickly at Constable Ogilvie. "Ah, the infamous Mr. O'Connor!" he declared. "Yes, I heard something to that effect. We have had recent dealings with the said Mr. O'Connor."

"So you will know why we are concerned?"

"Well, I can assure you, Reverend Mother, that he won't find out from us where she is, if that's what's worrying you."

"That is what's worrying me."

There was silence, and Whitley frowned. "We are here to uphold the law and to see that rules are not broken," he said quietly. "If you don't trust us to do that, then our jobs mean nothing."

"Nobody is above the law, Chief Constable, as you said yourself, and nobody has broken any law, to my knowledge."

They stared at each other for a moment before Whitley spoke. "We seem to be at a stalemate here, Reverend Mother." He paused. "You obviously do not wish us to see the young woman in question, and as she has not actually broken any laws, I will report to the Press that she is well and being cared for by the Church." He looked at Ogilvie, whose expression showed relief. "You will bear witness to this, Constable Ogilvie?"

"Indeed, sir."

The Reverend Mother couldn't help but notice the relief on the young man's face, and she smiled to herself. She had no doubt that here was a trustworthy policeman.

"One more thing," Whitley was saying. "She has a child, I believe?"

"Yes."

"O'Connor's perhaps?"

"Oh, I wouldn't think so."

"Hm." Whitley stepped back on to the gravel path. "Good day to you Reverend Mother. Come, Ogilvie."

The Reverend Mother watched as they walked the length of the path to the gate. She had no doubt that Chief Constable Whitley would let slip to O'Connor what had just transpired at her door. He was not a man to back down so easily. She smiled as she closed the big door.

"Well, Phyllis, did you hear all that?" She spoke to the empty corridor.

Phyllis stepped out of a shadowy doorway, nodding as she walked towards the Reverend Mother.

"I certainly did." Her thin features were flushed to a bright crimson. "The nerve of the man!"

"Yes, but I think he took the bait, child, so we need to get you and Hope ready to pay a visit to Audrey Maitland's place. You do know where it is?"

"Yes. Been there many times back when me an' Billy…"

"Yes, yes!" A note of irritation grew in the Reverend Mother's tone. "I don't need to know all that." She took Phyllis by the arm. "If you go at first light, there should be nobody about." She smiled triumphantly. "I want you to stay there until you hear from me that the coast is clear. I shall await the visit of the notorious Mr. O'Connor."

"Notorious?" Phyllis's face creased as she puzzled over the comment.

"By all accounts," said the Reverend Mother. "I'll find out for myself very soon, I should think."

*

The following morning, unrecognisable in a long black gown and hooded cape, and wheeling a heavy pram, Phyllis made her way swiftly down the hill and in the direction of the Maitland cottage. Dawn was spreading its crimson arms across the sky when she trundled the heavy pram through Audrey's gate. As the Reverend Mother had suspected, she had seen nobody on the streets, and sighed with relief as she knocked tentatively on the peeling front door.

It took a few minutes before she heard footsteps along the passage inside, and the door opened slowly. Audrey's face appeared, surrounded by the white frills of a mop cap. Her look of shock was soon replaced with a broad smile as she realised who was standing on her verandah.

"Phyllis, love, come in, come in!" she muttered, as she opened the door wide.

"Hello, Mrs. Maitland." Phyllis pointed behind her. "I've got Hope in the pram."

"I'll get Billy to bring the pram in. You get the child and take her through to the kitchen. It should be warm in a jiffy, when I stoke the fire. Billy!" She called behind her. "Out of bed, quick! We've got visitors."

Billy appeared at his bedroom door, fair hair tousled and blinking the sleep from his eyes. He was tying a dressing gown around his middle, and through the haze of interrupted sleep he managed to take stock of the situation.

"Phyllis! Crikey, the Reverend Mother doesn't muck about!" Billy followed Phyllis outside to where the pram was standing on the front path.

Phyllis lifted the child out, and Billy quickly pulled the heavy pram across the verandah and through the front door.

Once they were all inside, Audrey shut the door, bolting it on the inside. Phyllis saw the action and frowned.

"That's to keep undesirables out, Phyllis." Audrey smiled reassuringly at the girl.

"You mean Sid?"

"Yes, I do mean Sid." Audrey tightened her dressing gown cord. "Now down to the kitchen, both of you, and I'll get you some breakfast. I presume you haven't had any yet?"

"No. We was too early for breakfast."

Billy, having wheeled the big pram out to the back vestibule, stood at the kitchen door and watched his mother fussing around Phyllis and the child. He had to go to work soon, and he hoped his mother knew what she was doing. Sid O'Connor was not a man to be trifled with, and if he caught wind of what was happening with Phyllis and the child, they could all be in danger, his mother included. As he ran his fingers through his tousled hair, he looked up to see Phyllis watching him. He smiled tightly.

"I'm sorry," she mouthed.

"I don't want either of ya leavin' this house while I'm at work," he rasped, "an' don't go answerin' the front door. Mum?"

"I heard you, Billy." Audrey glared at him. "Now get dressed while I fix you some breakfast."

Billy headed for his room to get dressed. *This could turn out to be a very interesting day* he mused.

Sid O'Connor Meets His Match

The Reverend Mother didn't have to wait long before receiving a visit from Sid O'Connor. It was that same afternoon when she spotted a stranger hovering around the big gates. She watched from her office window as he dropped a cigarette butt on the gravel at his feet and ground it out with his boot.

"Filthy habit!" She shuddered as she saw him remove his cap and scratch his head.

He spent some time gazing around him before he slowly made his way towards the imposing front door. The Reverend Mother smiled to herself as she closed the curtains.

"Well, Mr. O'Connor, we get to meet at last." She picked up a large brass bell from the desk and moved swiftly from the room, gliding silently along the length of the corridor to the front door. There she held the bell behind her back and waited for his knock.

It took several minutes before she heard the brass knocker hit the door with a hollow thud. She waited for an appropriate length of time before pulling the latch and letting the door swing open. The young man stood with one foot on the step, and he pulled off his dirty cap as the Reverend Mother stared out at him.

"Yes?" She stood at her full height of five foot eight inches and stared down at the grubby figure standing before her. "Who are you and what do you want?"

"Me name's Sid O'Connor – er- Miss – Sister," he stuttered.

"Is it indeed?" purred the Reverend Mother, her eyes glinting. "It's Reverend Mother to you, young man. I have been expecting you."

"Have ya?" Sid blinked at the imposing figure looming over him.

"I have."

Sid managed to recover his composure and his thin features twisted into a sneer as he spoke.

"Well, you'll know why I'm 'ere, won't ya, - Reverend Mother?"

"Yes, I know why you're here."

There was silence and Sid frowned.

"Well, where is she?" he muttered, shuffling from one foot to the other.

"You mean Phyllis?"

"Course I mean Phyllis! Who else?"

The Reverend Mother scowled as she thought about this. Finally, she smiled down at her visitor, and in hushed tones she gave him her answer.

"At this moment, young man, I'm not sure where Phyllis might be. She could be in the laundry, or she could be out the back in the vegetable garden, or perhaps she's taking a nap."

"What?" Sid put his other foot up on the step. "Are you havin' me on?"

"Having you on? Certainly not! This is a big place, Mr. O'Connor. I can't be expected to know where everybody is at a given time."

Sid stepped forward menacingly. "You'd better tell me where she is, or I'll…"

"Or you'll what, Mr. O'Connor?" The Reverend Mother raised the bell in front of her. "One shake of this, young man, and you will be surrounded by so many black clad women, your head will spin."

Sid moved back off the step, looking around as he did so. "I don't see nobody," he sneered.

"Oh, you will if you don't move away quietly, and go about your business elsewhere."

Sid made a move forward.

"One shake!"

Sid stepped back. He glared at the black clad figure looming above him and stabbed a tobacco-stained finger in her direction.

"This ain't finished, Reverend Mother!" he spat venomously. "I don't give in that easy."

Sid spun on one foot and stalked off along the gravel path towards the gate.

"And neither do I, Mr. O'Connor! Neither do I!"

The door slammed and the Reverend Mother leaned against it momentarily, taking in a deep breath. This wasn't over and she knew it. With a deep sigh, she made her way to the office, closing the door behind her. There were always dramas in this place, and she was beginning to tire of the constant seeking for answers to her girls' problems. There had never been a problem like young Hope before, and it troubled her that no matter what was done for Phyllis, the child was not going to change. She would always be the way she was, even though she was such a loving child.

The Reverend Mother smiled as she picked up a pile of mail from her cluttered desk. It was time to see how many debt collectors she could expect at the door. She shuffled through the envelopes until she came to one postmarked Sydney. Smiling, she grabbed a small wooden letter opener, and tore the top of the envelope. A single page emerged and the spidery handwriting she recognised at once.

"Ah, Clarissa, what news do you have for me?"

Her expression was soft as she unfolded the paper and leaned against the desk to read it. As young women they had shared the excitement of travelling to the Congo to minister to those unfortunate individuals who were afflicted with all the flesh-eating horrors of leprosy. Both had only lasted twelve months before returning home to go their own separate ways. Clarissa had taken her vows and remained in Sydney, where she had eventually become the Reverend Mother at the Convent for the Sisters of mercy. They had corresponded regularly over the years and were both content with their lot.

My dear Ponty, the letter began.

This brought another smile to the Reverend Mother's face as she remembered their young days as Margery Pontefract and Clarissa Sawyer. It was so long ago. She sighed.

> *My dear Ponty, (Sister Angelica)*
> *I haven't written for some time, and much shame to me. I received your recent letter, and I may be able to help you.*
> *I have in my cloister, a dedicated nun who has not put a foot wrong in my estimation, but who has only recently made a startling confession to our Parish priest, and I feel that she needs to have a change of environment. I wondered if I might suggest sending her to you, as you are obviously in need of more workers to look after the children where you are. She is Sister Miriam to us, and a kinder person you would not meet. She has a reason for wanting to be down in your area, and I will explain...*

The Reverend Mother's sharp features stretched even further as she read what her dear friend had to say about Sister Miriam.

"My goodness!" she breathed to the silent room. "What should I do about that, I wonder?" She clucked her tongue as she slowly folded the paper and slipped it back into the envelope. "There is no escape from the ways of the world, no matter how hard we try. I will write back straight away."

Phyllis and Audrey

The front door had closed behind Billy, leaving Audrey and Phyllis staring at each other, while the child, Hope, pulled at her mother's skirt and made a grunting sound. Phyllis looked down at her.

"Are you hungry, Hope?" she asked softly. The child grunted again, and Phyllis looked up at Audrey. "She might like some toast, Audrey, if that's alright."

"Yes, certainly." Audrey picked up the big bread knife from the table and began to slice the loaf that stood beside it. "Now that Billy's gone, we can eat." Audrey then opened the firebox and began to spread the coals. "Ah, that should do nicely." She smiled down at Hope. "I'll make you some toast, little one. How would you like that? With jam?"

"Yes, that would be nice, thank you, Audrey." Phyllis answered while Hope still clung to her skirts.

Audrey grabbed the large wire toasting fork from beside the stove and after skewering the bread, held it over the coals.

Soon the bread was golden and ready to be spread with a little butter and jam. Audrey cut it into fingers as Phyllis sat Hope on a chair. They watched as she picked up a finger of toast and stuffed it into her mouth.

"No, Hope!" Phyllis grabbed the chubby fingers as they reached for another piece. "Finish what ya have in ya mouth first!" She looked apologetically at Audrey.

Audrey smiled as she cut more slices from the bread. "Does she talk at all, Phyllis?" she asked quietly, seeing the young mother's distress.

"No. She just makes noises when she wants somethin'."

"Has anyone tried to teach her?" Audrey skewered another slice of bread to the toasting fork.

"Yes. The nuns have tried, but she just gets angry and starts to scream."

Audrey looked at the child happily stuffing slices of toast into her mouth and frowned. "You don't think she could be deaf, do you?"

"Deaf?" Phyllis looked horrified. "No, I don't think so."

"Let me try something." Audrey moved behind the child and clapped her hands. There was no reaction from Hope, who continued with her toast. Audrey tried again, this time beside the child. There was still no indication that she had heard the sound. "I'd say she's deaf."

Phyllis blinked, and tears welled in her eyes. "Why, Mrs. Maitland? Why is she like this?"

Audrey took her arm gently and sat her at the table. "Some things are beyond explanation, Phyllis. My husband, Reginald, was deaf. It was the working with machinery that caused his, but we worked out a way of communicating with each other by using hand signals."

"Hand signals?" Phyllis wiped her eyes on the sleeve of her black cardigan.

"Yes." Audrey sat beside her. "It was different with my Reginald, of course, because he could talk, but after he lost his hearing, he had to get the gist of what we were saying by watching our lips or we would use our hands to indicate certain words."

Phyllis nodded uncertainly. "I don't want 'er taken away from me, Mrs. Maitland. Hope's all I got." She paused, sniffing loudly. "D'ya think ya c'n help 'er? I mean, she's quite adorable most o' the time."

"I can try," said Audrey, as the child held out her plate.

"She wants more," said Phyllis.

"And that's the sort of thing I mean!" exclaimed Audrey, her eyes gleaming. "Hope has her own way of expressing herself. All we have to do is build on it – add to her vocabulary."

"Her what?"

"Her – her understanding."

"Oh. Are you sure?" said Phyllis uncertainly.

Audrey clasped her by the hand. "Yes! We will do this for Hope, Phyllis. Nobody is going to take that child away from you! Nobody!" Satisfied that she'd solved one problem, Audrey stood up. "Now I must get dressed and head down to the shops for some milk powder and flour." She laughed. "Before we run out of bread!"

"But Billy said we wasn't t' leave the 'ouse."

"Fiddle faddle!" chortled Audrey. "Sid O'Connor doesn't scare me, my girl!"

Phyllis shivered. "'E should."

"Don't worry about me, love." Audrey patted Phyllis's shoulder. "I won't be gone long. You'll be safe here, as long as you keep the doors locked. Make Hope some more toast, and eat some yourself, girl. Don't want you fading away to a shadow." With that Audrey made a hasty exit.

*

Audrey hurried along the deserted street, a shopping basket on one arm and an umbrella in the other hand. The morning had deteriorated rapidly, and she guessed that rain was on the horizon. The corner shop at the end of her road was empty when she entered. The little bell above the door tinkled merrily to announce her arrival. She saw Mr. Shaw peering out from the room behind the counter. He smiled as he saw her and wiped his hands on his calico apron.

"Good morning, Mrs. Maitland!" His greeting was warm and loud, and his brown eyes twinkled behind their thick spectacles.

"Good morning, Mr. Shaw." Audrey was breathless and stood for a moment just inside the door.

"Are you alright, Mrs. Maitland?" Mr. Shaw bustled from behind the counter and placed a sturdy chair beside her. "Sit down, my dear. You look a little peaky."

"I'm afraid I hurried, and I'm out of breath." Audrey sat heavily. "I'll be alright in a moment."

"What can I get you?"

"I need some milk powder and some bread flour."

The rotund Mr. Shaw grinned. "Has Billy been eating more than his share?" He laughed loudly.

"No." Audrey cringed at the sound.

It was true that Mr. Shaw kept a record of all his customers' purchases and knew to the last ounce what each used in a week. This was Audrey's second visit, and she knew he'd want to know why.

As she was contemplating a satisfactory answer, the doorbell tinkled, and Jess DuBois appeared. Audrey smiled, hoping that the relief was not visible on her face. Jess had always been a good friend to her, and she knew that if she had to talk to anybody about her current situation, it would be to Jess. She had experienced firsthand what Sid O'Connor was capable of.

"Hello, Jess," she breathed, grateful for the distraction.

"Hello, Audrey." Jess smiled at her. "You're out early."

Audrey flashed a quick glance in Mr. Shaw's direction, but he was busy scooping flour into a bag.

"I'm trying to beat the rain," said Audrey quickly.

"Have you got time to come in for a quick cup of tea, on your way home?" Jess asked politely.

"Um- not today, Jess, thanks all the same. I've got to get back." Audrey stood up.

"Oh! Is everything alright, Audrey?"

"Yes! Yes!"

"Billy's eating her out of house and home." Mr. Shaw grinned from behind the counter.

Audrey scowled as he placed her bags on the top of the counter. Picking them up she put them in her basket. "Could you put these on the account, please Mr. Shaw?" she said stiffly. "Billy'll get paid at the end of the week, and then I'll fix you up."

Mr. Shaw shrugged grudgingly. "Very well, Mrs. Maitland."

Audrey nodded to them both and scurried out the door, setting the bell jingling erratically. Jess and Mr. Shaw looked at each other as the door closed.

"She usually stops for a chat," sighed Mr. Shaw, adjusting his spectacles.

"She doesn't usually knock back a cup of tea, either," rejoined Jess. "Is everything alright with her, do you think?"

"I couldn't possibly say." Mr. Shaw shrugged his heavy shoulders. "But that's her second visit this week and that *is* unusual. Now, what can I get you, Mrs. DuBois?"

"Oh, half a pound of tea and half a pound of sugar, please Mr. Shaw."

"Coming right up." Jess watched as Mr. Shaw deftly weighed out the exact amount of tea on his large scales and poured it into a paper bag. He did the same with the sugar, and handed them across the counter. "Will there be anything else?"

"I'd better have a box of Bex powders, please. Beau's sister, Charlotte, is home again from the hospital, and may need those."

"Oh? I'm sorry, Mrs. DuBois. I didn't know she'd been in the hospital. Serious, was it?"

Jess laughed softly. "She was climbing a ladder and fell, breaking her ankle."

Mr. Shaw tut-tutted loudly. "Women climbing ladders? Unheard of in my day!" He leaned conspiratorially on the counter. "You know, it's the war that's changed everything and everybody. Women never had to do such things before the war, and…"

"She won't be doing it again for a while, I can assure you," Jess cut in quickly. "Now, what do I owe you, Mr. Shaw?"

Mr. Shaw adjusted his glasses and reached below the counter for his accounting book. He opened it noisily. "That'll be four shillings, thanks, Mrs. DuBois."

Jess counted out the shillings and handed them across the counter. "Thank-you, Mr. Shaw." She placed the items in a string bag. "Now I'd better hurry before it *does* decide to rain." She smiled.

"My bones are telling me that it will before the day's out," said Mr. Shaw, nodding his head sagely.

Jess walked out on to the footpath. The sky certainly looked like it could unleash a deluge from the dark clouds that were gathering. She frowned as she looked along the street and could just make out Audrey's figure trudging slowly in the direction of her house. Making up her mind to pay Audrey a visit, Jess hurried towards her own home.

*

Audrey arrived home just as a loud clap of thunder rent the air and sent the neighbourhood dogs into a frenzy of barking. She shut the front door behind her and with a sigh, removed her coat and scarf. Heavy drops of rain began to fall on the tin roof and within seconds the noise was deafening. Audrey padded along to the kitchen, where Phyllis was washing dishes in the sink. She turned as Audrey entered.

"You got home just in time, Mrs. Maitland!" Phyllis shouted above the noise.

"I certainly did." Audrey looked across at Hope, who was sitting at the table and playing placidly with a set of small wooden blocks. "Hope obviously can't hear the rain," she mused, almost to herself.

Phyllis looked across at her daughter. "No, she can't. Up at the orphanage we don't hear the rain on the roof, so I've never noticed that before."

Audrey dropped her basket on the table, and Hope looked up, her chubby face registering surprise. Audrey picked the basket up and dropped it once more on to the table. A slow grin spread over Hope's features, and she banged a hand on the table. Phyllis gasped.

"D'ya think she heard that, Mrs. Maitland?"

"I'm not sure, Phyllis. Maybe she felt the vibration." Audrey banged her fist twice on the table.

Hope, whose hand was still flat on the table, copied the sound, leaving the two women open-mouthed with amazement.

"She sensed the vibration," said Audrey slowly. "Maybe she's not completely deaf. Has she seen a doctor?"

"No."

"I think we should take her to Doctor DuBois," said Audrey matter-of-factly, "and the sooner the better."

"Who's Doctor DuBois?"

Remembering that Phyllis had spent the past three years shut away from the world, Audrey tried to explain a little of Beau's past.

"Oh yeah," said Phyllis, "I remember 'im. 'E worked in the Grey Goose for a while. Had a big scar on 'is face."

"Yes, he did. He got that during the war." Audrey paused. "He married Mrs. Stanley."

"He what?"

"Oh. Something else you haven't caught up with, Phyllis. Mr. Stanley didn't come home from the war. He died of the flu just after the Armistice."

"Did 'e?" Audrey saw tears in Phyllis's eyes. "Such a nice man 'e was."

"Yes, he was." Audrey took a deep breath, remembering the loss of her own son, Frank. "Anyway, that's what happens during war." She flicked her hand across her eyes.

"D'ya think 'e c'n help my Hope?"

"I don't know, Phyllis, but it's worth a try."

Hope for Hope

A knock on the front door startled Audrey and Phyllis as they sat chopping vegetables for the evening meal. Hope had gone for a nap, and the house was quiet. They looked at one another and waited. The knock sounded again.

"It's not Sid," said Phyllis slowly. "It's not loud enough."

Audrey stood as the knock sounded again. She headed along the passage to the front door.

"Who's there?" she called out.

"It's Jess, Audrey," came the reply.

Audrey breathed a sigh of relief and opened the door. "Come in, Jess," she said quickly, ushering her visitor inside and locking the door once more.

"Is everything alright, Audrey?" Jess frowned as she saw the door being locked.

"Come into the kitchen, Jess, and I'll tell you all about it."

Mystified, Jess followed Audrey to the kitchen, where she saw Phyllis Powell.

"Oh!" was all she said.

"Hello, Mrs. Stanley," said Phyllis quietly. Realising what she had done, she quickly shook her head. "I'm sorry – I meant - hello Mrs. DuBois."

"Hello, Phyllis," said Jess, sensing the girl's embarrassment. "And it's alright. It happens all the time." She smiled at the young woman. "It's been a long time since we saw you."

"Yeah, I know. I didn't mean f' everyone to be worried about me. I had t'get away from Sid."

"Sit down, Jess." Audrey pulled out a chair. "I'll make you a cup of tea."

"There's no need, Audrey. I've just finished lunch," said Jess hurriedly. "When I saw you at the shop this morning, I sensed something was amiss, so I waited for the rain to stop before coming to check on you."

Audrey laughed wryly. "So now you know."

Jess looked at Phyllis. "I thought you were at the orphanage."

"I was, until this mornin'. The Reverend Mother's expectin' a visit from Sid, so she wanted me an' Hope out o' the way. Mrs. Maitland kindly said we could come 'ere."

"So you have your daughter with you?"

"Yeah." Phyllis looked down at her hands. "Hope's not like other children, Mrs. – DuBois."

"Please call me Jess." Jess placed a hand over Phyllis's. "Why do you say that?" She looked quickly up at Audrey. "What's wrong with her?"

There was silence until Audrey spoke. "She's what's called a Mongoloid child."

"Oh." Jess understood and her heart ached for the young mother. "I see."

"No-one's goin' t'take 'er away from me!" declared Phyllis vehemently.

"No, of course not." Jess shot a worried glance in Audrey's direction.

Audrey moved the kettle across the stove to where it began to sing loudly. "I'm going to make that cup of tea, Jess. You'll probably need it when I tell you the whole story."

"Very well." Jess glanced up at the clock. "As long as I'm home by three for Lottie's next feed."

"You've got a baby?" Phyllis stared at Jess in wonder, making her smile.

"Yes, Phyllis, I have. Her name's Charlotte, but we call her Lottie, because Beau's sister, whose name is also Charlotte, is living with us at present."

"Oh." Phyllis laughed uneasily.

"Charlotte is looking after the little one?" asked Audrey as she poured three cups of tea.

"No." It was Jess's turn to laugh. "Charlotte is recovering from a broken ankle, so Izzy has Lottie and Grace."

Audrey shook her head. "It's all too complicated for me." She replaced the kettle and sat heavily beside Jess. "Let's tell Jess about Hope, Phyllis." She smiled softly. "She might have some suggestions as to what we should do."

Jess looked from one to the other as Phyllis recounted her story of the love she had for the child who should have, by rights, been placed in an institution. Jess listened, wide-eyed, as the girl expressed her fervent wish to have her checked by a doctor for the deafness that had just been discovered.

"Would your 'usband see 'er, Jess?"

"I'm sure he would, Phyllis." Jess clasped Phyllis's hand. "You know, with the war and so many men returning home deaf from the close proximity to guns and canon fire, doctors are looking for ways to help them. Beau has worked with returned soldiers who have suffered all sorts of trauma as a result of the war, so I feel sure he would be willing to see what can be done for your little one." She saw tears well in Phyllis's eyes. "I'll talk with him tonight."

"Thanks, Jess. You don't know what that means t'me."

Jess stared across at Audrey, whose eyes had also welled with tears. This was going to be a difficult situation for Phyllis, whatever the outcome.

*

Later that evening, when the children were all in bed, and Charlotte had retired to the sleep-out, Jess sank into the couch in front of the lounge fire and sighed heavily. Beau, who had been placing another log on the fire, looked up at her.

"That was a big sigh, Jess. What's wrong?"

"I need to talk to you, Beau."

"What about?" Beau placed the poker against the wall, and sat beside Jess, drawing her against him.

Jess nestled into the crook of his arm and smiled up at him. "We haven't done this for some time, Beau," she said as she rested her head against his shoulder. "I miss our evening cuddles."

"Life has changed, Jess." Beau kissed the top of her head. "Now, what do you want to talk to me about? You'd better make it quick, before I fall asleep."

"I saw Phyllis Powell today."

Any weariness that Beau had been experiencing suddenly evaporated. He sat upright. "Where?"

"At Audrey's."

"What was she doing there?"

"Hiding from Sid."

"What did she have to say for herself?"

"A lot, Beau." Jess shook her head slowly. "She has a problem with her child, and I promised her that I would talk to you about it."

"A medical problem?"

"In a way." Jess paused. "She is a Mongoloid child, Beau."

Beau sucked in his breath. "Oh. She should have been institutionalised, Jess."

"In a way I suppose she has been, up at the orphanage."

"What does Phyllis want me to do?"

"She has just discovered that Hope is deaf, but Audrey seems to think that she can sense vibration, and so uses her own method of communication. I told them about the work being done to help returned soldiers who are now deaf, and I wondered whether you can perhaps see the child, to determine whether there's any hope for her." Jess smiled suddenly. "Hope for Hope, you could say."

"Hope for Hope," Beau repeated softly. "I can certainly see her." He looked earnestly into Jess's eyes. "But don't get your hopes up too high, Jess. The child was quite obviously born deaf."

"Thank-you, Beau." Jess held his face between her hands and kissed him. "I knew you'd try." She looked up at him quizzically. "It might be a good idea if you see her at Audrey's. Phyllis is trying to avoid being discovered by Sid."

Beau grinned. "Very well. I shall go and see her first thing tomorrow."

*

True to his word, Beau knocked on Audrey's door at eight-thirty the following morning. He heard the shuffle of footsteps along the passage, and then Audrey's voice.

"Who's there?"

"It's Beau, Audrey."

He heard the sound of the latch being pulled, and the door opened slowly, revealing Audrey in her dressing gown and mop cap. She smiled at him.

"Good morning, Doctor DuBois."

"Jess has sent me to have a look at Phyllis's child."

"Yes, come in. They're both still here."

Beau stepped into the narrow passage, and Audrey swiftly locked the door after him.

"I'm not taking any chances," she said as way of explanation, when he frowned at her. "Sid O'Connor could be lurking anywhere."

"True," said Beau as he followed her to the kitchen.

Phyllis sat at the table, handing Hope thin slices of toast. She looked up as Beau entered and smiled.

"Hello, Doctor DuBois," she said huskily. "I'm glad you've come."

Beau smiled as he placed his black bag on the table. "Jess insisted," he said as he ran a professional eye over the child sitting quietly, eating her breakfast. "So, what do you think I can do to help you, Phyllis?"

"Well," Phyllis pushed her fair hair away from her eyes, "I'd like ya t'check Hope's ears, please."

Beau pulled out a chair and sat beside the child, who turned pale blue eyes on him. A smile spread across her round features, and she lifted a hand to touch the scar on his face.

"Hope!" stuttered Phyllis, horrified. "Don't do that!" She grabbed the child's hand and pulled it away. Colour suffused her face. "I'm sorry, Doctor DuBois!"

"No need to be, Phyllis," said Beau quietly. "It happens all the time, and it's actually a distraction for my young patients." Beau reached into his bag. "Has Hope had her ears checked before?"

"No."

"It could just be that they are blocked."

"Blocked?"

"Yes, with a build-up of wax. It happens sometimes that the ear has a problem ridding itself of wax and may need a little help. So, if Hope will let me, I'd like to look into her ears and see what's going on." Beau removed a large black scope from his bag, and Phyllis's eyes widened. "It's alright. It won't hurt. It's called an otoscope and has a magnifying glass whereby I can see into the ear canal." Phyllis nodded dumbly. "Can you distract Hope, while I put the scope in her ear?"

Phyllis turned the child's attention back to her toast, while Beau began his inspection of her ears. Finally, he looked up and placed the scope back in the bag.

"When did you actually notice that Hope was not responding to sound?"

"I hadn't." Phyllis shrugged her shoulders. "It was Mrs. Maitland who noticed it yesterday."

"And you hadn't noticed anything wrong before that?"

"No. She don't talk, an' only makes gruntin' sounds when she wants somethin'."

"I'd like to have her checked at the surgery, by my associate, but I have a feeling that the problem can be easily solved. Her ear canals are very narrow, and I suspect are blocked, which means that everything sounds muffled. I'd also like to check her Eustachian tubes while she's there."

"Her what?" Phyllis looked bemused.

Beau smiled. "The problem could be further down, behind her nose," he said, as a way of explanation.

"Oh."

"She didn't hear the rain yesterday," said Audrey, who had been listening intently, "but she sensed the vibration when I banged on the table where her hands were."

"Are you happy for her to be checked out at the surgery?" Beau looked from Audrey to Phyllis.

They both nodded.

Beau closed his bag and stood up. "I'll get back to you when I can arrange for Doctor Simmons to see her. It could be in a day or two."

"How are we goin' t'get there?" asked Phyllis anxiously.

Beau thought quickly. "I'll – I'll send a car for you." No doubt he could persuade Charles to act as chauffeur. He was at a loose end these days.

"Thank-you, Beau," said Audrey breathlessly. "Can you stop for a cup of tea?"

"No, thanks all the same, Audrey. I have surgery at ten." Beau picked up his bag. "It wouldn't hurt you to have a check-up either, Audrey." He smiled.

"I know. I have been feeling a little breathless lately."

"Then come and see me," said Beau, before turning to Phyllis, who was looking on anxiously. "We'll look after your little one, Phyllis."

Beau smiled at the trio once more before taking his leave. As he swung his leg across the bar of his bicycle, he reflected on how fortunate he was to have a child who was free from disability. Phyllis had chosen to encumber herself with a child whose problems were not going to go away, and he had to admire her for that. The Phyllis he had known three years ago, was not the same one he had seen today. The old one had gone and left a very caring mother in her place. He would do what he could for her and the child.

*

Charlotte gazed silently at her brother as she sat in the big armchair, her plastered foot resting on a stool. Beau was arranging kindling and newspaper in the grate, ready to set a match to it. She watched his movements as he carefully placed the sticks in order of size. Everything Beau did was meticulous; he left nothing to chance. As she watched him, she silently mourned the loss of all the years they had not seen each other, and she had a sudden desire to reach out and touch his head. Fortunately, or otherwise, he was too far away from her, and she was unable to rise from the chair.

As if sensing her watching him, Beau turned suddenly, and their eyes met.

"What is it, Charlotte?" His voice cracked slightly. "Are you uncomfortable?"

"No," she answered briskly. "However, I was wondering why you feel the need to light a fire. The evening isn't cold."

Beau sat back on his haunches. "I like the comfort of a fire, Charlotte."

"Comfort." Charlotte repeated the word slowly. "It's not a word I know much about, Beau. There was no such thing at the Convent."

Beau struck a match and set it to the paper, where it immediately flared into life. "I gathered that," he said slowly, watching the flame gather momentum. "Was it really necessary to be cold all the time?"

"You get used to it, Beau." Charlotte winced as she moved her foot on the stool. "After a while you no longer feel it." She gave a short laugh. "If you did, there was always the kitchen, where the only fire burned. Kitchen duties were very popular in the winter."

Beau stared into the flames as the kindling crackled in the heat. "I don't think I'd ever been in such a cold place, if you discount the frontline, of course." He reached for a larger piece of wood and placed it carefully over the crackling kindling.

"Yes," said Charlotte absently. "That must have been truly awful." She stared at the back of his head. "We've not talked much about those years of your life, Beau."

"No." Beau brushed his hands together before standing and leaning on the mantel. "They're best forgotten, Charlotte." He smiled grimly.

At that moment, Jess walked into the lounge, closing the door quietly behind her. "You'll be pleased to know that all the children are in bed." Her smile changed to a frown as she saw the serious expressions on the faces of Beau and Charlotte. "Is everything alright?" she began.

Beau relaxed. "Everything's fine, Jess." He smiled fondly at the woman who had made life bearable for him. "Charlotte and I were just discussing the benefits of having a fire for warmth."

"Oh." Jess looked at Charlotte. "I don't see any point in being cold if you don't have to be." She picked up the knitting that lay on the couch, before settling into the depths of the brown cushions.

"What are you knitting?" asked Charlotte absently.

"A jumper for Ben," said Jess, as she unwound a length of green wool.

Silence followed, broken only by the crackle of the fire and the click of Jess's knitting needles. Beau sat beside his wife and stretched out his legs towards the fire. He closed his eyes. It had been a long day, beginning with his visit to see Phyllis's little girl. He pondered over that and his subsequent discussion with Raymond Simmons about her possible prognosis. Raymond had agreed to see Hope in two days' time, so Beau had arranged with Charles to collect them in his car. Now he only had to tell Phyllis of the arrangement and pray that she had no unwelcome visitor in the meantime.

"What's the problem with this child you went to see this morning, Beau?" Charlotte's voice interrupted his thoughts.

Beau stared across at his sister. "I'm not sure, Charlotte. She appears to be deaf, but nobody has realised it until now."

"How old is she?"

"She's three."

Charlotte shrugged. "I suppose that's possible." She paused. "And she's lived with her mother at the orphanage all this time?"

Beau nodded. "Yes, for most of that time."

"That seems a strange arrangement."

"The nuns look after mothers as well as children," said Jess, resting from her knitting. "The mothers work in the laundry which services the town."

"Oh? Who are the nuns?"

"They're the sisters of the Good Shepherd."

Charlotte shook her head. "I don't know of them. Perhaps I'll pay them a visit."

"Why?" Beau sat up straight.

"Curiosity, my dear brother, nothing else." Charlotte smiled at Beau's tight-lipped features. "Relax, Beau! I'm not thinking of joining the Order."

Beau sat back against the cushions. "Good!" was all he said.

They lapsed into silence once more, each one busy with their own thoughts. It was Charlotte who broke the silence.

"I still think it's worth a visit." She spoke as though talking to herself.

"Charlotte!" Jess and Beau chorused together.

Charlotte blinked at them as though seeing them for the first time. "What?"

"So you *are* going to visit the orphanage?" Jess's knitting needles had stopped.

"Why not." Charlotte shrugged. "What harm can it do?"

Beau watched his sister intently as he spoke. "Do you miss the cloistered life, Charlotte?"

Charlotte was slow to answer, and when she did, the words were quiet and measured. "I miss the discipline and the structure, and... the friendships."

Jess openly stared at her, while Beau looked down at his hands as he contemplated what he was about to ask his sister. When he looked up, his eyes sought hers, compelling her to return his gaze.

"Charlotte, I am going to ask you something that you may not wish to hear, but I want you to answer me honestly."

Jess turned her gaze on him, wondering what was coming. Charlotte's brow creased, but her gaze never faltered.

"What do you want to ask me, Beau?"

"The child you had, Charlotte…did you actually see him?"

Charlotte blinked. "Yes, Beau," she whispered. "Sister Miriam brought him to me. *He was dead!*"

"Where is he buried?" continued Beau doggedly.

Charlotte was fighting for control of her emotions. "Outside the Convent wall."

"You mean outside consecrated ground?"

"Yes."

The silence in the room was palpable as they all stared at each other.

"I think that's criminal," said Jess tentatively. "He was a newborn baby."

"What did you call him?" asked Beau, his voice shaking.

"Michel." It was just a whisper. "I called him Michel Beauregarde."

Part Three

The Truth Will Out

Nick's Dilemma

Nick pounded on the door with the sign that read: JOE HUDSON - PRIVATE INVESTIGATOR.

Some of the gold-plated lettering had tarnished and several letters were unreadable. They were just like Joe, Nick reflected. He waited, knowing that Joe was inside. He could hear him moving about.

Nick had spent the morning aimlessly wandering the city, trying to get his head around what his parents had confessed to him the previous night. His whole world had been blown apart, and everything he had always known to be true, had been destroyed in those few minutes. He was no longer the person he thought he was, and everything his parents had taught him over the years, accounted for nothing. What was it his mother had always said to him when he was in any kind of trouble? "The truth will out, Nick." The truth will out! What did that mean? From where he was standing now, absolutely nothing! His whole life was a lie!

The door creaked open, and Joe stood blinking at him in the sudden light. A smile split his face as he saw Nick.

"Nick, my boy! You're back!" He pulled the door open wide and ushered Nick into the cramped space of his office. "Clear those papers off the chair and sit down, lad. I've been waiting to hear about your trip down south." He glanced at Nick and frowned. "Everything alright?"

"No, it's not, Joe." Nick ran his fingers through his thick hair.

Joe grabbed his jacket from where it had been flung across the back of his own chair and shrugged himself into it. "In that case, let's go to Gray's Hotel. You look as though you need a drink." He snatched up keys from the cluttered desk and took Nick by the arm. "Come on!"

Within minutes they were seated at a table in a secluded part of the Bar at Gray's, and Joe was ordering drinks. He glanced across at his friend and colleague, and for once no words of humour or sarcasm issued from his mouth. Nick looked troubled. Joe bit his lip as he contemplated what he should say to open the conversation.

"What seems to be the matter, Nick?"

Nick looked across at Joe, his dark eyes narrowing. "I don't know where to begin, Joe. It all seems so bizarre and impossible."

"What does?" probed Joe gently.

Nick pushed his knuckles into his eyes. "Everything." He shrugged helplessly as he looked up at Joe. "I am not the person I thought I was, Joe."

"What do you mean, Nick?"

A young waiter placed their drinks before them, smiled politely and moved off.

"I'll try to explain, but I don't know how I'll go." Nick curled his hands around the beer glass in front of him. "Before I left Bendigo, Beau DuBois asked to see me. He had a newspaper article he wanted me to see. It was old and faded, and the print was hard to read, but I got the gist of it." He took a sip of the amber fluid to moisten his dry mouth. "My father had defended his father in what I gathered to be a sexual assault case with a female patient."

"His father was a doctor?"

"Yes." Nick took another sip. "That in itself was rather a long shot. I mean, Beau having that article and me being in Bendigo all seems rather bizarre, don't you think?"

"It does, I suppose." Joe lifted his glass to his mouth, where it hovered for a moment. "Go on."

"I don't know whether I mentioned it to you, Joe, but Beau had taken a dislike to me the moment I set foot in the town, and I couldn't understand why, but now I think it was because he connected me to the lawyer who had exonerated his father twenty-five years ago."

Joe scowled. "That doesn't make sense, unless he thought his father was guilty."

"Exactly my thoughts, Joe."

"What did your father have to say about it, presuming he remembered the case?"

Nick shifted uncomfortably on his chair. "I confronted my father when I got home yesterday, and that's where the whole story came crashing around me. There was more to it than that one case, and a history between my father and Beau's father that goes back even further." He paused. "This is where I'm not sure where to begin."

"Take your time, Nick. I have nothing pressing at present." Joe settled back against his chair.

So over the course of several drinks, Joe sat listening to Nick spilling out the story that had been revealed to him the previous evening. It was punctuated with thumps on the table that set glasses rattling and curious eyes turning in their direction. However, Joe let Nick get it all out of his system, and once the words petered out, he leaned forward and grasped Nick by the hand. It was a shocking truth that had just been exposed and Joe felt deeply for his young colleague.

"I hope you feel better for that, Nick," he said as gently as he could.

Nick sighed. "I wouldn't say I feel better – it doesn't change anything, but I had to share it with somebody, and you are the closest person to me." He looked into Joe's blue eyes. "Please don't say anything to Amelia just yet. I need to pull myself together before I see her."

Joe smiled. "She's looking forward to seeing you, Nick. You two must have really hit it off."

"We did."

"Good." There was a long pause. "If I hadn't sent you on a mission to Bendigo, none of this would have surfaced." Joe was almost speaking to himself.

"No, it wouldn't have – not yet anyway. My mother always said to me – 'The truth will out, Nick.'" He laughed harshly. "How could she have said that to me, knowing what she did?"

"It might not be my place to say this, Nick, but I'm going to, anyway. Your mother probably acted out of a misguided sense of loyalty."

"Loyalty!" Nick stared at Joe. "Loyalty to whom? My father?"

Joe nodded.

"What they did was wrong, Joe, and nothing can ever make it right."

"I suppose you're right. Where do you go from here, Nick?"

"I don't know, Joe. Firstly, I must let it all sink in."

"I have a suggestion."

"Which is?"

"Have a talk to Clarence Bonner-Smythe. His daughter, Celia, was married to Beau DuBois once. Clarence could possibly tell you about the DuBois family."

"I might do that."

"I'll take you, if you like?"

"What, now?"

"While the iron's hot, Nick."

"Very well."

"Good." Joe smiled. "I'll just visit the restroom first. All that beer has to go somewhere."

Nick's Visit With Clarence

Nick and Joe ran for a tram just outside the hotel and sat in silence as it rattled its way along the city streets, tipping out commuters along the way and taking more on board. Conversations hummed around them until finally Joe tugged Nick's sleeve.

"Next stop is ours, Nick."

When the tram screeched to a halt, Joe was ready to jump out on to the road. Nick followed, barely making it to safety before the tram lurched forward once again.

"They don't stop for long!" shouted Joe above the noise of the wheels. "You have to be ready."

"I can see that!" Nick scowled after the departing tram. "It's dangerous, to say the least. What happens to older people who are slow?"

Joe shrugged. They had reached the footpath. "Safer for them to walk, I would say."

"Hm."

Nick had not travelled on a tram before - there had never been any need for it. His father had always... His brain slammed the door on that subject, and he concentrated on keeping pace with Joe. For a man of his size, he moved quickly.

They arrived at a row of fashionable red brick terraces and Joe bounded up the steps of a rather grand home – a little larger than the rest of the row. A shiny brass bell hung beside the door, and Joe gave it a tug. Within moments the door opened and a young woman with black cropped hair appeared. Large brown eyes stared out at them, unblinking.

"Yes?" she said finally.

Both men removed their hats. Joe smiled at the young woman as he twisted the brim of his hat.

"Hello, Celia," he said quietly. "You don't remember me?"

"Should I?" came the frosty response.

"Joe Hudson, Private Investigator?"

Recognition dawned on her pale haughty features. "Oh, yes!" she exclaimed. "What brings you here, Joe?" Her eyes swung across to Nick, standing quietly behind Joe.

"I'd like to speak with your father," said Joe, "and I'm glad you're here, too, Celia."

"I'm not here for long." Celia opened the door wide. "Father's in the front room. Who's your friend, Joe?"

"My apologies, Celia." Joe laughed self-consciously. "I'm forgetting my manners. Celia, this is my friend and colleague, Nick Armitage." He turned to Nick. "Nick, meet Celia DuBois."

Nick's eyebrows rose slightly as he held out his hand to the glamorous woman who bore the name DuBois. "I'm pleased to meet you —er -" He was at a loss.

Celia came to his rescue. "Celia Morley, actually," she said as she swung her gaze back to Joe, who registered surprise. "I'm pleased to meet you, Mr. Armitage."

The two men stepped into the cool passageway. Celia led the way to the lounge where Clarence sat in one of the red velvet armchairs, sipping on a glass of wine.

"Daddy, you have visitors," she said coolly. "Joe Hudson and his colleague, Nick Armitage."

"Joe!" Clarence extricated himself from the chair, placed his glass on a small table and extended a hand to Joe. "What brings you here?" His eyes switched to Nick and they also shook hands.

"We need some information," began Joe, as Clarence ushered them to plush armchairs. "We thought you might be able to help, and Celia too, if you're not too busy."

Celia dropped gracefully on to a high-backed dining-chair and smoothed her black linen skirt. "I do need to be at the Clinic by two, so I have a few minutes. What is it you want to talk about, Joe?"

"About Beau's family – in particular his father."

There was silence as Clarence and Celia looked at one other.

"What do you want to know?" asked Celia, her voice husky. "I never knew Beau's parents. His mother died when Beau was a child, and his father died not long before we got together."

"I see." Joe brushed a hand through his greying hair. "And what of his sister? What do you know about her?"

"I didn't know Beau had a sister, until… recently." Celia stared blankly at her father.

Clarence leaned across his chair and patted Celia's hand. "Why do you want to know about Charlotte, or Sister Agnes as she was known for many years?"

Joe looked at Nick. "Perhaps you can tell them what you told me, Nick."

Clarence and Celia looked expectantly in Nick's direction, and he heard Celia say quietly:

"Don't tell me the DuBois family has more secrets?"

Nick licked his dry lips. "I met Beau recently, while Joe had me on a job down in Bendigo. He showed me a newspaper article about his father from twenty-five years ago. My father, Hugh Armitage, was the defence lawyer for Doctor DuBois in a case involving a female patient."

Celia sat up straight, her face tight. "And?"

"My father apparently had the charges dropped."

"On what grounds?"

"Insufficient evidence, according to father." Nick cleared his throat. "But I believe Beau thinks his father was guilty."

Celia laughed harshly. "After what he did to his own daughter, I would say he probably was guilty."

"I questioned my father about it," said Nick, "and was not prepared for the answers he gave me. It seems that the association between my family and Doctor DuBois goes back even further, and that's what I need to tell you about."

"Go on?" said Clarence, settling back on his chair. "I'm sure we can handle more secrets."

"I'm not so sure," whispered Celia, as she got up to pour herself a wine. "Drink, anyone?"

The three men shook their heads.

Nick leaned forward on his chair and clasped his hands together on his knees. "When I arrived in Bendigo, and met the people connected to the case that I was on, concerning a missing woman, Beau and his wife were on the list - not as suspects, but as people who may have had information." He waited as Celia resumed her seat. "Beau didn't take to me, right from the very first meeting, and I had no idea why. It wasn't until he showed me a newspaper article about his father, and my possible connection to that through the named Lawyer, Hugh Armitage, that I realised, or thought I did, that he blamed us in some way." He looked across at Celia, who was staring intently at him over the rim of her wine glass. "It wasn't until I returned to Sydney and spoke with my father about the whole sorry affair, that I learned there was more to this story – much more."

A heavy silence lay in the room, until Clarence broke it. "We're listening."

Nick glanced helplessly at Joe, who merely shrugged his shoulders.

"I have often wondered," Nick began, "why I bear no physical resemblance to either my father or my mother, but that was always explained as 'nature reaching into my family tree for an ancestor to copy'. I thought no more about it until now."

"My God!" said Celia slowly, as she leaned forward. "I know who you look like."

"You do?"

"Yes, but how…?"

"That's the part that has been hidden for all of my thirty-two years."

"You're – you're Beau's brother." It was a barely audible statement from Celia. "But how…?"

"Tell us, lad," rasped Clarence, his eyes on Nick's face.

Nick sat back on his chair with a little sigh of resignation. "Very well."

When Nick had finished speaking, there was a deathly hush in the room, broken only by the loud ticking of the clock above the mantel.

"Does Beau know?" asked Celia finally.

"No," breathed Nick. "I only found out myself last night."

"Do you think he suspects?"

"Oh, without a doubt."

"What are you going to do now?"

"I'm not sure that there's anything I *can* do." Nick spread his hands. "I – I thought you might be able to fill me in on some of the family history."

Celia shook her head. "As I've already said, I know very little about Beau's family."

"A visit to the Convent might be a place to start," said Clarence, his expression bleak.

"Yes, perhaps you're right." Joe looked at Nick. "What do *you* think, Nick?"

He nodded slowly. "What about the family home?"

"It's no longer there," said Clarence. "It was pulled down not long after Charlotte found Beau hiding there, trying to come to terms with what he'd just discovered about his father." He stared at Nick. "You *do* know about that, I presume, Nick?"

"I only know what Beau's wife told me. It must have been a terrible experience for everyone."

"Yes, it was," said Celia quietly. "I gave Jess a hard time when I knew Beau was going to marry her."

"Water under the bridge, Celia," said Clarence gruffly. "Anyway, isn't it time you were heading for the Clinic?"

Celia looked up at the clock. It was ten minutes to two. "Yes." She stood up. "I'm afraid I have to go, gentlemen. Good luck with everything, Nick. You're going to need it." Celia headed for the door. "Let me know how you get on, - please?"

"Of course."

The three men waited until they heard the front door slam before looking solemnly at one another.

"If you don't mind, gentlemen," said Clarence, "I'd like to telephone my dear friend, Angela Rickard, and include her in this." And as if in answer to Nick's puzzled expression, "Angela was the instigator in the search for Beau. She is also a very dear friend to both Beau and Jess and could tell you the kind of man Beau is." He looked closely at Nick's drawn features. "Not all the DuBois men are of dubious character, Nick. Beau is a fine man, and you would do well to remember that."

As Clarence walked across the room to where the telephone hung on the wall, Nick stopped him. "Wait! Everything is happening too fast. If you don't mind, I'd like to delay my visit to the Convent for a day or so." He looked beseechingly at Joe. "I think I'd like to see Amelia before I unravel any more of this."

Joe looked at Clarence, who held the telephone receiver. "Amelia's my daughter," he said by way of explanation. "Maybe Nick's right."

"Very well, but I'd still like to talk to Angela about this. She does have a vested interest in Beau's life, and I'm sure she'll want to meet you, Nick, when you're ready." Clarence was already dialling the exchange.

Nick and Joe remained silent as Clarence gave the number to the girl on the other end of the line. There was silence for a few moments before they heard him say:

"Angela? It's Clarence, my dear… yes, I know it's not a good time to call you, but I have some news for you that I think you'll want to hear…Are you coming over for tea tonight…? Good, good… I'll tell you then… goodbye, my dear." He replaced the receiver. "I hope you don't mind, Nick."

"No, not at all."

"Would you like to come to tea tonight? Bring Amelia, by all means." Before Nick had a chance to answer, Clarence added: "Perhaps we could go out. I know of a very nice restaurant, Mario's, and I know Angela will be pleased." He turned to Joe. "The invitation includes you, Joe."

Joe shook his head. "Mario's? That's the one down on the quay, isn't it?" and as Clarence nodded. "I'm not the kind of person one takes to a flash restaurant, Clarence." He laughed. "Thanks all the same."

"Nick?"

Nick hesitated. "I'd like to talk with Amelia first."

"Certainly," said Clarence. "I'll make a reservation for seven o'clock anyway. If you make it, you make it."

"Thank-you." Nick stood and looked over at Joe. "Where is Amelia likely to be at this time of the day, Joe?"

"Your guess is as good as mine, Nick." Joe struggled out of the deep chair. "We'll go back to my office, and I'll call her workplace from there. Someone will know where she is."

Once Nick and Joe had said their goodbyes to Clarence, they set off along the street towards the city. Nick wanted to walk, to clear his head, and the thought of sitting on a crowded tram, surrounded by chattering people was too much for him to contemplate. Joe agreed, and together they stepped it out along the bitumen footpaths until they reached Joe's office block. Neither spoke as they walked – each preoccupied with their own thoughts on how quickly life could change, and not always for the better.

Nick now had a new identity to come to terms with, and as the can of worms had already been opened, he would not be able to ignore it – to pretend that it had never happened. It had happened. The previous chapters of his life had suddenly been erased, and his history rewritten. If he hadn't been sent to Bendigo, none of it would have surfaced, and his life would have been as it had always been – a lie.

They reached Joe's office building and climbed the stairs to the third floor. Joe put the key in the lock of his office door, and they stepped into the cramped space. Removing his coat, Joe flung it haphazardly across the back of a chair and reached for the telephone. He remembered the number Amelia had given him and dialled the operator. Nick stood waiting as Joe spoke to several people before finally getting on to Amelia.

"Yes, Amelia, it's - it's Joe… What do I want at this hour of the day? I want to see you. It's important… Yes… Can you come to my office?" Joe glanced quickly at Nick. "Yes, that would be good… Alright, I'll see you then." He replaced the receiver. "Amelia will be here in half an hour."

Nick sank on to the nearest chair, his legs unable to hold him. Joe pulled open a drawer in his desk and produced a small bottle of whisky. Scrabbling about in the drawer, he found two glasses, which he put on the desk.

"You need some of this, Nick." Joe proceeded to pour a small amount of neat whisky into the glasses and handed one across to Nick. "Get this down you, lad." He watched as Nick picked up the glass, which was grimy around the rim, and tipped the fiery liquid down his throat. He shuddered as it burned all the way down. Joe smiled at his reaction. Nick was not a seasoned drinker. "That should do the trick."

"What's Amelia going to say?" said Nick miserably.

"Well, if I know anything at all about my daughter, Nick, she'll try to find a positive." Joe poured himself another whisky and downed it in an instant.

Nick shuddered. "I don't know how you can drink that stuff, Joe."

"Lots of practise, Nick." Joe eased his bulk on to the chair behind his desk. "Lots of practise."

*

The door opened and Amelia appeared. She stepped into the room and frowned at the two sitting glumly staring into their empty glasses. Walking quickly to Nick, she planted a kiss on his cheek. The smile she received was less than enthusiastic. Amelia glanced across the desk to her father. Blue eyes met blue eyes and held for a moment before Amelia looked away. She pulled her tote bag from her shoulder and placed it on the cluttered desk. Hands on her slender hips, she faced Nick.

"I should go out and come in again," she said with forced cheerfulness. "I feel I've just walked into a morgue. Has somebody died?"

"In a manner of speaking," replied Nick, without looking up.

"And what's that supposed to mean?"

Nick remained silent.

Joe rubbed his fingers in his eyes. "We have something to tell you, Amelia," he said finally.

"For the record or off the record?" Amelia's tone was sharp as she looked from one to the other. Her eyes landed on the whisky bottle. "Do I need some of that to fortify me?"

"Joe looked up. "What?"

"The whisky, Joe! Do I need some to fortify me?"

Joe shook his head. "No, I shouldn't think so." He glanced across at Nick. "Do you want to tell her, Nick, or shall I?"

"You tell her, Joe."

Joe's gaze switched to his daughter. "This is off the record, Amelia."

Amelia pushed a pile of papers across the desk, and perched on the corner, her pale blue skirt pulling tight across her long legs. "Tell me, *off the record*, what the hell is going on?"

Joe sighed. "Nick's visit to Bendigo unearthed more than anyone could imagine," he began.

"Like what?"

"Like a whole new identity."

Amelia stared at Nick, whose eyes were still averted. "A new identity for whom?"

"Nick, I think you should tell her."

"Can somebody please tell me!" exploded Amelia.

Nick slowly placed his glass on the desk and looked into Amelia's angry blue eyes. "When you left Bendigo, Amelia, I had a visit from Beau DuBois." The name stuck in his throat. "He showed me an old newspaper cutting." He swallowed hard. "It was about his father and... my father and a connection which led to a secret being revealed that has changed my life completely."

"What secret?" Amelia was trying very hard to be patient. She wriggled forward on her perch.

"My father was a lawyer and Beau's father was a doctor."

"Yes, I get that."

Nick took a deep breath before plunging into the murky past. "The newspaper cutting was about my father defending Beau's father in a case involving a female patient. He was exonerated."

"So what's the problem?" Amelia was becoming exasperated.

"The problem, so I found out later from my father, goes back a few more years – back to when I was born..."

Amelia listened attentively as Nick revealed what his father had told him, and she didn't speak, even when his voice tailed off and once again, he was unable to meet her gaze.

Finally, she took a deep breath and reaching forward, took his hand. "I'm sorry I wasn't there for you, Nick," she said gently as she squeezed his fingers.

"It wouldn't have changed anything," sighed Nick.

"No, I know it wouldn't, but at least you would have had someone in your corner, so to speak." Amelia shook her head, making her short dark hair bounce. "That is truly unbelievable... How are your parents now that they have finally spoken out about this?"

Nick shrugged. "I don't know," he said bitterly. "I didn't hang around long enough to find out."

"You'll have to face them sooner or later, Nick," said Joe gruffly. "Maybe they deserve a little compassion. After all, it would have been a very difficult situation."

"Compassion!" spat Nick. "What compassion did they show all those years ago? It was a criminal act, and I'll *never* forgive them." He stared at the two watching him closely. "*Never*, do you hear me?"

Silence dragged across the room, as they all stared blankly at one another. Amelia was the first to speak when the scratching of the wall clock became intolerable.

"So what do you propose to do now, Nick?"

His eyes searched her face, as if he expected to find the answer there, but her blue eyes merely questioned him. He shrugged.

"I don't know," was all he said.

"I have a suggestion," said Joe as the silence lapsed again. "Clarence Bonner-Smythe has invited both of you for dinner at Mario's, (down on the quayside) tonight, and I think you should go."

Nick dragged his eyes away from Amelia's face. "I – I'm not sure that that's a good idea."

"I think it sounds wonderful, Nick!" Amelia's eyes were shining, as she reached once more for Nick's hand. "I've always wanted to go to Mario's – exquisite food, I believe."

"Yes, it's an excellent restaurant, but..."

"No 'buts', Nick – we're going." Amelia glanced at her father. "What time, Joe?"

"Seven, I think."

Amelia looked up at the ancient clock. It read 3:20. "Is that clock right, Joe?"

Joe pulled out his pocket watch, looked at it and up at the clock. "Yes, Amelia. I know it sounds rather arthritic, but it keeps perfect time."

Amelia smiled fondly at him. "Are you invited too, Joe?"

"Me?" Joe spluttered. "At Mario's? I don't think so, Amelia."

"But were you invited?" Amelia insisted, her blue eyes wide.

"Yes, I was, but..."

Amelia groaned. "Then we're all going, and that's the end of it!"

"I don't have a clean shirt," said Nick helplessly. "And I don't have any money on me."

Amelia brushed that aside. "We have a couple of hours to make you both respectable, so let's do this. We'll find a department store, and I don't want to hear any excuses from either of you."

Joe and Nick glanced at one another.

"Amelia has had the last word, I'm afraid, Nick. We'd better do as we are told."

Dinner At Mario's

At seven o'clock the trio crossed the drawbridge over the water and into Mario's. The lights from the restaurant shimmered in the water beneath them, as they trod carefully on the planks. Amelia had miraculously managed to have the two men suitably attired for the occasion, in crisp white shirts and formal black blazers. She was satisfied that they looked presentable enough for the fashionable crowd who would be milling around Mario's. Her final words to Joe had been to make sure he remembered his manners, and if he wasn't sure what cutlery to use, to follow Nick's lead. Joe had snorted at this and muttered something like "I have dined with the hoi polloi before, Amelia." Both Nick and Amelia had smiled at that, and Amelia had spontaneously kissed her father's cheek.

Amelia had chosen to wear a silky off-the-shoulder gown of a rich peacock blue, which skimmed her slight figure and brought out the colour in her eyes. She secretly noted the stunned look on Nick's face when she had appeared at the door of Joe's office, where the two men had been left to get ready. Her cheeks flushed.

She took Nick's arm now, as they stepped into the doorway of the restaurant. The happy buzz of many conversations greeted them as they waited to be shown their table. A young man in a black satin waistcoat and carrying a bundle of menus greeted them cordially.

"Good evening, sirs and madam." He smiled, showing white, even teeth. "Do you have a booking?"

"Mr Bonner-Smythe is expecting us, I believe," said Joe quickly, after a discreet nudge from Amelia.

The young man's face lit up. "Oh, yes. Follow me, please."

They followed him as he scurried between the tables until he came to one that looked out over the harbour. Light reflections shimmered and wavered on the gently moving water, and Clarence and Angela sat watching as the last ferry passed by on its way to the quay.

Clarence rose from his seat as his visitors approached, his smile warm as he reached out a hand to first Joe and then Nick, before acknowledging Amelia. Angela's smile was also warm as she beckoned Amelia to sit beside her.

Introductions over, they took the menus from the hovering waiter and began to peruse them. Amelia, seated beside her father, sensed his horror at the prices, and nudged her foot against his. Joe looked up sharply and met her stern gaze.

"It won't hurt your pocket for once," she whispered.

"How do you know?" he whispered back.

Clarence, sensing an issue, spoke across the table. "Tonight is on me," he said quietly.

All eyes looked at him.

"That's very generous of you, Clarence," said Joe gruffly, "but we can't let you do that."

"Nonsense!" Clarence waved a hand dismissively. "It will be my pleasure." He smiled indulgently at Angela as he spoke.

Realising that it would be bad manners to argue, Joe accepted the offer graciously.

"Thank-you, Clarence."

"That's settled! Now, does everyone eat lobster?" There was a murmur of consent. "Good! Lobster it shall be." He signalled a waiter who was hovering nearby.

After the waiter had received the meal orders, they all settled back to wait. Clarence looked at the three sitting opposite him and was immediately reminded of the meal he had shared with Beau and Jess on the evening before their marriage. That was the night he had carried the heartfelt letter of apology from Celia to Jess, after all the trouble she had caused. He realised that that had been a turning point in Celia's life. Her husband, Matthew, was desperately ill, and if she was to make a success of his medical Clinic and Serendipity Lodge (where many returned soldiers had been rehabilitated) then she needed to stop thinking about herself. Clarence had supported her through this, and Matthew's ultimate death, and he was pleased to see that at last Celia had gone from selfish to selfless, almost. There would always be certain traits in her character that would flare up from time to time, because she was too much like her mother, but he was satisfied that she was finally on the right track.

Clarence looked across the table with its snowy white linen cloth and caught Nick's eye. He smiled.

"Well, Nick, I have filled Angela in on your extraordinary story, and I'm hoping she can put your mind to rest about Beau. She hasn't known him as long as we have, but she might have snippets of information that we don't have."

Nick looked into Angela's warm brown eyes, and immediately felt drawn to her. He wondered fleetingly about her relationship with Clarence, because she was obviously a lot younger than him, but that thought vanished as Angela began to speak.

"Nick, I have to say that I was deeply shocked when Clarence told me what had happened to you recently. Having seen Beau's trauma first-hand when he discovered the truth about his father, I can fully understand your – grief I suppose you could call it." She smiled sadly. "I have a patisserie just a few blocks from here, and Beau rented a room next door for a while. I got to know him, because he would come in for breakfast every morning and we developed a friendship." She giggled. "We had this little joke between the two of us. Because he has a French name, and I sell French pastries, we would greet each other in French. 'Bonjour!' he would say, and I would reply 'Bonjour, monsieur!' So it would go on, and customers used to look sideways at us." She sighed. "I do miss those days."

"Tell Nick about Jess's visit," prompted Clarence.

"Oh, yes, when Beau told me his fiancé was coming from Bendigo for a visit, I was curious to know what kind of woman he had chosen. I had already met Celia, his ex-wife." She cast a sidelong glance at Clarence.

"Angela wasn't impressed with Celia," laughed Clarence. "They still don't see eye to eye, but fortunately we have called an uneasy truce."

"Yes." Angela raised her eyebrows. "I met Jess and was immediately drawn to her. She was sweet and kind and just what Beau needed. I could see that they were very much besotted with one another." She paused. "When Jess caught the Spanish Flu, Beau was absolutely devastated that he might lose her, and he fought for her life like a man possessed. She came through it, all thanks to Beau. That was when they decided that they would get married straight away, and not waste any more time. I helped them with their plans, and it was a beautiful wedding, out at serendipity Lodge, where Beau was working." Angela leaned forward and looked straight into Nick's eyes. "If you want to know what kind of man Beau is, I can tell you categorically that you will not find a finer more honest man in this world. I would stake my life on him, and I know Jess would agree." She spread her hands. "What more can I tell you? What went on in the past has gone and there's nothing can be done about it, but you have a chance now to get to know some very fine people. I know them all, and I'm proud to call them friends. You are still the same person, Nick, whatever name you choose to go by."

There was silence around the table as Angela's words sank in, and they all had a chance to ponder on it when their meals arrived. It was time to eat the delicious seafood that Clarence had ordered - shrimp cocktails followed by whole lobsters. There was much cracking of shells as each person picked a way towards the soft white flesh. Laughter increased as juice spurted on to the pristine tablecloth. Even Joe felt more relaxed than he thought he might have, as he tucked a large white table napkin under his chin. Conversation was down to a few words muttered about the quality of the food, and the courses continued until finally a tangy orange soufflé cleansed their palates, and they all sat back, well sated and content.

"I must say that was the finest meal I've had in a long time," said Joe loudly, as he made a final sweep across his chin with the napkin.

"I'm pleased to hear you say that Joe." Clarence sat back on his chair and folded his napkin carefully on the side plate. "We're never disappointed here, are we, Angela?" He beamed at her.

"No, Clarence, we're not." Angela returned his smile, which was not lost on those around them.

Amelia turned to Nick as Clarence summoned the waiter.

"What do you plan on doing tonight, Nick? Are you going home?"

"How can I?" He turned to Joe. "I might doss with you tonight, Joe, and then maybe tomorrow I'll feel like going back – but only to collect a few personal things."

Joe shrugged. "Suit yourself, Nick. You're welcome to stay with me, but you'll have to face your parents sooner or later."

"I know, but I need a little time to think – to let it all sink in."

"Are you going to speak to Beau?" The question came from Angela.

"Yes, I'll call him tomorrow."

"Good. He needs to know."

"So does Charlotte," muttered Nick.

"Talk to Beau first." Angela smiled softly.

An awkward silence ensued, broken finally by Clarence. "I've just ordered coffee," he said quietly.

Conversation took a turn to more general topics as coffee was served and the evening wound down. Angela lifted the mood by talking about business at the patisserie, and how the patrons were beginning to come back after the flu epidemic. Clarence smiled indulgently at her as she spoke, and his adoration of her was obvious to all those listening. She missed the camaraderie that she'd had with Beau, but she giggled as she talked about the man who was now living in Beau's apartment. He was an Irishman with a good set of lungs and an unending supply of Irish songs that he shared with the neighbourhood. Angela's cheeky imitation of his accent brought smiles all around, and even Nick was amused.

Clarence was the first to push his chair back from the table, and with a sigh, rose to his feet.

"I have a big day tomorrow, out at Serendipity," he said as he pushed in his chair, "so if you don't mind, Angela and I will be on our way."

Joe removed the napkin from his shirt collar and placed it carefully on the table. "Thank-you, Clarence, for a wonderful evening." He held out his hand, which was gripped firmly. "One day I will return the favour."

Clarence laughed softly. "You're very welcome, Joe." His eyes flicked to Nick, who was also rising from his seat. "I hope you can get all this sorted out amicably, Nick."

"Yes, so do I." Nick smiled ruefully.

"Would you good folk like a ride to wherever you're going? I have the car parked nearby."

"Nick and I will walk, thanks all the same, Clarence," said Amelia quickly as she smiled apologetically at Nick.

Clarence nodded. "And you, Joe? Can I drop you off at home?"

Joe nodded, sensing that Amelia wanted to be alone with Nick. "Thank-you, Clarence, that would be very much appreciated." He glanced at Amelia and received a grateful smile in response.

Minutes later, after having said their goodbyes, Nick and Amelia stepped it out along the quayside, their footsteps echoing in the quiet of the evening. Amelia had draped a black woollen shawl around her shoulders as the sea breeze was cool, and she tucked her arm in Nick's as they walked.

There was silence between them for some moments, until they reached the end of the promenade way, and were faced with a rocky climb up to the road. Amelia pulled Nick to a halt, and turning him to face her, wrapped her arms around him. Nick sighed as he pressed his face into her sweet-smelling neck and circled her waist with his hands.

"It's so good to see you, Nick," murmured Amelia.

"Even under these circumstances?" responded Nick slowly, lifting his head.

"Yes, even under these circumstances." Amelia looked into his eyes. "This hasn't made the slightest bit of difference, Nick, to the man you are. You're Nick Armitage, and as far as I'm concerned, that will never change."

"But you know what my parents did, Amelia. I can't condone that, what-ever the circumstances."

"I know you can't, Nick, but you can't change it, either. There's no way *you* can make it right."

"No, unfortunately."

"Go and see your parents tomorrow." Amelia pulled her arms from around Nick and placed her hands against his chest. A slow smile spread across her face. "Are you really going to doss with Joe tonight?"

Nick shrugged. "Where else can I go?"

"I have a suggestion." Her blue eyes searched his.

"And what is that?"

"You can doss with me."

Nick was silent for a moment. "Amelia, I don't think that's a very good idea."

"Why not?" she demanded, her blue eyes glittering in the semi darkness.

Nick sighed. "I'm not very good company at the moment."

Amelia's smile was seductive. "We can change that," she whispered eagerly.

"What will Joe say?"

Amelia placed her hands on her hips. "Nick, I am twenty-eight years old, and Joe has had nothing to do with my life for a very long time. I don't care what Joe says!" She paused. "Besides, my place is a lot tidier than Joe's."

Nick grinned for the first time that night. "I'm sure it is," he muttered.

"Is that a 'yes'?"

"Alright, it's a 'yes'."

Amelia wrapped her arms around his neck. "You won't be sorry, Nick Armitage," she murmured against his lips.

*

After detouring to check in with Joe, who (incidentally) was not surprised by the turn of events, Nick and Amelia walked the several blocks to Amelia's apartment. It was in a slightly more up-market area of the city, where trees lined the streets and gaslights had been replaced with electricity. The apartment was a semi-detached red brick terrace with a double storey and wrought iron balcony.

Amelia unlocked the front door and they stepped into the long narrow passage that led to a staircase. Along one side of the passage, Nick saw a lounge, with comfortable dark blue fabric armchairs, and a dining room set with a polished table and six straight-backed dining chairs. Beyond the staircase he spotted the door to the kitchen and another door, which he presumed led to a bathroom. It was all very compact and neat and so typical of Amelia.

The one thing that puzzled him was that it was not so very far away from Joe's place of residence, and yet the two had hardly seen each other over the years. That was a shame, because from what Nick had seen of the two of them together, there was a certain camaraderie and affection.

Amelia kicked her high-heeled shoes off at the foot of the stairs, threw her shawl across the banister and turned to Nick.

"Does it meet with your approval?" she asked provocatively.

"It's very nice."

"A bit of a step up from Joe's place, don't you think?"

Nick smiled. "You are two very different individuals," was all he said, in defence of his colleague.

"Hm," murmured Amelia. "You *would* say that." She took his hand. "Come on, I'll show you what's upstairs."

Nick followed her up the narrow carpeted staircase, knowing full well what was upstairs. Off the landing were two bedrooms and another bathroom, all tastefully decorated in pinks, trimmed with a deep blue. They stood together awkwardly in the doorway of the bedroom where a large double bed dominated the small space. Nick looked down at Amelia's eager upturned face, and a slight smile curved his lips. He had been too busy over the past few years to take much notice of girls, and his experience with them had happened long ago, during his college years. Should he make this clear to Amelia, or just let nature take its course?

As if reading his mind, Amelia laughed up at him. "Should I take the first step, Nick?" Her fingers lingered on the buttons of his shirt.

"That won't be necessary," he whispered huskily, as his sudden desire for her banished his misgivings.

Scooping her up in his arms, Nick carried her across the room to the big bed, and there he laid her gently on the covers. As his hands fumbled with the soft silken fabric of her dress, Amelia was undoing his belt. The air was suddenly electric as clothing was removed and their bodies came together in that perfect moment of sexual unity.

Hearts hammering together, they lay in that euphoric state for several minutes before Amelia reluctantly stirred. She smoothed her hands over the thick black hairs of Nick's chest and sighed deeply.

"I don't know what you were worried about," she murmured.

Nick laughed. "It's been a long time," he admitted. "In fact it's been a very long time."

"No girlfriends?"

"No, not since college."

"Saving yourself, were you?"

"No. I just didn't have the time." He gazed into those aquamarine eyes. "And of course, the right girl didn't come along, until now."

"Until now?"

"You heard me." His arms tightened around her slender body, and she snuggled into him.

"For me, too," she whispered against his chest.

*

The following morning, Amelia was up and dressed while Nick still slept. She crept into the bedroom, carrying her shoes, and leaned over him.

"Nick," she breathed into his ear. There was no movement from Nick, so she tried again. "Nick!"

He stirred and lifted his face from the pillow. Turning his head slightly, he blinked up at Amelia.

"What time is it?" he asked, groggy with sleep.

"It's eight-thirty," whispered Amelia, "and I have to go to work."

"Oh." Nick struggled into a sitting position.

"It's alright." Amelia placed a hand on his chest. "You can stay there, but unfortunately I have to go." She smiled. "Thank-you for last night, Nick."

"Satisfactory?" Nick grinned ruefully.

"More than satisfactory." She pulled on her high-heeled shoes. "Oh, and Nick?"

"Yes." Nick rubbed his hands through his tousled hair.

"Please go and see your parents today. Yes?"

Nick looked into those mesmerizing eyes, and knew he was cornered. "Yes, I will."

"Thank-you, Nick." Amelia brushed a quick kiss across his mouth. "I'll see you tonight?"

Nick nodded. "Hey, what about a proper kiss?"

Amelia smiled from the doorway. "I don't want to smudge my lipstick."

She blew him a kiss and then was gone.

Nick groaned and rolled over on to his back. He wasn't looking forward to returning to the family home, but he knew he had to, after storming out of there the previous night. What could he possibly say that would mollify the situation? He closed his eyes and his mother's ravaged face drifted before his consciousness. *"Please, Nick, try to understand,"* was all she said as he stared, disbelieving, at the both of them. Try to understand? How could he?

Nick lay for a few moments before throwing back the blankets. His thoughts turned to Amelia and all the sweetness of the previous night. He groaned and swinging his legs over the edge of the bed, stood up and scratched his head.

After dressing in the same clothes he'd worn the previous evening, Nick wandered around Amelia's home, familiarizing himself with the layout. There were two bedrooms and a small bathroom upstairs, all neat and tidy, like Amelia, except for the big bed of course. Nick looked at it ruefully. Making beds was not one of his strong points, but he figured if he wanted to stay on the right side of Amelia, then he'd better straighten the covers and plump up the pillows. He stood back and surveyed his handiwork. It looked satisfactory to him.

Hunger sent him downstairs, and he foraged in the kitchen for something to eat. There was nothing, and Nick wondered what Amelia survived on. She must have eaten before she left for work, but there was no evidence that she had. Nick shrugged and after finding the front door keys on the kitchen table, headed out and down the steps to the street. If he wanted to eat, he would have to find some shops close by, or prevail upon his mother to feed him. He didn't want to do that, so he wandered along the street to see what he could find.

Several blocks closer to the inner city, Nick found a patisserie and pulled open the wire door. The air inside was pungent with the smell of freshly baked bread, and Nick's hunger pangs increased. People were lined up in front of the counter and business was brisk. Nick joined the queue, as he searched in his pockets for some change. His wallet was at his parents' place, and all he could find in loose change was five shillings. That might buy him a sandwich and a cup of tea, he mused.

It was his turn to be served and he looked up to find himself staring into Angela Rickard's brown eyes. She smiled widely; her cheeks flushed with the warmth from the ovens.

"Nick!" she exclaimed. "This is a surprise. Where did you spring from?"

"I – er – I stayed in town last night," stuttered Nick, "and not being able to find any food in the cupboards, I came looking for some breakfast."

"You've come to the right place," laughed Angela. "What would you like?"

"Well - er - that's the problem, Angela." Nick lowered his voice. "I have left my wallet out at my parents' place and find I have only five shillings to my name. I hope that will buy a sandwich and a cup of tea."

Angela grinned. "It certainly will, Nick. If you'd like to find a table, I'll see that you get breakfast."

Nick handed over the five shillings in loose change, and grinning sheepishly, made his way to the back of the shop where small tables were laid with red and white checked tablecloths. Nick found a secluded one and sat down. For a moment he wanted to hide. He had no money; his clothes were rumpled and he was masquerading under a name that was not his. How much worse could things get?

It was no longer than five minutes, before Nick looked up to see Angela hovering over him, a tray in her hands.

"Here you are, Nick." She placed the tray on the table. "Wrap yourself around this."

"Thank-you, Angela. I am indebted to you, I'm sure." The tray contained a plate with thick toasted sandwiches and a large mug of tea.

Angela pulled out the chair opposite and sat facing Nick. "It'll fill a hole," she said lightly.

Nick bit into a toasted cheese and ham sandwich and nodded his satisfaction. "Good," he muttered.

Angela smiled before becoming serious as she leaned towards him. "I'm sorry I couldn't be of any more help last night, Nick."

Nick finished what was in his mouth and wiped it with a napkin before he spoke. "That's alright, Angela. I'm not expecting miracles." He shrugged. "I have to face my parents again today and…"

"And you're not looking forward to that?"

"Nick sighed. "No."

"Well, you've all had time to think about it, so hopefully you can now have a rational conversation."

Nick stared into Angela's sympathetic brown eyes. "I'll have to tell them that I must talk to Beau. They might not want me to do that, but it's important, because I'm certain he has already put two and two together."

"And made four?"

"Possibly."

Angela reached over and took his hand, squeezing it tightly. "Beau will understand that this is not your fault, Nick."

"It doesn't make it any easier, Angela."

"I know, but the sooner it's done, the better for everyone now."

"Yes, I suppose you're right." Nick laughed harshly. "Do you know, Angela, I feel like a homeless, nameless vagrant at this moment?"

"No, you're not, Nick! You're just – finding your way through life."

"Yeah, the hard way."

Angela stood up. "Well, anyway, finish your breakfast before you go doing anything else. I'd better attend to the counter." She moved away. "Let me know what happens, Nick."

Nick nodded, turning back to his sandwich. Yes, he'd better fuel himself to be ready for whatever was going to happen.

Nick Faces His Parents

Nick walked slowly up the gravel drive towards the house that he'd lived in all his life. Suddenly it looked strange to him, and the welcome mat at the door belied the way he was feeling. He rang the doorbell as though he were a stranger. His mother appeared and stared at him through the wire door.

"Nick," was all she said.

"Hello, mother." Nick waited for her to open the door.

"Come in," said his mother eventually.

Nick stepped over the threshold. "I've come back for some of my things," he said tightly.

"Oh."

There was an awkward silence as they stared at each other.

"Where's father?"

"He's out walking with the dog."

Nick grunted. "I see." He headed for his bedroom.

"Nick!" He stopped. "Nick, please try to understand that what we did was for your welfare."

He turned. "My welfare?"

"Yes." It was just a whisper.

"No, mother." Nick's tone was icy. "What you did was wrong."

"We saved you, Nick."

"Saved me from what?"

"We saved you from a very uncertain future, Nick." Beatrice wiped her eyes on her apron.

"And you think I should be grateful for that?" Nick knew his tone was rising, but he'd only just started. "I'm going to talk to Beau. He has a right to know what happened."

Beatrice moaned. "No, Nick, please don't do that."

"Why not! I'm sure he's guessed the truth anyway."

Beatrice swayed and had to lean against the wall. Nick struggled with the anger that was rising in him, and concern for his mother. As her knees crumpled beneath her, forcing her to the floor, Nick strode forward. Grasping her beneath the arms, he lifted her effortlessly, and helped her into the cane chair that stood beside the phone table in the hallway. Beatrice looked up at him, her face streaked with tears.

"I'm begging you, Nick," she murmured.

"They have to know, mother," said Nick quietly.

There was silence before Beatrice spoke. "I know they do, Nick, but…"

She was interrupted by the appearance of Ralph bounding through the front door, followed by Hugh. The dog made straight for Nick, leaping and bounding around him in a frenzy of excitement.

"Down, Ralph!" Nick pushed the dog away.

Hugh removed his hat as he walked through the door and stopped as he saw Beatrice and Nick in the hallway. He frowned.

"What's going on?" He looked from one to the other. "Nick? Beatrice?"

"It's alright, father," said Nick tersely. "I've come home for some of my things and then I won't bother you again."

"What are you talking about?" Hugh hung his hat on the brass hook near the telephone.

"I need some space to think about what you told me, and I can't stay here."

"Where will you live?" Beatrice murmured.

"I don't know yet. I'll have to think about my options."

"Don't be foolish, Nick," said Hugh abruptly. "We are still your parents."

"According to some paperwork, perhaps, but we all know how that came about, and I have to make amends somehow."

"And how do you propose to do that?"

Beatrice interrupted. "He wants to talk to Beauregarde."

"How is that going to help?" snapped Hugh.

"Beau already suspects that there is a connection. It's time he knew how close that connection is."

"What will happen then?" whispered Beatrice.

"I don't know." Nick shrugged. "It depends how forgiving he is."

"Can't this wait, Nick, until we've had time to adjust to it?"

"No, mother, it can't. Too much time has gone by already." Nick sighed heavily. "Now if you will excuse me, I will gather up a few things and get out of your way."

As Nick turned, he heard his mother sobbing into her apron. Stealing himself, he walked the length of the passage to his room and closed the door behind him. He collapsed against it, feelings of guilt, hurt, anger and sorrow curdling inside him. His decision had been made, and he would have to live with it, whatever the consequences.

Mindlessly he gathered up clothes from his wardrobe and threw them into a battered suitcase that he'd had since his days at college. Scooping up his wallet and fobwatch from the bedside table, he stuffed them into his trouser pocket. There was nothing else he needed, so without a backward glance, he left the room.

Hugh and Beatrice were still near the door, but Beatrice had risen from the chair and Hugh was comforting her. As Nick made to walk past, Hugh grabbed him by the arm.

"I want you to think about what you are doing, Nick," he said calmly. "No good can come of this."

"Father, the can has already been opened. I have to follow it through."

"Think about what this is doing to your mother."

Nick stared at Beatrice's tear-stained face. "I'm sorry, but there's nothing I can do about that."

He walked past them, and out the wire door on to the verandah. Ralph jumped up on him as he made his way down the front steps.

"No, Ralph!" he chastised. "Stay!"

Nick crossed the front patch of lawn and on to the gravel path that led away from the house. Ralph stared forlornly after him. His parents didn't see the bitter tears he was swallowing as, back straight, he headed down the gravel path to the road.

As Beatrice tried to follow Nick, Hugh kept a restraining hand on her arm.

"No, Beatrice, let him go," he said helplessly. "What's done is done."

"He is still my son," whispered Beatrice bitterly. "I can't let him go like this."

"He has to find his own way back to the past." Hugh sighed heavily. "There will be consequences for all of us, and I think we knew that, Beatrice, when we made the decision to do what we did."

"*You* made the decision, Hugh!" Beatrice pulled away from his grip.

With faltering steps, Beatrice made her way along the passage towards the kitchen. Hugh made no attempt to follow her. Instead, he turned and watched Nick's retreating figure until he disappeared from view. His shoulders slumped. Beatrice was right, and the consequences would be all his.

*

Nick caught a tram back into the city and found himself at Joe's door. He knocked loudly. There was no answer. He put down his suitcase and sat on it. Joe probably wasn't very far away. Nick pulled his watch from his pocket. It was almost midday, which would be lunchtime for Joe, and almost certainly he would be at Gray's. He could wait, or he could go in search of his employer, which meant lugging his suitcase with him. Maybe he should catch a tram to Amelia's, drop off his case, and then head back to Gray's?

He still had Amelia's keys, so he decided that he would do that. The only trouble was that Amelia might think he was moving in permanently. He couldn't do that to her. He had to find a place of his own. Anyway, he could explain everything to her that evening, when he returned her keys.

Nick headed back on to the busy street, and bearing left, made his way in the direction of Amelia's terrace, hoping that a tram would come rattling by. He was lucky and managed to get on board one going in the right direction. He knew that getting off with a suitcase was going to be tricky, and not being familiar with the tramstops to know which one was his, Nick remained near the door.

Finally, the tram screeched to a halt in front of a Church that Nick recognised, so he jumped off with his case, making it to the footpath unscathed.

He wasn't sure that these public forms of transport were entirely safe.

Nick unlocked the door of Amelia's terrace, and walked in. He was surprised to see that Amelia had arrived home in his absence. Her shoes were at the foot of the stairs. He called out.

"Amelia!"

Amelia appeared at the head of the stairs. "Hello, Nick." She smiled down at him.

"I didn't expect to see you here." Nick dropped his suitcase and took the stairs two at a time.

"I have a spare set of keys," she explained, as he bent to kiss her cheek. "I always come home for lunch." She looked past him to his case on the floor at the foot of the stairs. Nick followed her glance.

"I need somewhere to put it," said Nick quickly. "I tried Joe's, but he wasn't home."

"That's alright, Nick." Amelia patted his arm. "You can stay here as long as you like. How about some lunch? I'm going to make a sandwich."

"Yes, please." It seemed a long time since he had eaten. "I had some breakfast at Angela's patisserie. It was very nice, and I couldn't find anything here."

Amelia laughed as she hurried down the stairs. "Sorry, Nick, but I don't have breakfast."

"You don't have breakfast?" Nick followed her down the stairs.

"No. I don't have time usually."

"You should, you know."

"No lectures, Nick." Amelia pushed her feet into her discarded shoes.

"Alright." Nick raised his hands in defeat, as he followed her to the kitchen.

"What would you like?" Amelia emptied the string bag that lay on the table. "You can have cheese, egg, tomato or just butter on your bread." She smiled at him. "Take your pick."

Nick grimaced. "Or we can go to Angela's place? It's only a couple of blocks away." He looked at Amelia hopefully.

Amelia looked at her watch. "Alright. You win." She picked up her set of keys from the table and shoved them into her handbag. "You can tell me all about your visit with your parents while we walk."

"There's not much to tell," said Nick as he followed Amelia out the front door and on to the street.

"Lead the way, while I listen."

As their footsteps echoed on the bitumen footpath, Nick told Amelia of his brief encounter with his parents, and what he had said to them. When he had finished, they continued walking in silence.

Amelia broke the spell. "So you're going to speak to Beau?"

"I have to. My silence is not going to make it all go away. Beau has his suspicions anyway."

"You have to do what you think is best, Nick."

"Best for whom?" Nick thought of his mother. "Not everybody, that's for certain."

"No, it will be painful for some."

They had reached Angela's patisserie. Nick opened the wire door and followed Amelia into the warmth of the shop. Angela spotted them from behind the counter and smiled warmly.

"Back again, Nick? Hello, Amelia."

Nick approached the counter. "Yes, back again, Angela. We'd like something tasty for lunch, and I do have money this time."

Amelia dug him in the ribs. "I don't have anything to Nick's liking at my place," she laughed.

"I see." Angela glanced from one to the other. "Well, why don't you both find a table and I'll see what I have to tempt you. I have some freshly baked beef pies."

"Sounds wonderful. We'll have one each, thanks Angela, and a pot of tea, please."

Amelia opened her mouth to protest, but Nick took her arm and guided her to the table he had occupied earlier.

"Angela's pies look very moreish," he whispered. "You might not want to stop at one."

"We'll see." Amelia sat down at the table and looked around her. The atmosphere in the little shop was vibrating with the happy sound of voices, as customers bought their loaves and chatted with Angela. "It's certainly a friendly place," she mused, almost to herself.

"It is," said Nick. "I can see why Beau frequented the place."

"When are you going to speak with him, Nick?"

"When we've had lunch, I'll track Joe down, and make a call from his place."

Amelia smiled. "Good." She paused. "I'll have to go back to work. When you've finished what you have to do, go back to my place… and Nick?"

"Yes?"

"I'll cook tea for us if you can get the stove going." She grimaced. "I don't use it very often."

"Do you have any wood?" queried Nick.

"There's some in the back yard – not a lot, but there should be enough."

Nick's brow furrowed. "I have a feeling you don't look after yourself very well, Miss Hudson."

"Well enough."

"Hm."

Angela arrived with a laden tray, which she placed carefully on the table. "Enjoy your lunch." She beamed at them before heading back to the counter.

"Thank-you, Angela!" called Nick to her retreating back.

"She's nice," said Amelia as she removed the cups and saucers from the tray and began pouring the tea.

"She is. I wonder what the story is with her and Clarence?"

Amelia looked up quickly. "It's not our business, Nick."

"I know. I'm just curious." Nick removed the plates and cutlery from the tray and placed it on the floor beside his chair. "I have met his daughter, and she's much the same age as Angela." He attacked his pie with the knife and fork.

Amelia shook her head. "You investigators have to find a story in everything, don't you?"

"Not much different to a reporter," answered Nick, before placing the fork in his mouth.

"Touche!" Amelia followed suit with the pie, suddenly realising that she was hungry.

They were silent while they ate. Nick was the first to put down his knife and fork and wipe his mouth with the linen napkin.

"That was delicious, wouldn't you agree?"

"It was." Amelia took a sip of her tea. "You can bring Joe along with you tonight, if you like."

"I can?" Nick was surprised.

"Yes. He is my father, Nick."

"I know, but…"

"But we haven't always seen eye to eye, that's true." She shrugged. "Maybe I'm maturing and want to reconnect – maybe."

"Alright. I'll drag him along."

"Good!" Amelia stood up, brushing crumbs from her skirt. "I must go, Nick. Thank-you for the lunch, and I'll see you and Joe later." She pushed in her chair. "You know, Nick, if this story was 'for the record', I could quickly go from being a humble female reporter, to a high-profile journalist."

"But it isn't 'for the record', Amelia." Nick's eyes narrowed as he stared at her.

"I know, and there's not much chance of me being anything more than a humble reporter, but it was a nice thought." She smiled at him. "Don't worry, Nick, I'm not going to say anything unless you want me to." She sighed. "Today I must interview an old lady whose cat has returned, after being missing for six weeks. Exciting, isn't it?" She rolled her eyes.

"Yes, it certainly is, now off you go, Amelia. You don't want to keep the old lady waiting."

"I'd be ruining my reputation. I'll see you later today, Nick."

Nick stood briefly as Amelia headed for the door. As he resumed his seat, Angela approached and picked up the tray.

"All finished?" She began to stack the empty crockery and used cutlery on the tray.

"Yes, thank-you, Angela. It was very nice."

"You're welcome, Nick, or as I used to say to Beau – 'Je vous en prie.'"

"I don't speak French, Angela."

"Neither do I – just a phrase here and there." Angela laughed.

"I'm going to talk to Beau this afternoon."

Angela's expression became serious. "You're doing the right thing, Nick." She picked up the tray. "I never cease to be amazed at how life twists and turns in the most extraordinary ways."

"It doesn't please everybody though, Angela."

"No, unfortunately."

*

Nick finally caught up with Joe, as he wandered slowly along the street, in the direction of Joe's residence. He was in an inner-city suburb, and the terraces were crowded together, rather like narrow brick sentinels, all supporting each other in a wavering line along the edge of the Parramatta River. Children played hopscotch in the street; chalk lines scratched into the asphalt. Nick ducked his head as a ball headed in his direction, narrowly missing him.

"Sorry, mister!" called out a young lad of about twelve, dressed in short pants and a grubby fairaisle pullover.

"So you should be, Harold." Nick turned to see Joe retrieving the ball, which he threw to the young lad before catching up with Nick. "They've got nowhere else to play." He grinned apologetically.

"No harm done." Nick shrugged as he fell into step with Joe.

"It's not what you'd call the best end of town, but it's close to my office, and I only spend as much time here as I have to. Anyway, you didn't come here to talk about my neighbourhood."

"No."

They had reached Joe's front door, and he shoved a key in the lock. "Come in."

Nick stepped into the hallway, and instantly inhaled the stale smell of dampness and tobacco smoke. He stifled a cough, but Joe noticed.

"Sorry, mate," he apologised. "The place is closed most of the time. It probably needs an airing."

Joe led the way into the cluttered sitting room, which was in much the same state as his office. He pushed a pile of papers off the shabby sunken couch and gestured for Nick to sit.

Nick felt the springs beneath him, and he shifted uncomfortably.

"Sorry," laughed Joe. "Can I get you a cup of tea, or something stronger?"

Nick shook his head. "No thanks, Joe. I'm here to make a call to Beau DuBois."

"Ah, I see." Joe removed another pile of papers from a one-time grand red velvet wing-backed chair and sat heavily. "You want to tell him the good news, eh?" The chair creaked beneath his weight.

"Good news?" Nick laughed harshly. "It depends on the way you look at it."

"Yes indeed." Joe scratched his head. "What do you think he'll say?"

"I have no idea, Joe, but he won't be entirely surprised."

"No, I don't suppose he will be." Joe stood up. "We'll have to go around to my office to make that call. I don't have a telephone here." He laughed. "The Private Investigative business is not that lucrative, Nick. Come on, it's only a short walk."

Within minutes the two were climbing the stairs to Joe's office. Nick suddenly realised that he didn't have a direct number for Beau. He only had a number for the Grey Goose.

"Joe, have you got Beau's home number? I did notice that they had a telephone in the hallway."

"I think so." Joe shuffled amongst the pile of papers on his desk, before rummaging in the drawers. It took a few minutes, but he eventually came up with the right piece of paper. "Here it is!"

"Joe, you need to do something about your filing system," said Nick, taking the scrap of paper from his employer's hand. "How do you know where anything is?"

Joe grinned. "I can usually put my hand on what I need."

Nick shook his head as he walked across to the telephone. He straightened out the piece of paper, before lifting the receiver and turning the handle. A bright female voice came through the line.

Nick went through the exchange to the Bendigo exchange, and eventually he heard the ringing on the other end. He waited. It was Jess's voice that answered. "Hello. Jess DuBois speaking."

"Jess, it's Nick Armitage."

There was a delay before he heard her voice again. "Nick! Oh, you've arrived in Sydney then?"

"Yes, I've been here a couple of days. Is Beau at home? I need to talk to him."

"No, he's at the surgery today. Can I give him a message?"

"I'd rather not, Jess. I need to speak with him."

"Oh. He will be home this evening, if that's any help."

"This line is not clear, Jess, so I'll hang up and try later. You did say he'd be home this evening?"

"Yes."

There was a delay. "Thanks Jess. 'Bye for now."

Nick hung up the receiver. "Beau won't be home until this evening. I think that's what Jess said."

"You'll have to try him again then." Joe picked up his keys from the desk. "Come on, we'll go to Gray's for a drink."

Nick followed Joe out on to the street and fell into step beside him.

"By the way, Joe, Amelia has invited you for tea tonight."

Joe stopped in his tracks and stared at Nick. "She's what?"

"She's invited you for tea."

Joe laughed. "Well, well! So, the old man is not so bad after all?"

"It seems that way."

"Don't tell me she's going to cook?"

Nick shrugged as they continued walking. "I don't know. We'll see, shall we?"

Joe was still chuckling when they reached Gray's Hotel and walked through to the bar.

*

Jess replaced the receiver and stood for a moment in the passage, contemplating Nick's phone call. What could he want after only being gone for two days? It must be important if he didn't want to relay a message. Perhaps he'd spoken to his father and found out something about the courtcase all those years ago? Jess heard a noise at the other end of the passage and saw Charlotte leaning on her crutches.

"Who was that, Jess?"

"It was Nick Armitage."

"What did he want?" Charlotte made her slow way towards Jess.

"I don't know, Charlotte. He wants to speak with Beau. He's going to call again this evening."

Charlotte was silent for a moment. "Perhaps he's found out something."

"My thoughts exactly, but we mustn't pre-empt this. It could be something else entirely."

"Maybe." Charlotte's face told Jess that she doubted that.

Jess patted her on the arm. "Come on, let's get some tea ready for the hungry hordes when they all arrive home." She smiled at Charlotte's drawn face. "We'll find out in good time what Nick has to say, and in the meantime, is that Lottie I hear bellowing for her aunt?"

"I believe it is."

Beau's decision

Jess and Charlotte stood silently in the passage, listening to Beau as he spoke to Nick. One side of a conversation is not always conclusive, but they conceded that the subject was serious, and personal, as Beau's expression was haggard and he stared, unblinking, at the two women.

Finally, he replaced the receiver and his head was lowered as he stood silently, staring at the telephone.

"Well?" said Charlotte sharply. "What was that all about?"

Beau rubbed his hands across his forehead. "I must go to Sydney," he said huskily.

"Why?" Charlotte moved towards him on her crutches. "What did Nick have to say?"

Beau sidestepped Charlotte and moved into the bedroom. "Where's my suitcase, Jess?"

Charlotte followed. "Tell me what's going on, Beau!"

"I can't." Beau was at the wardrobe, pulling shirts and trousers from their hangers. "Not yet."

Jess appeared in the doorway and could sense the tension between Beau and his sister. She moved swiftly to the big double bed, and kneeling, pulled a case out from beneath it. "Here it is, Beau."

Beau hauled the case on to the bed and began throwing his clothes into it. Jess quietly began to fold the clothing neatly, as he would have done had he not been so agitated. Charlotte stood tall on her crutches, glaring at him as he searched in drawers for underwear.

"Beau! Stop what you are doing and talk to me! Please!"

Jess stood back as Charlotte confronted her brother. Beau straightened his back, and his face was set in hard lines as he stared at his sister.

"You will know, Charlotte, as soon as I find out the truth for myself. I need to be absolutely sure of the facts before I pass on any information." His voice trembled. "I'm sorry." He clicked the catches of the case before looking at his watch. "If I go now, I'll catch the last train to Melbourne." He looked at Jess. "Let Raymond Simmons know, Jess, that I'll be away from the surgery for a few days." He smiled wanly. "Anything else will have to wait."

"Do you have to go right now, Beau?" asked Jess "What about Phyllis and her child? Aren't you supposed to see them tomorrow?"

"Raymond is going to deal with that." Beau picked up his case. "Fortunately, everything has been arranged. Charles is going to take Phyllis and Hope to the surgery tomorrow afternoon."

Jess moved swiftly to his side. She had a feeling of déjà vu as she kissed him. "Take care, Beau, and let us know the minute you arrive. Do you have money?"

"Yes." Beau looked down on her, and for a moment his eyes glistened. "I don't know how long I'll be gone, Jess." He turned to Charlotte, who was still glaring at him. "We will know the truth soon, Charlotte, I promise."

With that he grabbed his hat from the hook behind the door, jammed it on his head and strode away from the two women. They heard the front door slam behind him. Charlotte had tears in her eyes as she turned to face Jess.

"What is he not telling me, Jess?" she whispered.

"I don't know, Charlotte, but we're not going to solve anything standing here. We have children to feed," she said wearily. "And then I'd better give Raymond Simmons a call."

*

Beau ran across the pedestrian bridge just as the train whistle blew. Steam obscured his view as he raced along the platform, searching for an open door. A man saw his plight and a door opened just in time for him to jump on board, dragging his case behind him. He was gasping as he clung to a rail. The train shuddered beneath him, and a hand grasped his arm.

"That was a close one," he heard a man's voice say.

Beau nodded in response, unable to speak for the moment. The train gave a jolt and the two men were thrown against the carriage wall.

"Good grief!" exclaimed the stranger. "It's going to be a rough ride by the feel of things."

Beau regained his footing. "Just gathering speed, I'd say," he said hoarsely.

The stranger laughed. "More likely the engine driver wants to get home." He was a young man possibly in his early thirties, and sporting an impressive waxed moustache. His fair hair was immaculately groomed, with a centre parting. Tight curls formed a halo around his head. Beau noticed that he wore a striped college blazer and cream flannel trousers.

"Come on." The young man grinned at Beau. "Let's find a seat." He flung open the door to the carriage and made his way along the corridor, peering into each compartment as he went.

Beau followed, rather reluctantly. He would have preferred to have a compartment to himself, where he could think about what lay ahead for him in Sydney, but the young man seemed eager to have company.

"Here's an empty one." He slid the door open and stepped into the compartment, where he flopped down on one of the leather seats, breathing a sigh of relief.

Beau lifted his case on to the luggage rack above and sat opposite his companion.

"What takes you to Melbourne?" The young man glanced up at Beau's case. "Going home?"

"No," said Beau carefully. "I'm heading up to Sydney, hopefully on tomorrow morning's train."

"Oh!" The young man leaned forward, holding out his hand. "I'm sorry,

I should have introduced myself. My name's Warwick Somerton."

Beau shook the outstretched hand. "Beau DuBois."

"Nice to meet you, Beau. French, eh?" Warwick leaned back against the seat.

"Australian, actually, although my grandfather was French." Beau glanced at the insignia on Warwick's blazer. It read: Highview College. "Are you heading back to college?"

Warwick wrinkled his nose. "Yes. I have another year to finish my science degree, before I move on to university to do Medicine."

Beau gave a short laugh. "I wish you all the best with that. I'm a Medical practitioner. I studied in Sydney. It's a hard road if you want to be successful."

"I say! What a coincidence!" Warwick leaned forward again. "Any tips on how to survive?"

Beau shrugged. "Not really. Be prepared for the hard slog, and don't take it lightly. You'll never make it if you're not serious about what you are doing."

"You – er – you look as though you've been in an accident." Warwick nodded towards the scar on Beau's face.

"That was the war, Warwick. Enemy shrapnel left me with this scar and ruined my chances of continuing my career as a surgeon."

"What rotten luck." Warwick looked genuinely sympathetic. "I escaped the war."

"You were lucky." Beau didn't ask *how?* Many young men managed to escape the front line, and reasons were many and varied. This always left a bitter taste in Beau's mouth.

"I wouldn't say that exactly." Warwick's expression became serious. "There have been times when I've been spat upon and accused of *shirking my duty*." He shrugged. "Not to mention the white feathers that were pushed through my letterbox."

"That's a despicable thing to do."

"It wasn't either of those things. I… I failed my medical." He took a deep breath. "I've had a heart condition since I was a child, not that it has stopped me from doing things, but they wouldn't accept me in the army."

"Oh! I'm sorry."

"You were probably thinking the same thing as everybody else, am I right?" Warwick's hazel eyes bored into Beau.

"We should never assume, Warwick, but unfortunately as humans, we are very good at it." Beau smiled thinly.

"Yes, we are." Warwick was silent for a few moments. "What takes you to Sydney, Beau?"

Beau turned to look out the window at the landscape flashing by. "Family complications. I hope I'm not gone long."

"Are you married?"

Beau turned from the window. "Yes, I am."

"Children?"

Beau smiled. "My wife and I have one daughter and my wife has three children from a previous marriage, so that makes four, if my arithmetic is correct."

"Oh, I see. You have an *instant* family."

"You could say that. What about you, Warwick? Any female attachments?"

Warwick blushed and shifted his position on the seat. "No, not at this stage. Not a good idea while I'm studying."

Beau thought briefly about his own relationship with Celia during the time of his study, and all the distractions that had occurred then. "I agree. It's not a good idea," he said quietly.

Both men turned back to watch the moving landscape as twilight descended, and conversation lapsed for some time. Beau knew that he would have to find somewhere to sleep when he arrived in Melbourne, as the next train to Sydney did not depart until early in the morning. He had been so anxious to get answers to the questions that had crowded his brain that he had not thought out a travel plan. Jess, he knew, would be concerned about him, and his previous trip to Sydney would still be clear in her mind. She had gone through hell and back wondering what had become of him when he had disappeared into his own private hell. He could not put Jess through something like that again. And then there was Charlotte, the central figure in the traumatic events - what was she going to say when he told her what he had learned from Nick? He shuddered. Thirty-two years of deception was about to be laid bare, and lives would be forever changed.

*

The journey continued in relative silence, broken only by the occasional comment about the darkening scenery that flashed by, and eventually the lights of Melbourne came into view. Beau pulled his case down from the luggage rack as the train began to slow down and smiled at his companion.

"Good luck with your studies, Warwick," he said, as he held out a hand.

"Thank-you, Beau. I hope you sort out those family complications." He gripped Beau's hand.

Together they made their way along the corridor to the end of the carriage and there they waited until the wheels ground to a halt beside the long platform.

Warwick jumped off and Beau followed. Doors opened all along the length of the train and passengers stepped on to the platform to be greeted by those who were waiting for them. As Beau glanced along the length of the train, he saw Warwick being greeted warmly by a young man. They hugged, before Warwick turned and waved to Beau. Beau waved back before the two men disappeared into the crowd. He had a sudden feeling that

Warwick's interest may not lay in young ladies. He turned and headed for the booking office. It was none of his business.

After purchasing a ticket for the early morning Albury train and its crossover to the Sydney train, Beau went in search of food. He was hungry, having missed his tea. The cafeteria was still doing business, so he selected stewed beef and mashed potatoes and a cup of tea and went to find himself a table.

The meal was overcooked, but warm and filling. His next problem was to find somewhere to sleep, so he decided that instead of traipsing the streets, he would find a seat at the station, and hope that he could get some shut eye.

There was a travellers' lounge, and Beau made himself as comfortable as he could on a bench seat. Nobody came in to disturb him, and soon he was fast asleep.

*

Beau was awakened by the sensation of being shaken on the shoulder, and a voice sounded loud in his ear.

"Hey, mate! Wake up! If you're catching the Albury train, you'd better get a move on. She leaves in five minutes."

Beau shook himself awake and stumbled to his feet. It took a moment to get his bearings, before he grabbed his case and thanked the man in the dark blue railways uniform.

"Platform 2!" shouted the man as Beau hurried away.

He found platform two where the Albury train was issuing forth steam and the whistle sounded sharp in the early morning air. Beau climbed on board and felt in his pocket for the ticket. While he was checking the carriage number, a conductor came up behind him.

"Can I help you, sir?" he enquired politely.

"Er – yes," said Beau. "I need carriage four."

The conductor smiled. "Next one to your left, sir. This is carriage five. Enjoy your journey, sir."

"Thank-you."

Beau pushed his ticket back in his pocket and headed for carriage four. As he reached the door between the carriages, the train jerked suddenly, sending him off-balance. He waited before opening the door and stepping across the boards that covered the couplings. Closing the door behind him, he leaned on it for a moment.

The corridor was empty as he made his way along the carriage, searching for an unoccupied compartment. He found one and slid the door open. After placing his case on the luggage rack, Beau shut the door and settled on to the leather seat, glad of the solitude. He wanted to be alone with his thoughts, to digest what Nick had said to him, and to be prepared for what was to come when he reached Sydney. The raw truth would be exposed at last.

The Visit With Doctor Simmons

As Beau was rattling his way towards Sydney, Billy was standing on the verandah of his mother's house, with Phyllis and Hope. They were waiting for Charles to take them to the surgery, where Doctor Simmons was to check Hope's hearing.

Billy paced restlessly along the verandah, his hands thrust deep into the pockets of his best trousers, while Phyllis watched him silently. So far there had been no sign of Sid and no word from the Reverend Mother. It was as if Sid was somewhere lying in wait for the opportunity to confront them. Perhaps he knew of their movements and was waiting for them to make a wrong move?

"For goodness sake, Billy!" Phyllis was exasperated. "Stand still, will ya? He'll be 'ere soon."

Billy stopped pacing and faced her. His thin face was clean-shaven this morning and his fair hair had been combed down with oil.

"We're sittin' ducks out 'ere on the verandah, Phyllis. If Sid's lookin' for us, 'e'll sure find us."

"Sid's not lookin' for us, ya daft idiot. 'E'da found us by now, if 'e was lookin'."

"Nah! I've known Sid a long time, Phyllis. 'E's bidin' 'is time, that's what 'e's doin'."

"Well, you wearin' out ya boot leather is not goin' t' help."

At that moment Charles arrived in his grey Chevrolet. Billy grabbed Hope from Phyllis's arms and hurried to the gate. Phyllis sighed heavily and followed him. Charles was out of the car, holding open the door for them. Billy pushed Hope into the rear seat, and turned to help Phyllis, who was holding up her skirts before stepping on the running board.

"Good mornin', Mr. Stanley," said Billy hurriedly. "It's good of ya to do this for us."

"Think nothing of it, Billy," said Charles congenially. "It's my pleasure."

Phyllis flashed him a smile as she seated herself on the rigid leather seat, and Charles lifted his hat.

Within seconds they were bouncing their way along the dirt road until they reached the main thoroughfare. Mitchell Street was heavy with traffic as they headed down towards the fountain, and Charles had to stop several times to avoid colliding with horse-driven carts.

"It's market day today," he muttered to nobody in particular. "No wonder the place is crowded."

He negotiated the big car around the fountain, and along the Pall Mall until he reached the street that would take them up the hill to the surgery. Billy sat tapping his foot nervously as Charles shifted down the gears to take the hill without stalling.

Phyllis nudged Billy as the car shuddered and smiled at his obvious distress.

"What's wrong, Billy?" she whispered.

"I coulda walked as fast," muttered Billy, grabbing hold of the door as the car hit a pothole.

"Sorry!" yelled Charles above the noise of the engine.

Hope, wedged between Billy and Phyllis, squealed with delight as they bounced about on the back seat. Her chubby hands flapped in the air, and her head moved from side to side.

"Well, Hope's enjoyin' the ride, even if you're not, Billy!" laughed Phyllis, taking hold of her daughter's hands and pumping them up and down.

Billy merely grunted. This was nearly as bad as the trucks he'd ridden in during the war. At least he had never had the sensation of being thrown out on to the muddy tracks.

Finally, the car came to a halt, and Charles pulled on the brake.

"I'm going to have to speak to Council about the state of the roads," he said apologetically, climbing out of the driver's seat.

Billy scrambled out and reached for Hope. Her bottom lip quivered as she was swung into his arms, and she bellowed angrily.

"That's enough, Hope!" Phyllis took hold of Charles's hand as he helped her from the vehicle and smiled apologetically at him. "Hope enjoyed the rough ride," she murmured.

The gate that led to the surgery stood open before them, and Billy hitched the squirming Hope more securely in his arms.

"Thanks, Mr. Stanley," he muttered hoarsely. "No need for you t'wait for us. We don't know 'ow long we'll be."

"Are you sure?" Charles looked at his watch. "I can come back in an hour or so."

"Nah! We'll be right, thanks." Billy stepped through the gate and headed up the path to the surgery.

Charles looked at Phyllis. "If you need me, ask Norma Allen, the nurse, to call me," he said quietly.

Phyllis nodded. "I will. Thanks, Mr. Stanley."

Charles watched as Phyllis walked quickly after Billy, holding her skirts up from the muddy path. He looked skyward. There had been substantial rain overnight, and it looked as though the elements had not finished yet. He frowned, hoping that Billy would be considerate of Phyllis and the little one.

Billy rapped on the large brass knocker and waited. Within moments the newly painted door opened and a nurse, dressed in a blue uniform and white starched cap, stood before them. Her smile was wide as she stepped aside to let Billy and Phyllis pass.

"Good afternoon," she said brightly. "You must be Phyllis Powell, and this, I presume, is Hope?" She tickled Hope's palm as the child held out an arm towards her. Then her gaze switched to Billy. "And you are…?"

"Billy Maitland, ma'am," murmured Billy hoarsely.

The bright brown eyes studied him thoughtfully. "The child's father?"

"Er – yes, ma'am," said Billy quickly.

Phyllis looked sharply in his direction but said nothing.

"Good. I'm Norma Allen. Come this way, and I'll show you the waiting room. Doctor Simmons shouldn't be very long."

They followed Norma along the passage, where the grey linoleum squeaked beneath their feet, and she motioned them into a large airy room. The smell reminded Billy of the dressing stations during the war, and he coughed involuntarily. Norma laughed gaily.

"The smell is rather strong, isn't it? Our cleaning lady is new on the job, and I'm afraid she was rather heavy-handed with the phenyl."

"It reminded me of the war," muttered Billy.

"Oh, I see." Norma looked closely at him as he sat on one of the many straight-backed chairs that circled the room. "It wasn't easy for you boys." She paused, remembering the loss of her own husband during those terrible years. "And your voice? Was that the war?"

"Yeah. Gas." Billy shrugged. "I was one of the lucky ones."

Norma nodded. "I'll call you when Doctor Simmons is ready to see you."

"Thanks," muttered Billy.

Left alone, Phyllis sat beside Billy and swung around to face him. She stared at him for a few moments before speaking.

"You told the nurse that you're Hope's dad, Billy. Does that mean you wanna be 'er dad or were you just bein' polite?"

"I wanna be 'er dad, Phyllis." He frowned as he looked at Hope. "It's real hard t'tell, isn't it, who she belongs to?"

Phyllis smiled. "You'll make a good dad, Billy." She tucked her arm through his.

"Let's not get too comfortable with this, Phyllis. We still 'ave t'face Sid, ya know?"

"I know." Phyllis's brow puckered. "I'm surprised we 'aven't 'eard from the Reverend Mother yet."

"Sid'll just be coverin' all bases, I suspect." Billy sighed. "I wish it was all sorted."

"Y'll have t'make an honest woman of me, Billy, ya know that, don't ya?"

"Eh?"

"Y'll have t'marry me, Billy."

Billy was silent as he stared at Phyllis. Her eyes were shining.

"Yeah, I reckon I will," he said slowly.

Footsteps sounded in the passage outside the waiting room, and Norma

Allen appeared in the doorway. She smiled and gestured for them to follow her.

"Doctor Simmons will see you now," she said, leading the way to the doctor's surgery.

Tapping lightly on the door, she waited for the signal to enter.

"Come in."

Norma opened the door. "Miss Powell and Mr. Maitland, doctor," she said, ushering them ahead of her.

"Thank-you, nurse."

The door swished shut behind her and Phyllis and Billy found themselves facing Doctor Simmons. He sat behind his enormous desk, a manila folder open in front of him, and studied them over the top of heavy-framed spectacles. Billy shuffled nervously, but Phyllis lifted her chin high and met his gaze defiantly. Hope, held tightly in Billy's arms, grunted as she stretched an arm out towards the strange man who sat looking at them.

Raymond Simmons cleared his throat. "Sit down, please." He indicated the two chairs that Norma had placed before his desk.

When they were seated, he removed his spectacles, sat back on his big leather chair and folded his hands on the desk in front of him.

"Doctor DuBois has spoken to me about your... situation, and..."

"Our situation?" Phyllis glared at him. "What d'you mean?"

Raymond cleared his throat once more. "I'm sorry. That didn't come out right. What I meant to say was –er – your child's problem with her ears."

"Oh." Phyllis relaxed slightly. "Yeah, she can't 'ear properly."

Raymond nodded. "What I would like to do is examine her ears to establish whether the problem is merely a case of a build-up of wax, or whether there's something more going on there." He smiled at Hope, who was still stretching out her arms towards him. "I have a young child myself, and I know how upsetting it is when something is wrong with him."

"'E's not like Hope though, is 'e, doctor?" Phyllis was trembling. "I mean, 'e's normal, isn't 'e?"

"There, there, Phyllis, don't get all het up." Billy patted her arm anxiously. "Doctor Simmons wants t'help us, ain't that right, doctor?"

"Yes, Billy, I do, and it has nothing to do with anything, other than Hope's ears." Raymond stood and moved to the door and opened it. "Nurse Allen, could you come in here, please?"

Norma appeared at the door. "What is it, doctor?"

Raymond turned to the anxious couple. "Would you agree to your daughter going with Nurse Allen?"

Phyllis's eyes widened. "Where to? Where you takin' 'er?"

"Just along the corridor to another room, where I have equipment set up."

Phyllis and Billy looked at each other.

"Ya don't want us there?" Billy was frowning.

Norma crossed the room and held out her arms for Hope. "It's much easier if the parents aren't there, Mr. Maitland. It's less stressful for everybody." She smiled at Billy.

Reluctantly he handed the child to her and watched as Hope was carried from the room. As the door shut quietly behind them, he turned to Phyllis. Her eyes were wide and fearful.

"What do you think they're goin' t'do to 'er, Billy?" Her voice wobbled dangerously.

"I dunno, Phyllis." He patted her arm gently. "Let's wait an' see, shall we?"

Phyllis sat on the edge of the chair, every nerve attuned to hearing her little girl's bellow of fear, but there was only silence. It stretched on for several minutes, and slowly her body relaxed. She smiled at Billy and reached for his hand.

"Did ya mean it about marryin' me, Billy?" Her hazel eyes were moist.

"Course I did, Phyllis." He smiled. "Mum wants a grandchild."

Phyllis's smile suddenly became a frown. "Is that the only reason, Billy?"

He sighed. "No, Phyllis. I wanna do the right thing by ya, an' if anybody has any objections, then they might just feel the weight o'my fist."

"Ya mean Sid?"

"Course I mean Sid." He paused. "Are ya sure ya dunno who Hope's father is?"

Phyllis brushed his fingers lightly. "Such a lot was happenin' 'round that time, Billy, what with you goin' off t'fight an' all, that I can't honestly remember, but I don't *want* it t'be Sid. He's nothin' but trouble." She took a shaky breath. "So, if you really wanna be 'er dad, then that's alright with me."

Billy leaned over and kissed her trembling mouth. "An' it's alright with me."

At that moment the door opened, and Norma Allen appeared with Hope. The child was clutching a rag doll in her hands, and Norma was smiling. Billy and Phyllis leapt to their feet.

"The problem has been solved," said Norma warmly. "Doctor Simmons will be in shortly to explain what he did, and what he wants you to do in the future." She smiled down at the child in her arms.

"So she'll be alright? She'll be able t'hear?"

Norma handed Hope across to Billy. "The doctor will explain it shortly." She moved towards the door. "Now if you'll excuse me, I have a wound to dress."

With a swish of starched uniform, she was gone. Billy and Phyllis looked at each other, and Hope let out a grunting sound. Her blue eyes widened with surprise, and she repeated the sound, a little louder. A grin spread across her round features, and as she opened her mouth to let forth again, Phyllis quickly placed a hand across her face.

"She can hear, Billy!" She laughed. "Hope can hear!"

"It's a bloody miracle!" Billy whooped with delight.

"It's not exactly a miracle." Doctor Simmons appeared in the doorway. "It was a simple matter of wax removal." He moved behind his desk and began to write on a slip of paper. "What you need to do now, is get these ear drops from the pharmacy, and apply two drops to Hope's ears once a week. That will keep the wax soft, and it will be easy to remove. She needs to see me in three months' time, or earlier, if you think her hearing has diminished."

"Why is she like this, Doctor?" asked Phyllis.

"Her ear canals are very narrow, and so wax builds up quickly."

"What did ya do?" asked Billy.

"Water, Mr. Maitland."

"Water!" Phyllis wrinkled her nose. "But I thought we weren't supposed t'get water in our ears."

Raymond smiled. "You're right, Miss Powell, but sometimes, when it's done correctly, water can be very beneficial, as in Hope's case." He could see that Phyllis wasn't entirely sure about his answer. "I used a syringe, and out came the wax."

"Oh!" Phyllis giggled nervously. "No wonder ya didn't want us in there."

"No." Raymond handed her the slip of paper. "If there's nothing else I can help you with, I must get on."

"Thank-you, Doctor," said Billy earnestly. "We're very grateful."

"I'm glad it was nothing worse."

"So are we." Billy kissed Hope's forehead. "Come on, let's go and give mum the good news."

"Oh, before you go, there's something else I'd like you to do, Miss Powell." Raymond was scribbling on another slip of paper. "Here is the address and the meeting times of a group from the Red Cross. It is run by my wife, Louise, and they help young mothers, such as yourself, with all sorts of childhood problems." He shrugged. "I would like you to avail yourself of the help, even if it's only for someone to talk to…" he broke off.

"Thank-you, Doctor." Phyllis smiled as she took the slip of paper. "I'll do that."

"Good. Good."

As they stepped outside the front door, Phyllis grabbed Billy's arm.

"Shouldn't we get the nurse t' telephone Mr. Stanley?"

"Nah! Let's walk." Billy grinned. "I didn't enjoy the ride before, so I'm happy t'walk. An' we c'n stop off at the pharmacy an' get these drops f'r Hope."

"Ya'll have t'carry 'er."

"I don't care. We might go t' the park an'ave fish'n'chips. What d'ya reckon?"

"Oh, Billy!" Phyllis was ecstatic. "D'ya know how long it is since I've 'ad fish'n'chips?"

"A long time I reckon."

"A bloody long time!" Phyllis slipped her hand beneath his arm. "Let's go!"

Confrontation

It wasn't long before Phyllis and Billy were sprawled on the grass at the Rosalind Park, a newspaper full of steaming fish and chips open in front of them. Hope was content to stomp on the grass, as she made loud noises and laughed merrily. People passing by watched her with curiosity, unaware of the life-changing moment that had only recently taken place. Phyllis noted their sympathy as they turned their attention to her. She wanted to shout out to them that she didn't want their pity. She loved her little girl, just the way she was. Hope would no longer be kept shut away from the world, and she and Billy would make a life for her that she deserved.

It was while Phyllis was silently promising her daughter the very best she could give, that the moment suddenly turned sour. A familiar voice sounded above her, and she froze.

"Well, what do we 'ave 'ere?" It was Sid. "'Appy families, eh?"

Billy leapt to his feet, fists clenched. "What d'you want, O'Connor?" he rasped, his voice cracking.

Sid was staring at the child who was gazing up at him. His eyes narrowed, and he stabbed a tobacco-stained finger at her.

"Is this Hope?" he muttered harshly.

Phyllis stood shakily and squaring her shoulders, glared at him. "Yeah, that's Hope."

"What's wrong with 'er?" His top lip curled.

"None o' your business, O'Connor," snarled Billy, "so piss off an' leave us alone."

"She's a mongol," he said contemptuously. "She's not right in the 'ead."

Billy stepped closer. "No, Sid, it's you who ain't right in the 'ead, an' if ya know what's good for ya, you'll piss off, an' not bother us again."

A crowd was gathering as the two men confronted each other. Sid laughed mirthlessly as he flicked his gaze over the silent onlookers and then back to Phyllis.

"Thought she was my brat, didn't ya? Well, I don't want nothin' t'do with 'er. She ain't mine, I c'n see that plain as day." He spat on the grass. "One thing before I go though." His red-rimmed eyes glared at Billy. "I got somethin' for ya, Billy." His right arm shot out, and he caught Billy on the chin with his fist. Unprepared, Billy staggered back, blood oozing from a split in his lip. "Remember the last fight we 'ad, Billy? I was the one taken by surprise then." He danced on his toes, fists clenched. "Come on! Ya got balls or what?"

Billy lunged as anger swept through his body. Sid O'Connor was not going to get the better of him, now or at any time. He swung a punch, but Sid ducked, laughing as he danced out of the way. Billy regained his balance, and breathing quickly, put his mind to work rather than his fists. He began to circle, watching for Sid to make a wrong move.

By now quite a crowd had gathered, and Phyllis pulled Hope out of the way. The child was sobbing hysterically, and Phyllis gathered her against her skirts.

"Somebody get the police!" Phyllis screamed, as Billy and Sid became locked together in battle.

Somebody had had the foresight to run up the hill to the police barracks, and while Sid and Billy writhed on the ground, grunting and abusing one another, the sound of a police whistle cut through the air. Running footsteps could be heard pounding down the hill. Within moments, the two men were jerked apart, each still abusing the other, as strong arms dragged them from the scene.

The crowd began to disperse as Billy and Sid were marched unceremoniously up the hill towards the police barracks. Phyllis lifted Hope into her arms and ran after them. She was sobbing by the time she reached the massive wall of the barracks. Billy and Sid were led through the gates and along a path to the rooms that served as a police station and temporary lock-up. Phyllis followed and was met at the door by a burly police constable who barred her way.

"You can't go in there, missus," he said, not unkindly.

"Why not?" Phyllis was breathing hard, and Hope was making it difficult for her by squirming in her arms. "I need t'be in there. That's my man been taken in, an' it wasn't 'is fault." She hiccoughed loudly. "It was Sid O'Connor what started it."

"Was it indeed? Sidney O'Connor, huh?"

"Yes! Now please let me in. I was there when the fight started."

"Started by Mr. O'Connor?"

"Yeah! That's what I said!"

"What's your name, missus?"

"Phyllis Powell."

"Oh! Wait here. I'll speak with the Chief Constable."

Phyllis leaned against the wall as the constable disappeared from view. Suddenly she felt very tired, and the tears weren't far away. Hope patted her face and grunted.

"Oh, Hope," Phyllis murmured despondently. "This ain't never goin' t'be over."

The constable reappeared and smiled at her. "You can sit inside, missus." Phyllis followed gratefully and was ushered to a chair by the door. "Wait here, missus."

Phyllis sank on to the hard-backed chair, and cradled Hope in her arms. They should have telephoned for Charles to pick them up, and none of this would have happened. What a day it was turning out to be.

*

Meanwhile, Senior Constable Whitley had entered a small room where Sid O'Connor sat awaiting his fate.

"Well, well, well! If it isn't the notorious Mr. O'Connor! You're a thorn in my side, O'Connor, and one day I'm going to put you away for good." The Senior Constable sat heavily and pulled a file across the table towards him. "What have you done this time?" He looked up as the burly constable entered the room. "Disturbing the peace again, I'll be bound."

"He was brawling with a Mr. Maitland, sir," said the constable, as he stood with feet apart and arms folded across his chest.

"Mr. Maitland, eh? You two are always at it. What was it about this time?"

"Nothin' important," muttered Sid belligerently.

"Nothing important, eh? Well I happen to think differently. Miss Phyllis Powell is in the waiting room, and I'll be interested to hear what she has to say." Whitley's eyebrows beetled. "Who threw the first punch?" Sid was silent. "Who threw the first punch, Mr. O'Connor?"

"The lady says it was Sid O'Connor," interrupted the constable.

"*The lady says it was Sid O'Connor,*" parroted Whitley. "Is that right?"

"'E had it comin'."

Whitley stared at Sid for a long moment, his heavy jaw working. "No, Mr. O'Connor, I suggest to you that you couldn't bear to see Mr. Maitland with Miss Powell, and…"

"Nah! That's where you're wrong! I want nothin' more t'do with 'er…"

"*And*" continued Whitley as though he hadn't been interrupted, "you thought you'd finish the argument and take the woman and child (that you reckon is yours) and disappear."

Sid leaned forward and thumped a fist on the table. "That child is not mine," he growled.

"Oh?" Whitley frowned. "What makes you so sure now?"

"She's not right in the 'ead," hissed Sid. "She's a mongol."

Whitley looked up at the constable. "What's he saying, Constable Osborn?"

The constable shrugged. "I don't know, sir."

Whitley looked back at Sid and frowned. "You're saying now that you are not the father of Miss Powell's child?"

"That's what I'm sayin'." Sid sat back smugly. "Billy c'n 'ave 'er."

Whitley was silent while he contemplated an answer. "Well, it doesn't alter the fact that you caused a fight to break out on public land, and for that I am going to put you in the lock-up for twenty-four hours. Let's see if that cools your ardour."

"Fair go!" whined Sid. "Nobody got 'urt."

"Maybe not, but it's time you learned your lesson, Mr. O'Connor." Whitley smirked as he thought of something else. "By the way, your three friends are going to do some serious time for committing those robberies."

"I 'ad nothin' t'do with those!" Sid's expression tightened. "Ya can't pin nothin' on me!"

"Not this time." Whitley's tone was menacing. "I will eventually, Mr. O'Connor." He slammed the file closed in front of him. "Take him away, constable, and then bring Miss Powell into the interview room with Mr. Maitland. It's time this quarrel came to an end."

*

Billy sat with his arms folded, waiting for the appearance of Senior Constable Whitley. He could hear the rumble of voices coming from a room nearby but was unable to distinguish what was being said. Sid would be justifying his actions, no doubt, and shifting the blame away from himself. There was no doubt that he was extremely good at that and had had a lot of practise.

Billy was concerned for Phyllis and Hope. They had suffered enough over the years, and if he could, he would make it up to them. Could he trust that Sid was no longer interested in winning the war for Phyllis's child? Yes, that was what it had become – a war. Billy smiled. Hope's condition - the condition that made her unique - had obviously shocked Sid. Bless her. Unwittingly, the child had solved the problem.

The door opened and Phyllis rushed in, followed by Senior Constable Whitley. Billy jumped to his feet, and ushered Phyllis on to his chair. She was breathless and Hope was crying.

Whitley sat opposite and studied the trio before him. He pursed his lips before opening the manila folder in front of him.

"I think we can close the file on a certain missing person, don't you?" he said slowly, raising his eyes to look at Phyllis.

"Yes," she said softly.

"And I think I can safely say that Mr. O'Connor will not be bothering you again." He smiled at the child in Phyllis's arms.

"That's good," cut in Billy.

Whitley turned his steely gaze on Billy. "And that brings me to you, Mr. Maitland." He cleared his throat noisily. "I don't want to see you in this place again. If I do, you can expect the same treatment as Mr. O'Connor." He smiled unexpectedly. "A night in the lock-up."

"You won't be seein' me again," said Billy hurriedly. "I got family responsibilities now." He smiled down at Phyllis.

"Good." Whitley breathed a sigh of relief. "On that note, it would be a good idea if you told the Reverend Mother of your plans. I don't fancy visiting that place again any time soon."

Phyllis smiled. "They looked after me an' Hope for three years."

"Yes, well, you won't need them now, I take it?"

Phyllis shook her head.

Whitley began to scribble something on the folder. "That will be all," he said absently.

"What about the fight, sir?" asked Billy, fearing that this had been forgotten.

"Oh, that?" Whitley grinned. "O'Connor's taken the rap for that. Now you'd better get out of here, before I change my mind." He turned back to his scribbling.

Billy grabbed Hope from Phyllis's arms and hurried her to the door. "Come on, Phyllis. We'd better tell mum what's been happenin' today. She won't believe us."

As the door closed behind them, the Chief Constable smiled to himself. He loved this job.

Beau's Arrival

Beau stood on the platform at Sydney Central Station and gazed about him. Everything was familiar, but he felt a sense of loss and bewilderment. People moved erratically around him, all seemingly in a hurry to reach whatever destination they were bound.

What was his destination? He wondered this as he tried to collect his scattered thoughts. He had left home in such a hurry that he given no thought to where he would stay or what he would do once he got to Sydney. Beau picked up his suitcase and headed for the exit on to George Street. Trams rattled by, and people rushed past him to catch the last trams of the day. He looked at his watch. It was six o'clock and the day had ended for most people in the city. Businesses were closing and he knew he had little chance of finding accommodation at this hour.

He headed away from Central Station in the direction he had always taken, towards the Clinic where he had worked with Matthew until his untimely death. Memories crowded in on him, and he walked quickly. Would Celia be at the Clinic at this hour? How much did she know of what was going on with his family?

His footsteps slowed as he approached the imposing block of offices, and he looked up to where he had often stood at the second-floor window, looking out across the harbour. There were no lights on. The façade was a blank wall of silence and approaching darkness.

Beau continued on up the hill, towards Angela's Patisserie. Would she still be there, clearing up after the day's trade, or would she have gone to Clarence's place? His head was fuddled. He had not slept during either leg of the journey from Melbourne, and he needed rest. His footsteps faltered as he came into view of Angela's place, and he prayed that she would be there. Angela had always been there for him in his times of need.

There was a light shining in the patisserie, and Beau sighed with relief. He tried the door. It was locked. He rapped loudly and waited. Glancing through the curtained window he could see Angela tidying up the display cabinet. He knocked again. This time she looked up, and he saw her hesitate. That was a natural reaction at this time of day.

"Angela!" he called out. "It's Beau!"

He saw the recognition on her face as she hurried towards the door. Beau heard her pulling back the lock, and then she appeared, flush-faced from the warmth of the patisserie.

"Beau!" she exclaimed, as she stepped aside to let him in. "What on earth are you doing here?"

Beau stumbled past her and dropped his case on the floor. "I didn't know where else to go," he muttered as he found himself in Angela's warm, pastry-scented embrace.

"That didn't answer my question, Beau." Angela leaned back and looked closely at him. "Why are you in Sydney? Where's Jess?" She touched his face. "You look like hell."

Beau removed his hat. "I feel like hell, to tell the truth, Angela. I've just come from the train, and if you could please get me a cup of tea, I'll explain what's happening, or try to."

"Of course, Beau! Come on through to the kitchen. You can talk while I make a pot of tea." Angela disappeared behind the counter and retrieved a tray of small cakes. "Something to go with the tea?"

Beau nodded half-heartedly, before following Angela's bustling figure out through a doorway covered with red velvet curtains, and into her kitchen and private lodgings.

He dropped on to a chair at the scrubbed pine table, and his head sank on to his hands. Angela watched him from where she stood at the big black oven, and she frowned. She had a fair idea why he was here, but to come at this hour and totally exhausted, was a worry.

"I'm sorry to do this to you, Angela," Beau muttered, raising his head. "I left home in such a hurry, I gave no thought to what time I would actually arrive."

Angela, who had moved the kettle across the stove to boil, pulled out the chair opposite Beau, and sat down.

"Start at the beginning, Beau," she said gently.

"How much do you know about what's going on with my family, Angela?"

Angela winced. "Probably most of it, Beau. Clarence had a visit from Nick recently, and he'd only just found out the awful truth about his life."

"I see." Beau looked up at Angela, his eyes red-rimmed. "You know as much as I do." He rubbed his fingers through his hair and groaned. "Nick telephoned me last night, and without thought, I rushed for the train station and headed for Melbourne." He grimaced. "I slept on a seat in the traveller's restroom, so that I could catch this morning's train to Sydney."

"Oh, Beau, you didn't? What has Jess got to say about all this?"

"I couldn't tell her, Angela." Beau sat back and spread his hands in a hopeless gesture. "I need to see these people face to face before I tell Jess what's going on."

"And Charlotte?"

The question hung in the air for several seconds before Beau shook his head.

"She knows nothing."

"She *needs* to know, Beau."

"I know, but I have to get my head around it first."

The kettle began to sing, so Angela busied herself making the pot of tea.

"The first thing you need to do, (after you've telephoned Jess to let her know that you have arrived) is have a good night's sleep, and then in the morning we can discuss what you should do next."

Beau smiled. In her usual kindly fashion, Angela was taking charge

"And where do you suppose I'll find a bed at this hour?"

"You'll stay here, of course." Her tone suggested that there would be no argument.

"I can't stay here, Angela," protested Beau.

"Why not? You've stayed here before."

"That was with Jess."

Angela laughed merrily. "I trust you, Beau. The bed is still made up, and if anyone has anything to say about this, I'll soon put them straight!" She pushed a cup of tea in Beau's direction. "Now drink this, have something to eat, telephone your poor wife, and then off you go to bed. I have some more tidying up to do before I retire."

"I am very grateful, Angela."

"It's the least I can do, Beau." Her expression became serious. "We've been through a lot of dramas together, Beau, and we'll get through this one, too."

"You're a true friend, Angela, and…"

Angela saw the tears of exhaustion forming behind Beau's eyes. "On second thoughts, Beau," she said hurriedly, "I'll telephone Jess, and let her know that I'm looking after you." She patted his hand. "You go to bed, and that's an order."

Beau didn't argue. He was too tired to make any sense, and Jess would understand. After draining his teacup, he stood slowly and picking up his suitcase, headed in the direction of the bedroom.

"Goodnight, Beau." Angela's voice followed him.

"Goodnight, Angela, and thanks once again."

His head had no sooner hit the pillow before Beau was sound asleep.

*

The following morning, Beau entered the kitchen to see Angela busy at the stove. The smell of bacon assailed his nostrils, and he realised that he was hungry.

"Good morning, Beau!" She sounded cheerful. "Sleep well?"

"I don't remember a thing, Angela."

"Good. Breakfast will be ready in a few moments. Sit yourself down."

Beau did as he was told. "What did Jess have to say?" he ventured finally.

Angela giggled. "She's mighty relieved to know that you are safe and pleased that I am in control."

"Is she?" Beau had to smile at Angela's response.

"I took the liberty of telephoning Clarence and telling him that you are here. He said to tell you that his car is at your disposal if you require it."

Angela placed a plate of bacon, eggs and tomatoes in front of him. "What do you propose to do first, Beau?"

Beau picked up his knife and fork. "I'll eat this first. Then I need to find Nick and visit his parents."

Angela nodded as she sat opposite Beau. "Good idea. I think I know where you will find Nick. He left his parents' home after they broke the news to him, and I believe he's staying with the Private Detective's daughter." Her brow furrowed.

"Amelia Hudson?"

"Yes, that's her name." Angela sprinkled her breakfast with a liberal shake of salt. "I have met her. She's a nice little thing. Clarence will be able to tell you more."

They ate their breakfast in silence, each one thinking of the repercussions that this was certainly going to have and the effect it was already having on so many lives.

Beau looked up to see Angela studying him.

"You'll have to go back out to the Convent, you know?" Her brown eyes held his.

"Yes. And that will probably be the most difficult part of this."

Angela placed her knife and fork on the plate. "It will bring back all those memories of what prompted your search for your sister. You have to be prepared for that, Beau." Angela leaned forward. "Just remember, you won't be alone this time."

Beau felt the memories beginning to seep into his brain. He saw himself hiding under the stairs of the home he had grown up in, trying to block out all the horror and misery that had been cast in his family's direction. He saw his sister's face as she had come to his rescue. After so many years of being apart, she had known where to find him. Now he had to face her with the rest of the truth. Was he strong enough to do it?

Angela was staring at him. "Are you alright, Beau?"

Beau shook off the memories. "I will be, Angela. I have to be."

"Yes, of course you do." Angela rose from the table. "Now, we'd better get ourselves moving if we want to find Nick."

"What about your shop? Shouldn't you be here?"

"That's all organised, Beau." She smiled at his puzzled expression. "The girls will take over today."

"Well, if you're sure."

"Besides, I promised Jess that I wouldn't let you out of my sight."

Beau had to smile at that. "Alright. I know when I'm defeated."

"Good. I'll do these dishes and we can get going." She looked up at the kitchen clock above the mantel. "We should be able to catch the next tram out to Clarence's place, if we hurry."

*

Within the next hour, Beau and Angela were knocking on Clarence's front door. He opened it immediately and ushered them into his spacious sitting room. As Angela passed him, he gave her a quick peck on the cheek. Beau noticed how her face suffused with colour and her brown eyes lit up. She was happy and he was pleased for her.

"I will say that it's good to see you, Beau," said Clarence, "although the circumstances are far from pleasant. Please sit down and I'll see if Hilda will make us some tea."

"That won't be necessary, Clarence," said Angela swiftly. "We've just finished breakfast." She smiled sweetly.

"Oh. Very well." Clarence turned to Beau, who was standing by the fireplace. "What's your plan, Beau? What do you want to do first? I hope you don't mind, but Angela has filled me in."

"Not at all, Clarence." Beau was fidgety. "Firstly, I'd like to find Nick."

"Ah! I'm a step ahead of you on that one, Beau. I've tracked down the man in question, and he's coming here." Clarence looked at his fob watch. "As a matter of fact he should be here soon. "

Angela giggled. "I think Clarence missed his vocation, Beau. He should have been a detective."

It was Clarence's turn to flush. "Really, Angela! I'm a successful businessman, so I suppose that means I'm organised. That's really all it comes down to." He laughed. "Next you'll have me working alongside Joe Hudson."

"Oh, I can't see that working," laughed Angela. "Mr Hudson is so…"

A knock at the front door interrupted what Angela was about to say, and Clarence hurried from the room. Beau and Angela heard muffled voices before Nick Armitage appeared in the doorway of the sitting room. He stood for a moment, as he and Beau made eye contact across the room. Then after rubbing a finger nervously across his chin, he walked towards Beau, his hand outstretched.

Beau saw the familiar move and stared at Nick. He felt rooted to the spot, and for a long moment his hand refused to reach out to take the younger man's. None of this was Nick's fault. Beau knew that. His mouth went dry as he looked into dark eyes that reminded him so much of his father, and he had to lick his lips before he could speak.

"Hello, Nick." He lifted his arm slowly, and the two men clasped hands. "I'm sure this is not what either of us want, but it seems that fate has decreed otherwise." Their hands dropped to their sides.

Nick cleared his throat. "When I first met you, Beau, (which doesn't seem that long ago) I got the impression that you didn't like me, and I couldn't understand why."

"Neither could I, Nick. There was something vaguely familiar about you, but I just couldn't put my finger on what it was."

"Of all the places for me to go, it had to be where you were. That's the part I can't understand."

Angela and Clarence stood silently, listening to the exchange. The two men had to get their feelings out of the way before they could move on to the next step.

"It was your name that triggered my search for that newspaper clipping. I'd heard the name Armitage before, and I had a feeling that it had something to do with my father." Beau shrugged. "I was right, and I needed to know if you were connected." Beau was silent as he contemplated what he would say next. "Your telephone call answered most of my questions, and the two and two I had in my brain, suddenly became four."

"And now you want my parents to clarify the whole story, so that you can tell…" He stopped.

"Yes, Nick. Yes, I do." Beau knew what Nick was about to say.

"Then we'd better go and do it."

Beau glanced at Clarence, who immediately stepped forward. "Take my car, by all means." He searched in his pockets and produced keys. "Here, it's all yours, Beau."

"I'm going too," said Angela, and at Clarence's stunned look in her direction, she added: "I promised Jess that I wouldn't let Beau out of my sight."

"Angela," said Clarence placatingly, "this is something that Beau and Nick need to do alone. This is really not our business." He looked beseechingly at Beau. "Tell her, Beau, that you will be perfectly safe with Nick."

Beau smiled at Angela. "Clarence is right, Angela. Nick and I need to do this alone."

Angela's shoulders slumped. "You mean I've taken a day off for nothing?"

Clarence patted her arm. "Not necessarily, m'dear. We could do a spot of shopping, you and I."

Angela groaned. "But we won't have a car."

"We don't need one, m'dear. We can catch a tram." He smiled indulgently down at Angela. "Now you two had better get going, while I have her on a short leash."

"Thank-you, Clarence." Beau smiled apologetically at Angela. "I will return, Angela, I promise."

"You'd better, or Jess will never forgive me!"

The Meeting

Beau drove while Nick gave him directions, and eventually they came to the long gravel driveway that led to the Armitage residence. Beau looked about him. The large sandstone house nestled snugly at the top of the hill, and the green paddocks swept down to where he saw water glistening in the sunlight. Beau could see that it was a well-maintained property.

A large redsetter bounded from the front verandah to meet them, and as Beau pulled the car to a halt, it barked excitedly. Nick climbed out, to be greeted by exuberant licking and furious wagging of the dog's thick red tail.

"Ralph!" chastised Nick, unsuccessfully pushing the dog away. "Get down!" He turned to Beau, who was climbing from the car. "As you can see, we have an obedient dog." He laughed as he wiped a hand across his wet chin.

Ralph circled the car, and began to sniff at Beau's trousers, before jumping up and placing his large paws on Beau's chest. Before Nick had time to reach the culprit, Beau felt a long wet tongue on his face.

"Ralph!" Nick grabbed the dog's collar and jerked him away from Beau. "I'm sorry, Beau. He is boisterous, but I rather think he likes you."

Beau pulled a handkerchief from his pocket and wiped his face. "That's alright. I've had worse things on my face."

Beau looked up to see a woman standing on the verandah. Nick turned to follow his gaze, and the smile died from his face. He released the dog's collar and stared at his mother. She was standing with her fists clenched at her side, and her thin features pulled into a tight expression. There was no warmth there, and Nick glanced at Beau to gauge his reaction.

Beau's face was a blank canvas – only his grey eyes had narrowed as he stared at the woman whose decision many years ago had changed the course of the lives of his family. He saw a tall, elegant figure, her grey hair pulled tightly back from her face, sharpening her features. Her back was erect, her chin thrust forward. Cool brown eyes bored into him.

Nick took a hesitant step forward. "Mother, this is…"

"I know who he is, Nicholas." Her voice was as sharp as her features. "We have been expecting you, Mr. DuBois."

Beau removed his hat. "Good morning, Mrs. Armitage." Beau's tone belied the fact that his heart was hammering loudly in his chest.

"You'd better come in." Beatrice Armitage stepped aside as Nick and Beau made their way up the steps and on to the verandah. "Go into the sitting room, Nick. I'll fetch your father."

Nick opened the screen door, and Beau followed him along a cool passage to the sitting room, where, in spite of the warm day, a fire crackled in the grate. Beau noted that the room was tastefully decorated with solid lounge chairs covered in green floral velvet. They bore no signs of being worn.

Heavy green velvet drapes were pulled back from the windows, letting in the morning sun.

Beau stood uncomfortably, waiting for the appearance of Hugh Armitage. He didn't have to wait long. Hugh walked through the doorway, and all of Beau's pent-up hatred for the man, shrivelled inside him. He saw a tall man whose face was grey in colour, and whose eyes were sunken into a face that at one time must have commanded authority. His shoulders were stooped beneath the blue-striped suit that he wore, and his thinning ginger hair flopped across his creased brow.

Hugh Armitage crossed the room and sank into one of the lounge chairs. Beatrice walked swiftly to his side and stood silently, as she watched her son and Beau DuBois standing awkwardly before the fire. Hugh waved his hands at them.

"Sit down, please," he muttered.

"I'd rather stand," said Beau stiffly.

Nick seated himself opposite his father, and for several moments there was silence, broken only by the crackle of burning wood.

"So," said Hugh eventually. "The past has come back to haunt us."

"You could say that, sir," began Beau tentatively, "and now I need to hear it from you. How could a man in your position think he could get away with something so profoundly - unlawful?" He stopped, his jaw working. "Tell me, please! I need to know."

Hugh reached out a shaking hand to Beatrice, who held it tightly. "What you have to understand, Mr. DuBois…"

"Doctor DuBois!" said Beau icily.

Beatrice Armitage shivered.

Hugh continued. "Doctor DuBois. We are talking about something that happened thirty odd years ago. The world was a very different place then. There were certain lines that could not be crossed."

Beau's eyes narrowed. "Like the lines my father crossed?"

"Yes."

"The lines you helped my father cross?" Beau's words hung in the air. "Why did you do that? Why would you risk your career?"

"Samuel DuBois was an evil man!" Beatrice's voice rang out. "He would have stopped at nothing to wreck Hugh's career…"

Hugh raised a hand to stop the outburst. "I was a young man, just starting out on my own when I met Doctor Samuel DuBois. He was a very personable man, and…"

"And you were very gullible," said Beatrice bitterly.

"Please, Beatrice, don't interrupt." Hugh breathed deeply. "He was a very personable man and he became our doctor. We formed a close relationship, and even had the occasional drink together." Hugh looked closely at Beau. "I never met your mother, but I was led to believe that she was an invalid, who took to her bed regularly."

Beau's jaw tightened. "Mother was never strong, and she died when I was very young, so I can't say what her problem was. In hindsight, I think she knew what my father was doing and was powerless to stop him."

Hugh nodded. "You may be right. However, let's get back to your father. He came to me one day, most upset that one of his patients had accused him of inappropriate behaviour. He denied it of course, and asked me to defend him, which I did." Hugh stopped and looked up at Beatrice. "It didn't end there and so I continued to defend him, although I knew that where there was smoke there was usually fire. He had me over a barrel. He knew that I was aware of his guilt, and that I could have done something to stop him. This went on for several years, and then of course his own daughter became pregnant." Hugh moaned. "His own daughter – how could he?" He waved his hand. "You know the rest, of course."

Beau looked at Nick. "You could have stopped him then."

"No, it was too late. I would have been ruined."

"Instead, you chose to ruin the life of an innocent girl."

Beatrice sobbed. "What kind of life would the child have? No! It was better this way."

"And my father never knew?"

"No." Beatrice stared at Beau. "As far as he was concerned the child was dead," she whispered.

"Your child?" Beau could not meet her stricken gaze.

Beatrice did not answer.

Beau leaned against the brick mantel, the heat from the fire scorching his legs. He felt the tears prick behind his eyelids and squeezed them shut. It was all making some bizarre kind of sense now, and he felt a certain amount of pity for these people who had been drawn in by the man who had also made his life a misery. He opened his eyes. Three people were staring at him.

"I'm sorry for what my father has put you through," he said slowly, "but there's still one person who needs to know all this, and that's my sister, Charlotte."

Beatrice, whose tense features had softened slightly, released Hugh's hand, and headed for the door.

"I'll make a pot of tea," she said quickly, before disappearing.

Hugh slumped in his chair. "I know we shouldn't have done what we did, but at the time, it seemed like the only thing to do." He gazed miserably at Nick. "I've always considered myself to be your father, Nick, and I loved you as though you were my own."

"I know." Nick's voice cracked. "But we must put things right, while there is still time." He looked at Beau. "Do you think Charlotte will be forgiving?"

Beau wiped a hand across his eyes. "She spent thirty-two years in a Convent, Nick. Forgiveness is probably something she dealt with daily."

Nick smiled weakly. "You're probably right."

"There's one thing I don't quite understand," said Beau, looking once more in Hugh's direction. "Why the Convent?"

Hugh looked towards the door. "In spite of how it appears to you, Doctor DuBois, this was not a pre-meditated act on our part. Our child was not due to be born when we were paying a visit to our dear friend, Sister Miriam." He shrugged. "I don't know what you'd call it – providence perhaps? But that's why we were there, and that's how it all unfolded."

"We need to pay a visit to the Convent, Nick."

"Yes, we do." Nick faced Hugh. "Do you and mother visit the Convent very often?"

"Once a year," said Beatrice, "I would visit, and put flowers on the grave. I was always careful not to let anyone see me."

Nick frowned. "Did it ever bother you that you were visiting a grave with the name of another child on it?"

"Yes, it did."

"And what of Sister Miriam? Did she have a hand in this?"

Beatrice looked quickly at Hugh. "Yes, she did."

"Did you continue to defend my father?" Beau said sharply, also looking in Hugh's direction.

"No." Hugh sighed. "Forgive me if my memory is a little hazy, but your mother had died around that time, and he withdrew into himself. Whether it was from remorse or guilt, we shall never know, but I had nothing more to do with him."

"So life went on as though nothing had happened?" Beau's question was more of a statement.

"I suppose it did."

"And you continued with your Law Practice?"

"Yes."

"And when my father died, you assumed that you would be safe – that your deception would never be discovered now? Am I correct?"

"Believe me, Doctor DuBois, I continued looking over my shoulder for many years. There was always the possibility that Sister Miriam would not be able to keep quiet." Hugh stopped as Beatrice returned, a tray of steaming teacups in her hands. "Then Nick happened to cross *your* path. What are the chances of that happening? I'd say only one in a million, wouldn't you? The whole thing blew up in our faces." Hugh gave a mirthless laugh. "The truth has a habit of revealing itself, don't you agree?"

Beatrice placed the tray on a small table beside Hugh and handed him a cup. "Be careful, dear, it's very hot." She looked up at Nick. "We knew then that it would have to come to an end. Dear Nick, we had tried so hard to protect you, and in spite of everything, you are still our son. You have been since the day you were born." She handed Nick a cup of tea. "I hope you can find it in your heart to forgive us. Your welfare has always been our primary concern. If *he* had been given access to you, then…" She shuddered. "I don't want to think about it."

Beatrice moved across to Beau. "Can you forgive us?"

Beau took the proffered cup of tea. "More to the point, Mrs. Armitage, will Charlotte forgive you?"

Beatrice nodded slowly. "Yes, of course. Maybe she won't."

"And Sister Miriam?" Beau looked at Beatrice over the rim of his cup. "Has she forgiven you for implicating her in your deception?"

"You'll have to ask her that yourself," whispered Beatrice, unable to meet his gaze.

"Oh, I intend doing just that."

Sister Miriam

Hugh and Beatrice stood on the verandah, watching as Beau and Nick drove slowly away from the property. Ralph bounded after the car as it headed down the gravel track, returning only when it had disappeared from view. Hugh placed an arm across his wife's shoulders and sighed heavily.

"Well, Beatrice, that wasn't as bad as it could have been."

"No." There was a moment's silence. "He seems like a very nice man."

"Hm. Not at all like his father, I would say."

"Did you notice a similarity between the two of them?"

Hugh shook his head. "No, I can't say I did. What similarity?"

"The expression in their eyes." Beatrice leaned her head against his shoulder.

"But their eyes are a different colour, Beatrice." Hugh was puzzled by this comparison.

"I know, but they have the same expression – sort of sad in a way."

"Sad?" Hugh shook his head. "No, I didn't see that, Beatrice."

"Hm." Beatrice was silent again. "I wonder what happened to his face?"

"I don't know, but he must have been a very handsome man, just like our Nick, before he was damaged." Hugh squeezed her shoulder. "Well, come on, my dear. We can't stand out here all day."

Beatrice turned to face him, her eyes wide and forlorn. "Do you think we've lost Nick forever, Hugh?"

"No." Hugh pulled her into his arms. "I don't believe so. Nick has to find himself first, and then he'll be back, you mark my words."

"I hope so, Hugh – I truly hope so."

*

It was late in the afternoon when Beau pulled the car to a halt at the gates of the Convent that was now very familiar to him. He shut off the engine.

"This is it, Nick," he said sombrely. "This is where we'll find Sister Miriam."

Nick stared at the grey edifice that loomed dark and forbidding behind the heavy iron gates. He shivered in the late afternoon sun.

"Is this where I was born?"

"Yes." Beau walked across the gravel to the gate. "This is where Charlotte spent thirty-two years of her life." He pulled hard on the heavy iron bell that hung beside the gate. It clanged loudly.

Nick stood beside him, and together they waited for the summons to be answered. It didn't take long before they saw a white-clad figure walk quickly from the building, and head in their direction. The novice peered at them from beneath her white veil, and her dark eyes were round with curiosity.

"Yes?" she queried politely.

"We wish to see the Reverend Mother, please." Beau smiled at the young woman, who looked no older than what his sister must have been when she entered the Order.

A frown etched her brow. "What business do you have with the Reverend Mother?"

Beau sighed. "It's personal," he said wearily, "and we need to see Sister Miriam."

"Sister Miriam?" Her expression became secretive, and she giggled. "She is being sent away!" she whispered conspiratorially. "None of the novices know why."

"Is she still here?" Nick asked quickly.

"Oh, yes." The young novice folded her arms across her ample chest and surveyed the two men standing beyond the gate.

"Then we must see her." Beau was becoming slightly irritated by the novice's procrastination.

"I'll have to speak with Reverend Mother first." The novice sniffed, and suddenly became formal. "Who will I say is calling?"

"Tell the Reverend Mother that it is Beau DuBois," said Beau with more patience than he felt. "She will know who I am."

The novice looked enquiringly at Nick. "And who are you, sir?" she asked primly.

"Nicholas Armitage."

"Very well. Wait here and I'll return."

They watched her solid figure scurry across the grass towards the heavy doors that led to the inner sanctum of the Convent. Nick reached for the gate and wrapped his fingers around two of the unyielding iron bars.

"It's like a prison, isn't it?" He shook the bars firmly. "What are they called, these nuns who live here?" Nick turned enquiring eyes on Beau.

"The Sisters of Mercy."

Nick laughed. "Sisters of Mercy?" he parroted. "I can't see any mercy in this place."

Beau smiled, remembering clearly the devoted attention he had received during his rehabilitation behind those walls. "There is mercy here, Nick." He looked at the younger man.

"Hm. If you say so, Beau."

They waited for several minutes before the doors to the Convent opened and the sturdy novice hurried towards them once more. This time she pulled a large key from somewhere beneath her habit and placed it in the lock that chained the gate shut.

"Reverend Mother will see you," she said curtly, swinging open the gate.

"Thank-you." Beau strode towards the building, glancing back as he said over his shoulder: "I know where to find her."

Nick hurried to keep pace with him, and together they entered the cold interior of the Convent. Their footsteps echoed on the flagstones as Beau headed towards the Reverend Mother's office. Suddenly remembering how cold it was in there, he pulled his jacket firmly around him.

Beau rapped on the door and waited for permission to enter.

"Come in," he heard.

Beau looked at Nick as he opened the creaking door.

"Ah! Doctor DuBois!" came a disembodied voice from behind the enormous desk. "We meet again."

"Reverend Mother." Beau removed his hat.

Nick blinked in the unaccustomed gloom and peered into the space from where the voice had come. She spoke again, and this time he could make out the shape of her veil and the white wimple around her face.

"What brings you here now that your sister has gone, Doctor DuBois?"

"I must speak with Sister Miriam."

"About what?" Her voice had a sharp edge.

Beau was silent, not knowing what to say.

"About my birth here thirty-two years ago," said Nick without expression.

They heard a sharp intake of breath, and the Reverend Mother rose from her chair. "I cannot let you see her," she said stiffly. "Sister Miriam is to be sent away from here, and in fact she leaves tomorrow. Now I must ask you to go and leave well alone."

"I am Nicholas Armitage," insisted Nick, "and I was born within these walls thirty-two years ago. Sister Miriam was there, because she knew my mother, and now I need to see her to…"

A strangled moan came from the Reverend Mother. "You will find her beyond the back wall of the Convent, tending to the children's graves there." She gulped. "Do not distress her, I implore you."

"Thank-you, Reverend Mother," said Beau quietly. "We will not forget your mercy. Come, Nick, it is time to finish what has been started."

*

The two men hurried past cultivated garden beds, receiving startled looks from the many black-clad figures working there. A small gate was visible in the wall that sheltered the garden from harsh winds, and they headed towards it. Swinging it open, Beau stepped into the outside world, and glanced from left to right. Nick followed him, pulling the gate shut after him.

"There's Sister Miriam," whispered Beau, seeing the black-clad figure squatting in the dirt some fifty yards to his left.

They approached slowly, so as not to frighten her. As they drew near, they heard her humming softly to herself as she worked with a small trowel in the heavy soil. She sensed their approach and looked up quickly. Beau stopped, bringing Nick to a halt beside him.

"Hello, Sister Miriam," he said softly.

Sister Miriam placed her trowel in the ground and stood slowly. A smile spread across her round features, and Beau heard her familiar Irish brogue.

"Well now, if it isn't the one and only Doctor DuBois. What brings you here?"

"We're here to see you, Sister."

"Are you now?" Brown eyes flicked across to Nick, and as if in slow motion, her expression changed to one of amazement. Her hands moved slowly to her face, and a tiny squeak issued from her mouth.

"As I live and breathe," she uttered. "You have to be Charlotte's boy."

"Yes," said Nick. "I'm Nicholas Armitage."

Sister Miriam walked slowly towards them, and placing her hands on Nick's arms, looked up into his face. "So you know?"

"I do." Nick smiled down at the woman who had been a part of the deception.

"Do you forgive me for what I did?"

Nick frowned. "You were only doing as you were told."

"Is that what your parents told you?" Sister Miriam stepped back a pace and her hands went once more to her face. "No, lad, it wasn't like that."

Nick's eyes narrowed, and as the nun began to tremble, he looked around for somewhere for her to sit. The only thing he saw was a fallen tree. He helped her across the grass and seated her on the log.

"What are you saying, Sister?"

Sister Miriam heaved a big sigh and ran her fingers across her face. "I'll tell you, lad, but not a word to Beatrice, do you understand?"

"Very well." Nick glanced at Beau. What more were they going to hear?

"It was a long time ago, lad, but it's as clear as if it were yesterday." Her smile was soft. "Beatrice had come to visit me (she did quite often) and she was in quite a state when the child decided to come. She panicked and I helped her to the birthing room, where a young lass was also waiting to deliver." She looked sadly at Beau. "That was your sister, Charlotte."

"I guessed that," muttered Beau.

"I was trained as a midwife, and I was on duty that day. It was a fearsome day. The rain was lashing the place like a crazy beast, and we couldn't send for a doctor, so I had to do my best with two bairns to deliver." She sighed as the memories rushed forth. "Beatrice's bairn came first, and I knew at once that he was dead. I wrapped him up and didn't show her. Then I attended to Charlotte, the young lass who had come to us with a terrible story of … what had happened to her. She delivered a beautiful boy, and I immediately wrapped him up and took him away. For you see, I had this idea in my head. There was my dear friend, Beatrice, who would probably never conceive again, and there was this young girl, abused and broken, but with a whole life of childbearing ahead of her, if that was what she wanted." She stopped, her eyes filling with tears. "I did the unthinkable. I switched the bairns."

"But my mother…"

"Yes. Beatrice and Hugh knew what I had done, but once I had shown Charlotte the dead bairn, it was too late to do anything about it." She looked up at Nick. "I knew you had a chance of living a good life with good people." She sighed. "And Charlotte? Once she had gotten over the initial shock, and had decided to join the Order, I knew she was safe. I would look after her for as long as she was here." She smiled. "Yes, it was wrong, and I have paid for that over the years, but Charlotte, who became Sister Agnes eventually, blossomed in a way that I felt justified my actions."

"So my parents went along with the deception, knowing that at any time it could be discovered?"

"Beatrice had wanted a child more than anything in this world." Sister Miriam's eyes hardened. "I gave her that chance, and in some ways I'm not sorry." She looked at Beau as she sighed. "And now they're wanting to send me away, because after all these years, I finally confessed my sin." She stood and moved slowly across to a tiny mound of earth against the brick wall of the Convent. Looking down at the tiny grave, she whispered: "But I'm not going anywhere. I'm staying with this bairn."

Beau and Nick stood beside her. "The Reverend Mother said that it's all organised, and that you're leaving tomorrow," said Beau.

"Did she now?" Sister Miriam smiled at him. "Do you know where she was sending me?"

"No."

"She was sending me to an orphanage in Bendigo."

"Bendigo?" The two men glanced at one another.

"Yes. That way the Reverend Mother said I would be close to Charlotte." Her voice shook. "No, that would not be the punishment I deserve, so I will live out my days here." She pointed to the wooden grave marker. "You see the name says Michel?"

"That was the name my sister gave her child – Michel Beauregarde," said Beau shakily.

"I know." Sister Miriam turned to Nick. "That should have been your name, Nicholas."

"I'll keep the name I've got," said Nick, as he bent and placed a trowel full of soil on the tiny grave.

"Beau?" Sister Miriam placed a hand on Beau's arm. "Is your sister aware of all this?"

"No, not yet. I will tell her the whole story when I return to Bendigo."

"Ask her not to hate me too much."

"Charlotte will not hate you, Sister Miriam. She will realise why you did it. I hope one day that you can forgive yourself."

"Perhaps."

Beau glanced up at the sky. The evening would be closing in very soon.

"Sister Miriam," he said gently. "We must go. It's a long drive down to the city, and it will soon be dark. Please take care, and we wish you well."

"Say 'hello' to that delightful wife of yours, Beau. You have a bairn now, I believe?"

"Yes, we have a daughter. We named her Charlotte after my sister. We call her Lottie."

"Very nice. Goodbye, Beau. Goodbye, Nicholas." Her eyes were full as she squeezed their hands.

Beau and Nick walked away, leaving Sister Miriam to attend the tiny grave. They hurried through the vegetable garden as the workers were starting to finish off their duties for the day. Neither spoke as they circled the building and crossed the grass to the main gates. Fortunately, they were still unlocked, so within minutes they were in the car. As they pulled away, they noticed a figure in white scurrying across the yard, a large key in her hands.

They drove in silence for some time before Nick ventured to say, "Do you think she'll be alright?"

"Sister Miriam?" Beau shrugged. "I couldn't say, Nick. That's quite a burden she's been carrying with her all these years."

"And my parents?" Nick shook his head. "That was a shock to hear the whole truth from Sister Miriam. Do you think it was the whole truth, Beau?"

"What does it matter now, Nick. The truth is sometimes simply how we see it." Beau swerved to dodge a pothole. "Our concern now is what we're going to tell all those who are waiting to hear what we've found out." The car shuddered on the rough road. "I'll have to turn the lights on soon, or we won't get home tonight." He laughed suddenly. "We have several women to pacify before we're much older."

Nick groaned. "Amelia will be wondering where on earth I've got to."

"So will Angela," laughed Beau. "Not to mention the reception we're going to get from Jess and Charlotte."

"I'm coming with you, Beau."

"To Bendigo?"

"Yes, if that's alright."

Beau smiled in the fading light. "I fully expected that you would, Nick."

"Amelia will probably want to come, too."

"Nick, Amelia will be very welcome." He pulled the car to a halt and climbed out. "Now I'd better turn on these lights, if I remember how to do it."

"Oh, that's easy." Nick jumped out of the car. "Here, let me show you, Uncle Beau."

Beau laughed. "I hadn't thought of that – nephew."

The Journey Home

The platform at Sydney Central Train Station was crowded as the hands of the great clock read ten to six. The morning was warm, but the usual fresh breeze managed to find its way between bustling passengers, as they juggled with luggage and farewelled loved ones.

Beau, Nick and Amelia stood together, waiting for the arrival of Clarence, Angela and Joe, who had promised to come and wave them off. Nick, being the tallest, stood on tiptoe as he searched the crowd for familiar faces. The first whistle sounded, reminding passengers that they should begin to board the train. Steam issued across the platform, making visibility difficult. Beau looked up anxiously at the clock.

"I don't think they're coming," he said, as he lifted his case in readiness to board the train.

"I can see them!" Nick raised his arms above the crowd and waved frantically.

Moments later, Joe appeared at his side, red-faced and breathing hard. Clarence and Angela appeared shortly after, and they all heaved sighs of relief.

"What kept you?" demanded Amelia, looking accusingly at Joe.

"It wasn't my fault," said Joe indignantly, before giving his daughter a hug. "We were held up by an overturned cart on the road. We had to wait while the horse was caught and pacified."

"Yes," agreed Clarence. "It was quite a to do, I must say. The poor animal was quite traumatised."

"We're here now," said Angela as she headed for Beau.

He placed his case on the platform before giving her a hug. "Goodbye, Angela," he murmured into her sweet-smelling dark hair. "Thank-you for being there for me once again."

"I'm glad everything has worked out, Beau, and I'm sure Charlotte will be so pleased once she gets over the shock. Nick is a wonderful man, and he will make things as easy as he can for her." Her eyes filled with tears. "You haven't seen the last of us, be sure of that. We'll take a trip to Bendigo, when you are all settled, won't we, Clarence?"

Clarence nodded his approval. "Definitely, m'dear."

Nick, who had overheard Angela's words, tapped her on the shoulder. "Amelia and I will be back, Angela. We won't be staying in Bendigo for long. Our work is here."

"Yes," interrupted Joe. "You need to return so that I can retire, Nick."

Nick stared at him. "You can't be serious, Joe."

"I'm very serious, Nick. When you return, we will discuss it fully and put a plan into action."

Amelia laughed. "You won't retire, Joe."

"We'll see about that." A second whistle sounded. "Now you'd better get on board, or the train will go without you."

There were more hugs, and a few tears from Angela.

"Give our love to everybody!" she called out as the three climbed aboard.

With a screech of metal, the wheels began to turn and another burst of steam covered the platform. Beau peered out of a greasy window to catch a last glimpse of his friends. He saw Clarence comforting Angela, while Joe stood with a hand raised almost in a salute. He owed them so much. Tears pricked behind his eyes, and he felt Nick's hand on his shoulder.

"Come on, let's go and find an empty compartment," he yelled over the noise of the train. "It's going to be a long day."

"And a long night." Beau wiped a hand across the greasy window, but their friends were out of sight now, and only an empty platform stretched away behind them.

"Well, I don't fancy sleeping on the station tonight," said Amelia, after having heard of Beau's uncomfortable night prior to his journey to Sydney. "It might have been a better plan to have travelled from Sydney overnight, as we have done before, Nick."

Nick grimaced. She was right, as usual, but Beau was anxious to get home after having spoken with Jess. Their arrival was going to be tumultuous, to say the least, because Beau had sworn Jess to secrecy about who would be accompanying him home.

They found an empty compartment and settled in for the duration of the journey to Albury. Amelia stretched out on one seat, leaving the two men to talk quietly together. She closed her eyes, and the movement of the train quickly sent her off to sleep. About an hour later Nick shook her gently and asked her if she would like some breakfast. He and Beau were heading to the buffet car. Amelia smiled up at him, as she remembered their first 'chance' meeting in the buffet car. Had it only been a few weeks ago? She felt as though she'd known Nick her whole life.

"Yes, Nick, I'm coming."

*

The day progressed slowly, as the three talked, slept, and ate intermittently. There was so much to catch up on, and Nick needed to know everything there was to know about this family he'd just discovered. He shed tears as Beau talked about his own childhood and the fear he had for his father. He was horrified as Beau told him what his sister had had to sacrifice to protect her younger brother. His fists clenched in anger as Beau told him how he had discovered part of the truth and had tried to hide himself from the shame of it all. Some of this Nick had heard from Jess, but in the re-telling, it became even more bizarre.

"What about your war experience?" Nick asked. "Do you want to tell us about that?"

Beau shrugged. "Not really. It was grim." He looked up into Nick's eyes, so like his father's but without that steely glint. "We didn't know what we were heading into, and as medical personnel, were unprepared for the shocking injuries we had to deal with. It was not just the physical traumas, but the emotional and mental scars that tipped some of us over the edge, including me." He ran a finger down his scarred cheek. "After this had happened, and I had been dragged back to safety, with my companion, I was a wreck, and had to be sent home." He stopped.

"I'm sorry if this hurts, Beau, but I must know what you went through."

"I know."

Beau smiled thinly as he sat back against the cool leather of the passenger seat. He closed his eyes as he related to Nick and Amelia his dramatic return to Australia from the Western Front, his time in an institution, and his eventual bid for freedom. They raised their eyebrows as he told of the months he spent tramping around the country, eking out a living by doing manual work for sympathetic folk who realised his situation. He went on to tell them that it was while looking for work that he had met Jess, and due to her empathy, his whole attitude had turned around, and he had worked for a time in the hotel where Nick and Amelia had stayed.

That was until Clarence and Celia had sent Joe looking for him and his peaceful life had been shattered once more. Not wanting to return to his old life, and feeling the pressure of his feelings for Jess, who was married to a soldier serving overseas, his desperation had led him to attempt to take his own life. Jess had found him in the bush, and he had been rushed to the hospital.

Amelia let out a gasp at that revelation, and her eyes filled with tears. "Oh, no! Beau, you must have been desperate to attempt something like that. You poor, poor man."

Beau took a deep breath at this point, as the memories washed over him. "I was sent back to Sydney with Celia, but unbeknown to me, Jess knew nothing of my whereabouts. I struggled with treatments for a time, and eventually found some sort of peace, working with my friend Matthew Morley, who ran a clinic for soldiers just like me. Incidentally, Mathew had married Celia in my absence. We were over, anyway, and she'd always had a certain fascination with Matthew."

"And Jess?" Amelia stared intently at him. "Tell us about Jess."

Beau rubbed his fingers across his face. "I didn't see her for twelve months, and in that time she had no idea where I was. Then I happened to be in Melbourne, so I decided to go and see her, to see how she was getting on. I found her and realised that my feelings for her had not changed. Her husband had been wounded overseas, and she didn't know where he had been sent." He shrugged. "I came back to Sydney, feeling lost and very much alone.

I continued working with Matthew, but it was always difficult with Celia there as well… Anyway, I had a letter from Jess's mother-in-law, Margaret." He looked up. "You didn't meet Margaret. She was a very special lady and very close to Jess. The letter said that her son, Jack, (Jess's husband) had died of the Spanish Flu, over in England, and that Jess was on the verge of collapse. As her friend, could I please help? I went immediately, and with Margaret's assistance we pulled Jess out of the black hole that she'd dug for herself." He smiled. "So that was the beginning for Jess and me."

Amelia shook her head in disbelief. "Oh, Beau, we had no idea."

"Oh, a lot of other things have happened, of course, but without Jess, I can honestly say that my life would not have been as happy as it is today. She is my rock… a safe place for me. Without her I probably wouldn't even be here now."

They were all silent as the home truths began to fall into place.

"And I wouldn't be dealing with this," said Nick with a brief smile. "I'd probably be at home playing tennis with my friends, with not a care in the world." He looked at Amelia. "And I wouldn't have met you, my lovely."

Amelia smiled across the carriage at him. "Now that would have been a tragedy," she murmured.

Homecoming

After the long, interrupted journey from Sydney to Melbourne, the trio managed to find lodgings in a hotel close by the station. It was not the Hilton, but the beds were clean, and they all managed to sleep, in spite of the noise of a party downstairs.

The following morning, after a meagre breakfast of tea and toast, they made their way to the station, in readiness to catch the ten-fifteen train to Bendigo and beyond to Swan Hill. The morning was clear after a downpour the previous night, and the roads were washed free of oil spills, horse manure, and other detritus caused by the movement of humans.

This was the final leg of their journey, and as the train rattled its way north, Nick was becoming increasingly nervous. Would he be received well by the woman who had given birth to him? She had always believed that he had died. Would she accept Sister Miriam's account of what had happened? These things tumbled through his brain, along with the final glimpse he had had of his parents, Hugh and Beatrice. They had looked so forlorn, knowing that they had been willing participants in the deception?

Amelia squeezed his hand as he sat beside her. He gazed into her large blue eyes and made up his mind that nothing he did was going to cause her heartache. Life was too precious for that.

"I love you," he mouthed silently.

"I love you, too," she mouthed back to him.

Beau, seated opposite in the crowded compartment, saw the exchange, and smiled to himself.

*

When the train finally came to a halt at the Bendigo station, there was a flurry of movement from the other passengers in the compartment. Beau, Nick and Amelia sat quietly until the compartment was empty, before reaching for their luggage.

"Well, this is it, Nick," said Beau, as he led the way along the corridor to the door of the carriage.

"Are they coming to meet us?" Nick was extremely anxious by now.

"No," said Beau, as he negotiated the steep step to the platform. "I thought it best if they wait at home for us."

"That's good. I don't fancy a public display of emotions."

"No. That's what I thought, too."

Nick helped Amelia on to the platform, and together they made their way up the steps of the pedestrian bridge and down the other side. Silently they walked the familiar streets that led past the Grey Goose, which was now resounding with the noise of the lunchtime crowd.

"I suppose Jean will be handing around her sandwiches," commented Nick, as they walked past the door to the Ladies Lounge.

"Definitely," answered Beau. "It's a tradition that everybody expects."

"It's served her well, obviously."

"Are we booking in there to stay for a few nights, Nick?" Amelia matched her long stride with his.

Nick smiled at her. "Of course. We'll give them a surprise, particularly Izzy."

Beau turned to look at him. "She was quite taken with you, Nick."

"What do you mean?" Nick laughed self-consciously.

"According to Jess, she thought you were quite charming."

Amelia laughed. "Did she now? Charming, eh?"

They were all still chuckling as they approached the house on Oleander Street. Nick's footsteps slowed, and he looked anxiously at Beau.

"Jess and Charlotte are on the verandah," he whispered.

Beau stopped at the gate, and his eyes travelled up to the two figures standing side by side at the top of the steps. Charlotte was leaning heavily on her crutches, staring unblinking at Nick.

After what seemed like a long time, Jess came slowly down the steps, and opening the gate, fell into Beau's arms.

"Welcome home," she whispered, before disengaging herself and turning to the two visitors. "Hello Nick." Jess gave him a quick hug. "Hello Amelia." She gave her a hug. "It's lovely to see you."

"What's going on, Beau?" Charlotte's voice floated down, loud and clear, from the verandah.

Beau led the way up the steps and gave his sister a quick peck on the cheek. "I have someone I'd like you to meet, Charlotte," he said in a low voice, "but I think we should all go inside first." He touched his sister on the arm and Charlotte turned and hopped into the house. "Into the kitchen, please Charlotte."

They all filed along the passage and into the kitchen, where Beau made sure Charlotte was seated, before indicating to Nick and Amelia that they should be seated also. Jess busied herself at the stove, moving the kettle across to boil, and reaching for the tea caddy. Baby Lottie made snuffling noises from her cot in the corner of the room. The rest of the house was quiet. The boys were at school and Grace was playing with Freya, so Jess felt comfortable that they were all out of earshot. She knew what Beau was about to say, and glancing at Charlotte now, Jess saw the uncertainty in her eyes. Did she have an idea of what was going on? She had never spoken about it to Jess.

Nick and Amelia sat staring across the table at Charlotte, while Beau sat beside her, his hands ready to clasp hers if necessary. He opened his mouth to speak, but Charlotte spoke first.

"What are you going to tell me, Beau?" She stared at Nick. "That Nick is our brother?"

There was silence for a long moment.

"No, Charlotte," said Beau finally. "Nick is not our brother... He is... your son."

Charlotte's fingernails scraped across the table, and she tried to stand. "No!" she cried. "He can't be! My baby died." She sat heavily, and tears welled in her grey eyes.

"No, Charlotte, he didn't. Your baby Michel Beauregarde did not die. He sits here before you, as large as life."

Charlotte shook her head in disbelief. "How?" she managed to squeak.

Nick reached across the table and placed his big hands over hers, while Beau continued.

"It's a long story, Charlotte, but finally I have all the pieces. Do you remember another woman who was giving birth at the same time as you?"

Charlotte frowned, and her hands turned and gripped Nick's. "Yes, I do."

"That woman was Nick's mother."

"I don't understand. Sister Miriam brought my baby to me and..." Charlotte stopped and swung her gaze around to Beau. "Are you saying that Sister Miriam...?" Her voice faltered.

"Sister Miriam swapped the babies, Charlotte. Mrs. Armitage's child was stillborn."

"Why?" Fresh tears welled in Charlotte's eyes. "Sister Miriam became my dearest friend, Beau. Why would she do that?"

"She did it out of love, Charlotte." Beau glanced across at Jess, who was also wiping her eyes. "She wanted your child to have the best possible chance in life."

"But I was his mother!"

"I know, and Sister Miriam knew that, but once the deed had been done, there was nothing she could do about it." Beau paused. "She begs your forgiveness."

"My forgiveness!" cried Charlotte bitterly. "For thirty-two years I have lived thinking that my child was buried outside the walls of the Convent. I'm not sure I can forgive something like that."

"If it's any consolation, Sister Miriam has made her confession, and now wants to live solely to care for the tiny grave outside the Convent wall. That is her punishment to herself."

Charlotte stared at Nick. "And the people who raised you, Nick – your parents – were they aware of what had happened?"

"Yes." Nick looked down at the table.

"Why couldn't they have said something?"

"They knew your father and what he was capable of."

"One more thing," said Charlotte slowly. "Did my father know of this deception?"

"No, apparently not."

Charlotte sat back on her chair, and her mouth twitched. "None of this would have come to light, if you hadn't come to Bendigo, Nick?"

"That's right."

"Your parents called you Nick?"

"Nicholas actually. Nicholas Hugh, after... my father."

"I have so many questions, but they can wait." Charlotte struggled to her feet. "I think the first thing I want to do is hold my son."

Nick pushed back his chair and skirted the table. Charlotte fell into his arms, letting her crutches clatter to the floor. Jess, Beau, and Amelia watched on as mother and son held each other for the first time.

"Carry me out to the sleep-out," said Charlotte finally. "I need to rest and come to terms with this." She laughed shakily as Nick picked her up in his arms. "This is not the first time you have carried me, Nick." Her eyes met his. "I don't suppose you want to change your name to Michel?"

"Nick will do very well," he laughed. "I don't know that I can call you 'mother,' either."

"No." Charlotte patted his chest. "Charlotte will do. And Nick, I will have to teach you how to walk quickly, or you'll never keep up with me."

"I'll wait until you're off the crutches," laughed Nick.

"The sleep-out is this way," directed Charlotte, while Nick glanced back at the three behind him. They were all smiling.

It would take time, but he felt sure that everything was going to be just fine.

Finale

The Ladies Lounge at the Grey Goose was buzzing with activity, as Jean hovered over the tables of food set out for her visitors. It was the evening before Nick and Amelia's return to Sydney, and the family had gathered with their friends, to say their farewells. Drinks were flowing and conversation was at an all-time high.

Jean, flush-faced with the pressure of keeping up with the food supply, stopped to wipe her perspiring face on her apron. The room was full, and she looked around at those who had gathered, pleased with the number who had turned up at such short notice.

Her gaze fell on Charles, resplendent in a grey suit, talking to Jess, who looked radiant in her favourite red dress. Their conversation was very animated, and Jean thought fleetingly of the Charles she had known for many years, and who had not impressed her with his pompous ways. He had mellowed, and she watched him now as he laughed with Jess. She knew that the loss of his beloved Margaret was still heavy on his heart, but he was getting on with life and filling it with his family.

Jean looked beyond Charles and Jess, to where Audrey Maitland was smiling widely as she held the small child, Hope, in her arms. Billy and Phyllis stood beside her, scrubbed up in their best clothes, and looking as happy as she had seen them. Life had taken a turn for them, and Jean felt confident that they would make a go of it. It seemed that Sid had done a back flip, and Jean would not have been surprised to hear that he had fled the town. This made her think of her own son, and the trouble he was in. She sighed. Well, he had made his bed and he could lie in it. She had no sympathy for him.

Her eyes rested on Charlotte, leaning on her crutches. She was deep in conversation with Beau as he inclined his head towards her. Their expressions were serious and intense, and Charlotte touched his arm gently. Jean watched as he led her away to a quiet corner of the room. They obviously had lots to talk about.

Doctor Raymond Simmons and his wife, Louise, stood to one side, drinks in their hands and their eyes on their small son, who was the same age as Jess's Lottie, and who sat contentedly at their feet. As Jean watched, Jess made her way across to them. She kissed Louise on the cheek and shook hands with Raymond. Then she squatted down beside their son. Jess laughed as she looked up at the proud parents, and her fingers tickled the child's chin. Jean noticed that even Raymond was smiling.

Jean wiped her face once more on her apron and turned her attention back to the food. As she did so, Izzy appeared at her side, her face also flushed with the excitement of the event and keeping up the food supply.

"It's all going well, Jean," she breathed, as she collected a trayful of empty platters. "Where are our guests of honour?" She looked around for Nick and

Amelia.

"They haven't come down yet," said Jean, looking around. She laughed. "It's almost like a wedding party, isn't it?"

"Yes," agreed Izzy, "and the bride and groom have yet to make their appearance." She giggled.

"Don't speak too soon, Izzy," said Jean conspiratorially. "You mark my words, those two will be married before the year is out."

Izzy sighed. "I agree, Jean. They seem made for each other."

At that moment Harry loomed beside them and placed an arm around Izzy's shoulder.

"What is it, Harry?" Izzy raised an eyebrow at him. "You look like the harbinger of doom."

"How perceptive of you, Isobel. Have you seen the children lately?"

Izzy groaned. "No, Harry. Where are they?"

"They're throwing stones in the fishpond. I told you at the time that it wasn't a good idea to have a fishpond where…"

"You deal with it, Harry! Can't you see I'm busy?" Izzy flounced towards the kitchen, her pink satin skirt rustling, and with that she was gone. They could hear her heels echoing purposefully on the linoleum in the passage.

Harry looked at Jean and shrugged helplessly.

"Bring them in, Harry," said Jean dryly. "Tell them there's food in here. That will bring the boys in, at least."

"I'm trying to man the bar, Jean!" protested Harry loudly. "Why does she always do this to me?"

Jean laughed. "Because, Harry, she knows you will do it. Izzy has you right around her little finger."

"I know!" Harry threw up his hands in mock defeat. "You don't have to tell me, Jean."

As Harry stomped from the room, Nick and Amelia entered, and a hush immediately settled on the group gathered there. To Jean's mind, Nick looked like the cat that had swallowed the cream, and she smiled. He was dressed in cream slacks with a pale blue shirt, and a navy jacket. His dark hair was brushed back, and for a moment, Jean could see Beau, as he might have been before the war had taken its toll on him. Only the eyes were different. Jean shook away the image and turned her attention to Amelia, elegant in a pencil-slim grey skirt, which revealed her slender ankles. She wore a pink chiffon blouse, with ruffles at the neck, and a long thigh-length grey jacket. Her short dark hair was brushed to its shiny fullness, and Jean could not help but notice how her blue eyes shone. She turned away, as she began to gather empty plates. Here was a girl in love, if Jean was not mistaken.

Conversation resumed as Nick and Amelia circuited the room, talking to everybody there. Jean watched them as they smiled and nodded, and she paused on her way to the kitchen, when she saw Amelia take Hope from Phyllis's arms and cuddle her affectionately. Jean sighed. She had no doubt that these two would be sadly missed.

Jean continued on her way to the kitchen, passing four grubby children and a very irate Harry on the way in.

"Jess is not going to be pleased," he grumbled.

"Oh well, they've had fun," muttered Jean, hiding a smile.

No, Jess would certainly not be pleased. Jean shuffled out to the kitchen. She needed to bring in more food, and that was something she prided herself on – she could feed a crowd.

*

When Jean returned to the Ladies Lounge with a tray of small, sweet tarts, Beau was calling for attention from the gathered crowd. Jean quietly placed her tray on the table and stood back to hear what he had to say. Charlotte stood leaning on her crutches beside him, and Nick stood close to her.

"Family and friends," he began, "as we all know, life can throw us some situations that have no connection to our past, or so we think." He smiled at Charlotte. "When I found my sister, or rather, when she found me, (a murmur went around the crowd) I thought that everything was finally in place, and our lives could continue, uninterrupted. After all, what was there left to interrupt life?" His eyes moved to Nick. "Nick came here on a mission, and that was to find Phyllis and her child. He did that, with Amelia's help, of course."

"Thank-you, Beau." Amelia laughed. "I'm glad I got a mention."

Beau smiled. "Most of you know by now, that I was not particularly taken with Nick, and made that blatantly obvious."

"Yes, you did, Beau," said Jess. "Shame on you."

"I've already apologised." Beau continued. "The past somehow has a way of catching up with us, and when I went searching for something that could possibly connect Nick to us, I found it." He paused and wiped a hand across his mouth. "I know I shouldn't speak ill of the dead but finding that old newspaper article opened up a whole can of worms for me, and I wanted to find out where the truth lay." He looked at Charlotte. "The truth lay in something that happened a long time ago, and all our questions have been answered." The blood rushed in his head, and he couldn't go on.

Charlotte took up the baton. "Thirty-two years ago, I gave birth to a son, and I was told that my infant had died. Another child was born that day – stillborn - and because I was a mere child myself, the midwife made the fatal decision to swap the babies, and my child became Nick Armitage." Her eyes were wet as she looked at Nick, and he gave her a swift hug. "My life became very different to the life that I expected to live, and although it was a fulfilling life, (you all know the story) there was always something missing. Now I have my son back and I don't want to waste another minute without him. That is why I have decided to go to Sydney with Nick and Amelia." Charlotte looked around the crowd. Her eyes rested on Jess, who was wiping her tear-streaked face. "Jess, I will never forget what you have done for me, and although I love my brother dearly, I now need to be with my son." There was hesitant applause while Charlotte found herself squeezed by both Nick and Beau. Finally, she managed to say:

"Besides, there are people I need to see in Sydney – people who need to know that although I don't fully understand the reasoning behind what they did, I will try to find it in my heart to forgive them." She stared at Nick.

"Thank-you, Charlotte." Nick's eyes were misted. "We both need to do that."

"Yes, Nick, we do."

Author's Acknowledgements.

When book three of the Forget Me Not series was finished, I have to admit that I was at a loss. I would have to give these characters up to settle their differences without me, I couldn't let that happen. They needed me, and besides, stories don't end; they continue to evolve. So I promptly pulled out the computer and began work on a fourth book.

At the same time, my husband, Tom, had just passed away, and that was extra incentive for me not to curl up in a ball and forget what was going on in the world. I needed to stay in a positive frame of mind, and knowing my characters so well, I adjusted to their needs and turned my attention to solving their problems.

I hope I have achieved this. I am learning all the time, and this journey just keeps getting better and better.

I am grateful to my readers for the positive vibes they send me when they've read my books. This keeps me going – knowing that the work I do is appreciated by so many.

Thank-you Valerie and Fran, for always being there to read my drafts and offer your suggestions and criticisms. This is a necessary part of the journey, and is greatly appreciated.

Thank-you , Joanne, for once again designing my cover and doing all those set-up tasks that I find are in the 'too hard' basket.

I won't make any promises as to what might follow book four. It will depend on how it is received. It may be time to find other characters and delve into their lives. Who knows?

In the meantime, I hope you enjoy Finding the Truth, and I look forward to your comments.

Valmai R. Harris

www.ingramcontent.com/pod-product-compliance
Lightning Source LLC
Chambersburg PA
CBHW022043290426
44109CB00014B/964